I Learned About
FLYING
From That

I Learned About
FLYING
From That

First-Hand Accounts of Mishaps
to Avoid from Real-Life Pilots

Volume 4

Edited by Robert Goyer

Illustrated by Barry Ross

filipacchi
publishing

First published in the United States of America
by Filipacchi Publishing
1633 Broadway
New York, NY 10019

Design: Patricia Fabricant

ISBN: 1-933231-24-6

Printed in China.

Contents

Foreword

WE ALL HAVE LEARNED *About Flying From That.* Since 1939 this feature in *Flying* Magazine has been the most popular and closely read article in the magazine. At first it may seem to be ghoulish to dwell so closely on near disasters that could have claimed the life of the writer, but that's not the way pilots think. The fact is that the pilots and aviation enthusiasts who read *Flying* Magazine are determined to learn from the mistakes and misfortune of others so they can avoid the same fate themselves.

Every *I Learned About Flying From That* article comes in "over the transom," as the saying goes in the publishing business. In other words, the articles are unsolicited and the magazine's staff has no idea when a submission will arrive. Every article is written by the pilot who had the experience of nearly crashing, or actually crashing and surviving in some cases. The magazine's staff edits the work for clarity, but the story is the pilot's alone.

Here at *Flying* we receive, on average, several submissions for *I Learned About Flying From That* each week. The flow of submissions is not uniform, of course, but they do arrive regularly. Clearly pilots are anxious to tell their story to warn others of a potential trap awaiting any aviator.

Because only one *I Learned About Flying From That* article appears in each issue of *Flying* most submissions are turned down. What we editors look for when selecting a submission is an event that a well-trained and careful pilot probably would not have expected before taking off. Many submissions deal with weather conditions that turned out to be somewhat worse than forecast, but there is little to learn from those. Weather forecasts are never perfect. Often pilots will write about errors they made during the preflight examination of the airplane, and those are typically rejected. What is there to learn from a pilot who, for example, fails to notice that the tow bar is still attached to the nose wheel before he taxis to the runway. Those are just dumb mistakes that anyone—pilot or not—already knows must be avoided.

The best *I Learned About Flying From That* tales—and the ones we editors select for publication—elicit one of two possible reactions after reading them: One reaction is "that poor sun of a gun, he sure drew the short straw and if that ever happens to me I'll be ready." The other reaction is "why didn't he think to. . . . fill in the blank." In either case the reader has learned about what can go wrong in the air, and also what can be done to prevent the emergency, or to deal with it after it happens.

Another crucial element of the *I Learned About Flying From That* feature is the work of illustration artist Barry Ross whose drawings have accompanied each article for more than 20 years. Barry is a very talented artist, but more importantly in this context, he is a pilot, airplane owner and aviation historian. Barry researches the aircraft involved in each article to be certain every detail of his illustration is accurate. He also contacts the writer to obtain photos of the people and aircraft so the likeness is correct down to the actual color of the paint on the aircraft. Several of Barry's illustrations are included here, and his work is in full color on the dust jacket.

I know that you will find the stories of near miss and luck in this book to be riveting, but I also know that, as *Flying* Magazine readers have for more than 65 years, you will in fact learn much from *I Learned About Flying From That.*

J. MAC MCCLELLAN
Editor-in-Chief, *Flying* Magazine

Introduction

THE FIRST *I Learned About Flying From That* that appeared in *Flying* in May of 1939 was a story by an Alaskan Tri-motor pilot, Garland Lincoln. In the tale Lincoln told about running his big Tin Goose out of fuel in soupy weather and about the subsequent and inevitable forced landing, which he had to execute by descending through a dense cloud layer to the mysterious terrain below. As you've already surmised, Lincoln got lucky and lived to tell the tale. And, as has since become tradition, at the end of the story he got to sum up the experience, declaring that flying blindly into an area of known bad weather wasn't a good idea.

With this kind of story anyone could predict a bad if not fatal outcome. That much hasn't changed in the almost 70 years that we've been operating this public aviation confession forum. And in this collection you'll read the story of a pilot who took off from a relatively short, high-elevation Utah strip on a hot summer day in a 180-hp Piper Arrow without checking the airplane's performance charts. And we've got the tale of an experienced and otherwise cautious airline pilot who decided to try to land despite a stiff but legal tailwind in a snowstorm with old and dubious braking-action reports. Some of these stories will make you scratch your head and wonder what exactly the pilot could have been thinking. And afterward, it might make you wonder what prompts pilots to publicly fess up like they do.

Some of the stories are flat out sobering, making you realize that, sometimes, no matter how thorough, cautious and experienced you are, bad things can still happen when you go flying. Like the engine quitting dead, a broken crankshaft, on a dark night over uncertain terrain. It's in a case like that when steady nerves, quick thinking, clever hunches and a hearty helping of good old fashioned dumb luck come in handy. Some of the stories here made me wish I were half the pilot the author was, and I had to wonder if I would have been up to a similar challenge.

It's hard to read *I Learned About Flying From That* without thinking about your own stories of foggy judgment, dim-witted decision making and ham-handed flying. Does any pilot not have a couple of this kind of tale to tell? I know that I've got a few, as do most of my friends. And who knows how many they're *not* telling.

One of the stories featured here has a special place in my heart. It's about a J-2 Cub pilot, just 22 years old, doing a little sightseeing over the Atlantic Ocean with his fiancée despite some blustery winds out of the west. The winds turned out to be so strong in fact that they began to blow the little Cub and its occupants out to sea. The main characters, in case you were wondering, are my mom and dad, now both 80 years old and living happily in Southern California. My dad's story of quick thinking and sure-handed flying makes for good reading, and it serves as a special reminder to me of how important it is to approach our flying with an eye to avoiding risks and a clarity of purpose in dealing with them when they do arise. If my dad hadn't made the right decisions, you might have one fewer story in this collection and an entirely different editor for it.

For even though we never know exactly what might happen to us when we go aloft, *I Learned About Flying From That* serves as a priceless catalog of hundreds of possibilities. While we can enjoy each one for the great story behind it, we can also file them away for later retrieval, perhaps at a time when we might really need the practical lessons behind them.

ROBERT GOYER

Barry Ross

WEATHER
WOES

ONE THING THAT BECOMES CLEAR in reading through hundreds of these stories is that while bad weather doesn't cause every accident or near accident, it's such a frequent factor that we'd be foolish not to think long and hard about how it might affect an upcoming flight or an upcoming leg.

While the weather isn't inherently evil, it can sometimes seem like it. The weather doesn't care about our plans or our lives. A bank of dense fog at our destination airport isn't going to part like the Red Sea in order to allow us a timely arrival. We're the ones who have to adjust. While that might seem like stating the obvious, many pilots fly as though the weather has their best interests at heart.

Even today, the weather still holds mythic sway over our imaginations, perhaps because its power beyond our ability to comprehend. Thunderstorms, lightning, mountain waves, severe wind shear, extreme turbulence: If you've ever wandered too close to any of these meteorological phenomena, you've seen firsthand how we are no match for the power of Mother Nature. Acceptance and avoidance (and sometimes a bit of luck) are key to making it safely to an airport.

That kind of acceptance was crucial to the pilot of a Cherokee whose destination airport lay on the other side of a freakishly big desert dust storm, the importance of which seemed completely lost on the air traffic controller that day. And to the pilot who ventured so close to a thunderstorm that it nearly tore his airplane apart, it was luck, steady nerves and a speedy getaway that saved the day.

Of course the lesson behind these stories is to not put yourself in such situations in the first place. Indeed, in nearly every one there were early signs that things weren't going quite as planned, but the pilots almost to a one chose to solider on. These pilots were all lucky. When it comes to flying in adverse weather, that kind of indecision will often prove a fatal mistake.

Making Progress Backwards

BILL JR. COULD LEVITATE. I saw it with my own eyes. There it was, hovering about six inches over the grass, dancing around in the wind against the tiedown ropes. Bill Jr. was a Piper J-2 Cub I sometimes borrowed from its owner. Powered by a 40-hp Lycoming "L" head single-ignition engine, and with a big 36-foot wingspan, the 700-pound airplane was an excellent slow flier. It would rise off the ground in winds as little as 25 mph, and take off at about the same speed.

The J-2 was fine with me. A year out of Naval Flight School, I was taking every chance I could to get up in the air. At that time, I was engaged to a girl who lived about 85 air miles away from my home in Northampton, Massachusetts. Tina was in her last year of nursing school at St. Joseph's Hospital in Lowell, Massachusetts. I flew out there in the J-2 Cub to visit her on our mutual days off—when I had enough money for gas, that is.

One gorgeous autumn day, I made plans to fly out to see her. The trip east was beautiful, and fast. A cold front had just blown through, and, as I figured it, the west wind was helping me and Bill Jr. along, with about a 25- to 30-mph push on the tail. Add that to the normal 55-60 mph indicated cruise speed, and we were really flying.

I landed at the airport in Dracut, a suburb of Lowell, tied down for the night, and spent an enjoyable evening with Tina and her hospitable family.

The following day dawned clear and cool, and the brisk west wind seemed to be blowing even harder than the day before. What a beautiful day to take my sweetheart for a flight, I thought. I preflighted the little Cub, glanced up to check the weather—not a cloud in the bright blue sky—and Tina and I climbed aboard.

Our takeoff roll into the wind was almost nonexistent. The tail came up, then *Bill Jr.* levitated. What a show-off. We made a leisurely sightseeing detour over the Lowell area, then followed the course of the Merrimac River, which intersects the city, then flows along until it empties into the ocean near the Massachusetts New–Hampshire border.

I had to be back at work later that evening, so soon it was time to drop off Tina and head home. I turned west, looked at the horizon and picked out a little peak I knew would take us back to Dracut, then poured what coals there were to the little four-banger.

As I looked toward the line of hills in the distance, my attention was drawn to the spectacular scenery. The tree-covered hills were covered with a blanket of red and gold leaves. And I just sat there in the cockpit, fat, dumb and happy, enjoying the thrill of being in the air on such a beautiful day with the woman I would soon marry.

My plan was to climb to 2,500 feet before leveling off. Eventually—it took me far too long—I noticed that the mountain on the horizon wasn't really getting closer. And the colorful foliage I'd been watching go by under the plane became tidal flats adjoining the seashore. I hadn't remembered anything like that around Lowell. Now there were breakers underneath *Bill Jr.*, and I suddenly realized what was happening: We were in the process of being blown backward out over the Atlantic Ocean.

Well, I had unknowingly done one thing correctly—I'd gained a little altitude, and now it was time to exchange my precious altitude for airspeed and penetration. I frantically scanned the shoreline for a suitable landing spot, but all I saw was miles of beach, all of it at a 90-degree angle to the strong west wind.

Then I saw a plane making a descending turn. My eyes followed it to a small field, which turned out to be Plum Island Airport, only about

1,000 feet from the beach. But it had a wind sock on it, and there were a few planes tied down, so I figured it would be safe to land there. Besides, I didn't really have much of a choice by that point.

I knew that if I had enough altitude I could get back down on the ground, and I hoped that as I got closer to the ground, the speed of the wind would diminish some. I pushed in full throttle and nosed *Bill Jr.* over into a fairly steep dive. It seemed to take forever, but finally the ground started moving in the right direction below us. Gradually the shore passed under the wings, and it was a race to see if we could make the runway before we ran out of altitude.

We made it, no sweat. I almost had room to make a pattern, but I didn't dare turn the plane downwind again. The wind was right down the runway, and as I flared to land, we actually came to a full stop—still in the air—and started flying backward a couple of feet above the ground at about four mph. I forgot to mention that *Bill Jr.* didn't even have a tailwheel; he had a nice tailskid, which seemed to work great as a brake when you were landing slightly backwards.

With the help of some local pilots, I got *Bill Jr.* tied down. Tina's father drove out and picked us up at the airport, and I got to spend another night in Lowell. By the next day, the winds had died enough to let me make a slow but successful return trip to Northampton.

My aborted trip home served as a good lesson for a young pilot. Given the winds aloft that day, a westbound trip in an airplane as slow as *Bill Jr.* just wasn't in the cards. In 50 years of flying since that trip, I've learned to know and respect the limitations of the airplane. I've also come to believe that a few extra horsepower never hurts, either.

Fly the Plane!

APRIL 21, 1999 looked like a beautiful day for a solo VFR flight from Baton Rouge, Louisiana, to Wichita, Kansas. Little did I know that before the day would end I would be fighting to stay inside my airplane over the mountains of northwest Arkansas.

Most of my 30 years of flying had been "flatland" flying, and my logbooks are filled with trips over the Gulf Coast, Oklahoma and Texas but very few over hilly terrain. The Kiamichi Mountain range between McAlester, Oklahoma, and my boyhood home in Paris, Texas, had hills, but I seldom ventured in their direction, and I did not consider them capable of causing the same problems I read about in flying in the western states. Formal training for "mountain flying" would have to wait until my travels ever took me to Colorado or points west. As a licensed pilot at 17, I was free to fly our J-3 Cub nearly anywhere I wanted to go, but my father, who was a CFI in northeast Texas for 25 years, always refused to let me take the Cub to Mena, Arkansas, insisting that I did not know what I would be getting myself into. Like most bulletproof 17-year-olds, I was confident that I could handle those little hills and was extremely put out by this restriction.

The weather briefing for the flight seemed innocent enough: good visibility, clear to scattered clouds with bases at 4,000 feet and winds aloft from between 200 and 220 degrees at between 25 and 35 knots. There was an advisory for occasional moderate turbulence below 6,000 feet. Perhaps the most unusual item in the briefing was the forecast for uncommonly strong surface winds in excess of 20 knots from the south and southwest all across the route, which did not cause me much concern because I knew my destination would provide a runway nearly aligned with the wind for landing.

The flight was proceeding according to plan. The Cardinal RG I was flying was running as smooth as a well-oiled clock; the GPS was showing the benefits of 15 to 20 knots of tailwind; and the ride at 6,500 feet was perfectly smooth. The first change in the flight plan was when the Center controller I was talking to advised that the Anne MOA in southern Arkansas had gone active and had several USAF jets maneuvering in it. I decided to turn to the east instead of the west because the easterly detour was shorter. After clearing the MOA, I turned toward Wichita and looked forward to arrival and supper.

This new course took me directly over Mena, Arkansas, and within a few miles of the Rich Mountain VOR, but no worry, I was still more than 3,500 feet higher than the highest crests in the area. The ride was still smooth when the VSI began indicating a rate of climb in excess of 1,500 fpm; the airplane felt like it was being propelled skyward by a rocket booster. What happened next, before I had time to do anything more than pull the power, would begin 10 minutes of the most hair-raising flying I had ever experienced.

The first sensation of trouble was the feeling of being hit over the head with a pipe, which was accompanied by a loud "bang," both doors blowing open and most of the gear in the cockpit flying around and exiting the airplane. The Cardinal rolled to the left and began careening downward. I did not know exactly what had happened, but the blood all over my face, clothes and cockpit and the severe pain in my head made me realize I was hurt, but how could that possibly happen with my seat belt/shoulder harness securely fastened? I was stunned but realized immediately that the first priority had to be recovering from the severe nose-down attitude and 60 degree bank that the airplane was in. My father's persistent admonition to "fly the plane" was ringing clearly through the confusion that surrounded me. The task at hand was to bring the wings level, ease the nose up and try to get the aircraft back under control in the midst of the turbulence that continued to slam it from side to side.

The numbing pain in my head didn't help my thinking any, and it was only after a couple of minutes that I realized that the reason I was bouncing all over the cockpit was that I was no longer belted into my seat! The shoulder harness was still looped around my right shoulder, so my initial thought was that the seat belt had come unbuckled, but when I reached for the belt on the door side of the seat I saw that the belt was still buckled and that the seat belt fitting had been ripped from the floor! Under normal flight conditions I would be unable to open the big doors on the Cardinal far enough to throw anything out, but as the airplane slewed left and right in the turbulence I saw just how far those doors could open in hammering turbulence. Believe me, this is not the view you want to see at 6,000 feet without a seat belt to keep you secure and inside the aircraft! I learned very quickly that you can fly just fine with one hand locked onto the bottom of the seat!

My headset was on the floor in front of the passenger seat, along with the lapboard and the charts clipped to it that had been in the right front seat. I recovered it and pressed the push-to-talk switch: "Center, this is 64V, I am in trouble and need vectors to the nearest airport!" The reassuring voice on the other end coolly responded with "Steer 310, 16 nm to 4,000-foot hard-surfaced runway." Only then did I realize that I had lost my eyeglasses. I could see the panel and instruments, but my now-uncorrected nearsighted condition posed yet another problem to overcome. The voice on the other end of the radio steered me to my destination, called out altitude alerts for the surrounding hills and put me exactly on the Poteau, Oklahoma, airport.

The pre-landing checklist (GUMP) was not without its own problems, for both the gear-up and gear-down indicator lights and the tachometer had failed in the turbulence. The helpful FBO at Poteau gave me the gear-down confirmation, and the landing into a 22-knot wind directly down the centerline of Runway 18 brought this harrowing event to a close. The FBO, Al Tecaro and Wanda Galland provided first aid and transported me to the local hospital where the ER staff sewed up the three-inch-long gash in my head.

Upon my return to the airfield I was stunned to see the damage the airplane had sustained: the seat belt fitting had been ripped from the floor, the overhead center console that had inflicted such a painful injury to me was smashed, and the famous Cessna Royalite trim around the pilot's door had been pulverized by my body being thrown against the doorframe during this wild ride. A small toolbox I carried in the baggage compartment that I had secured by wedging it under my clothing bag had smashed a basketball-sized hole in the rear window and had reduced the plastic bulkhead, dividing the baggage compartment from the tail cone into small pieces. Many items in the cockpit, including a coat lying on the backseat, the contents of the seat-back pockets and loose charts in my open flight case were never found. Surprisingly enough one snapshot I was carrying in a photo album lying on the backseat was ripped out of its holder, but I found it jammed in the gap between the stabilator and the fuselage, and I found my AWOL eyeglasses under the seat. What is perhaps most amazing is that there was no wrinkled skin on the aircraft, which I have concluded has one "built hell-for-stout" wing!

I really wanted to spend the night in familiar surroundings and decided that the airplane and I could handle a 45-minute flight to Paris, Texas, flying from the right seat. After I arrived in Paris, a friend came to pick me up, looked at the inside of the airplane and pointed out one item of damage that I had missed during my preflight inspection in Poteau: the battery box had been smashed by the force of the battery inside it, and the only thing holding the battery in the airplane was the battery cables! A comfortable bed, muscle relaxers and pain pills from the Poteau Hospital provided a good night's sleep.

The next morning a local A&P inspected the airplane for me to give a more complete assessment of the damage and helped secure the battery for an uneventful but slow trip back to Baton Rouge. The slow ride home gave me plenty of time to re-examine the decisions I had made that led up to the most harrowing 10 minutes I have ever spent in an airplane. Just what had I missed, and what could I learn from this experience?

First, mountain waves do exist in areas other than the leeward side of the Rocky Mountains, and they are not always neatly marked by the lens-shaped standing lenticular altocumulus clouds that are found in so many texts and training videos on aviation weather. I also realized that the presence of any unusual weather condition requires serious thought about the effects that may result from it. The next time I fly across the Plains with strong surface winds you can be sure I will think about far more than just the crosswind landing that may be required at the destination, and a consideration of the mountain wave or other turbulence that those strong winds can cause will be at the top of my list!

Next, I realized that had I given any thought to the query of the controller who suggested that I circumnavigate the Anne MOA, I would have recognized that the course I chose to go around to the east of the MOA would put me right over the leeward side of the biggest mountains in the area, while a deviation to the west would have put me on the upwind side of Rich Mountain and the other large hills; and I should have anticipated the considerable turbulence with the unusually strong surface winds out of the south and southwest.

I do agree now that sometimes it is better to be lucky than good, for it is only old-fashioned good luck that had my IAS within five knots of the maneuvering speed for the Cardinal when the hammer hit us, for there is no telling how this would have played out had I been flying lower and faster.

Finally, I learned the advice offered by that crusty old CFI dad of mine was right on both counts: the skies over Mena can be full of nasty surprises and all you really need to remember when problems mount is to "fly the plane!"

Arizona Dust Bowl

ARIZONA'S NEAR-PERFECT FLYING WEATHER can sometimes lull even experienced pilots into making mistakes that lead to dangerous situations. I recently learned that the hard way.

The Saturday of Mother's Day weekend, 1997, my wife and I flew our Cherokee 235 to Tucson International Airport from our home base at Falcon Field in Mesa in order to celebrate the holiday with her mother. The weather briefing I received before a midmorning departure indicated there would be convective activity in and around Tucson late in the afternoon. While that was a little unusual for early May, we planned to be headed home by 2:00 p.m. so I wasn't concerned.

After a pleasant lunch, we headed back to the airport. Ominously, thick black clouds were forming to the southeast of the city. It appeared the storm was going to be arriving at least two hours earlier than forecast. At first, I thought we would be able to depart Tucson and be on our way well ahead of the looming storm. However, by the time we turned into the executive terminal's parking lot, rain was starting to fall. Within minutes it was pouring. Heavy drops of water pounded the tarmac, creating a layer of white foam at ground level. Strong winds pushed the rain under the terminal's canopy where we had sought shelter. We ducked back inside and joined two other temporarily stranded pilots. We were all experienced desert fliers and figured that with the strong winds, the troublesome cell would pass quickly and we would soon be on our way.

We were wrong. The rain and winds continued unabated for nearly 30 minutes. Then, after the rain finally stopped, low ceilings obscured our normal route to the northwest along the nearby Catalina Mountains. We patiently bided our time until nearly four o'clock, when blue skies finally appeared to the west. One of the other pilots had just talked to Flight

Service and even printed out a color weather map. All indications were that the storm was stalled, but localized. By first proceeding west, it appeared, we could bypass the storm, then head northwest and find VFR conditions all the way back to the Phoenix area.

Ten minutes later we were in the air. We soon passed Ryan Field, which sat 10 miles southwest of Tucson International. Although there was some light rain in the vicinity, we had VFR conditions as far as we could see to the northwest. I leveled off at 4,500 feet and set the GPS direct FFZ.

Fifteen minutes later as we approached Coolidge, 30 miles southeast of Falcon Field, I noticed a brown haze at ground level to our west and northwest. It took me several minutes to realize it was a dust storm. As I watched, the storm intensified. The thick columns of brown dust billowing from the farmer's fields looked like smoke pouring from crevices in the earth's crust. I was still clearly VFR, but the dust clouds were headed northwest, right toward Phoenix.

Together, my wife and I considered our options. It was still VFR behind us and there were several airports to which we could return with no trouble, so I wasn't worried. Dust storms are fairly common in Arizona's desert and I'd easily flown around them before. I was concerned about how far to the northwest this storm extended, so I tuned in the ATIS for Williams Gateway Airport, which lay between me and Falcon Field. Unfortunately, the reservists who man the tower at this former air force base quit at four. I then tuned in Falcon's ATIS. The field was reporting winds one four zero at seven and visibility better than 10. No problem there. From what I could see out the windshield it appeared I could turn to the north and skirt the fringes of the dust storm before I turned west. There was no doubt we could beat the storm to Falcon, if it even extended that far; desert dust storms are typically short-lived. As I banked right, I switched to the Phoenix Approach frequency to find out what was happening at nearby airports. I listened to several transmissions. Everything seemed normal. Our plan should work and we'd be on the ground in less than 15 minutes.

I then glanced at my GPS. To my surprise we were registering 175 knots ground speed. I couldn't believe it. That's 45 knots better than I usually get! At first we were pleased because now we'd get home sooner. Our joy quickly turned to apprehension as we realized the high winds heralded a major storm. About this time I noticed a low-ridge line coming up under the nose of the plane. Having flown this route dozens of times before I knew there should be no mountains here. Where had they come from? The blowing dust was obscuring familiar landmarks. I wasn't sure where I was.

I reset the GPS for FFZ. Seconds later I received a new desired track indication that put Falcon nearly due north of me. That couldn't be right. I still should be southeast of Falcon, near Coolidge. At the same time I noticed the horizon was becoming more obscured in a darker brown haze. I could still see the distant mountains, but the dust clouds were now covering a greater portion of the sky.

This didn't look at all good. I decided I'd better contact Phoenix Approach to confirm my position. "Cherokee 2653 Tango, four thousand five hundred, VFR over Coolidge, requests flight following and vectors to Falcon," I radioed.

The controller responded with a transponder code. My wife dialed it in, then pushed the IDENT button.

Time passed slowly as I watched the growing dust clouds now in front of and below me. Finally, the controller came back. "53 Tango, I don't pick you up over Coolidge, but I do have a return over the San Tan Mountains."

I couldn't believe it. While I thought I was tracking north, the strong winds had carried me over the mountain range 12 miles north and west of Coolidge. But at least I now knew where I was. "That's me, sir. The wind causing the dust storm pushed me a little west."

The controller didn't seem concerned. "Twenty miles south of Falcon. Maintain present heading. Falcon reporting wind one four zero at seven, visibility 10. Descend to three thousand five hundred," he calmly instructed.

"Descend three thousand five hundred," I responded automatically.

I had less than 10 minutes flying time to Falcon. As we let down, the strong winds boiling over the mountain tops grabbed our Cherokee and sternly shook it. I glanced at my wife. She looked grim, with both of her arms straight down, her hands firmly gripping her seat's bottom. I managed a smile. "We'll be out of this in a minute or two," I told her with more confidence than I felt. Then I realized the dust was now above me, too.

"Approach, 53 Tango rapidly losing VFR conditions. Is Falcon still reporting VFR?" I asked, hoping I sounded calmer than I felt.

"Affirmative, sir, and Gateway is five miles and one o'clock."

Sure enough, the old airbase's three northwest-southwest parallel runways were right there, but they appeared to be shrouded by a brown curtain.

Our faithful Cherokee continued to shake as the turbulence rocked us back and forth, up and down. In front of me, the horizon continued to fade as the dust grew thicker. I now barely had three miles of visibility.

"53 Tango, descend to three thousand," I heard through my headset.

I instinctively started down. That proved to be a mistake. I was now surrounded by brown dust. The forward horizon was gone, the distant mountains a visual memory. As Gateway's runways disappeared beyond my right wing I called Approach.

"Sir, 53 Tango losing VFR. Say Falcon's conditions."

"Falcon still reporting wind one four zero at seven, visibility 10. Maintain present heading. Falcon seven miles."

That meant I'd be at Falcon in less than three minutes. From what I was being told I should punch out of this storm any second. But nothing changed. In fact, conditions were rapidly worsening. Then I realized the controller, safely ensconced in an air-conditioned, softly-lit, windowless room had no idea of what we were facing. He probably thought I was overreacting.

"Sir, 53 Tango has lost the horizon in blowing dust."

"Maintain present heading. Falcon six miles."

"Sir, 53 Tango's in the midst of a major dust storm. The horizon's gone."

"Maintain present heading. Maintain VFR. Falcon now five miles," he calmly repeated.

That was it. I couldn't see anything out the front but brown. The same conditions existed out the side windows. Below me, the subdivisions and cotton farmer's fields were growing indistinct. I made a decision.

"We're going back to Gateway," I announced to my wife. She nodded vigorously, the relief obvious in her face.

"Approach, I'm turning back to Gateway, Can you give me vectors?"

"53 Tango turn heading one four zero. Gateway four miles. Their tower is closed so I have no current weather."

I already knew what the current weather was—bad! I banked the plane into a standard rate turn, fighting the gusting winds, while my wife started to punch Gateway's identifier into the GPS. We both found our tasks difficult due to the continued turbulence. I silently thanked God I had gotten an instrument rating. I'm not sure I could have managed without it. I just kept thinking, fly the airplane and maintain altitude.

Finally, I rolled level about the same time the GPS displayed the new desired track. It matched my heading. While I configured the plane for a landing, my wife and I frantically searched ahead of us for one of Gateway's three runways. We didn't care which one popped into view first, we just wanted down.

With my ground speed now down to about 50 knots it seemed to take forever for the runway to come into view. Finally, my wife yelled, "There it is!"

Sure enough, the huge white figures 12R appeared out of the swirling dust. With the wind howling almost straight down the runway, I dropped in a second notch of flaps and cut the power. We seemed to stand still. Slowly the runway grew closer. I wasn't making much forward progress, but I was still headed toward terra firma. Visibility improved as I descended and I was soon over the tarmac. With the winds buffeting us about, we bumped once, then the tires grabbed the runway with an approving squeal that was immediately lost in the wind.

Neither of us spoke as we taxied to the ramp. It was hard for us to believe that things had deteriorated so rapidly. Not until I'd killed the engine did my wife speak. "I didn't think we were going to make it," she said. I didn't answer, but felt the same way. "I'm glad we're down," is all I could manage.

We exited our plane, securely tied her down as the wind-blown sand bit into our skin, then raced for the protection of the terminal. Our ordeal was over.

It quickly became apparent to me that I'd fallen victim to a situation I'd read about many times before—a series of mistakes, the compounding of which often leads to fatal accidents. First, I'd believed the weather data given to me by the FSS. Second, I'd failed to allow for wind drift and lost my positional awareness. Third, I'd assumed the approach controller knew what the weather was doing and understood my predicament. Fourth,

I'd assumed Falcon's ATIS was an accurate depiction of the current weather. Fifth, I should never have accepted the controller's instructions to descend; that only put me deeper into the belly of the storm. Instead, I should have insisted on a higher altitude. Most important, however, I vastly underestimated the scope of the dust storm. Rather than try to fly around it, I should have turned around earlier and returned to one of several Tucson area airports where we could have safely waited for the storm to run its course. And it was a big dust storm; the local nightly news programs lead their reports with stories of what had turned out to be the worst dust storm to hit metropolitan Phoenix in years.

Arizona does have great flying weather, but it can turn deadly serious if you let it.

Special Request

I SUSPECT THAT I WAS NOT ALONE in feeling a bit overwhelmed by the mass of information I had to memorize on the path to becoming a private pilot. As a seasoned pilot of all of a few months and hours past my check ride, I know now that everything I was learning on my way to my license was important in one way or another. But as a student pilot I sorted all that information into two fairly manageable piles: really important stuff I needed to know to keep myself from doing something stupid and crashing in the airplane, and less important stuff I needed to know to keep myself from doing something stupid and crashing on the FAA written exam.

The concept of special VFR fell into the latter category. Since at that stage of my training I had no intention of ever venturing into, let alone taking off or landing, in IFR conditions, I envisioned special VFR to be a tool that I would need only in case of extreme emergency, in particular, if the weather suddenly turned, trapping me away from the airport. I memorized the concept for the FAA exam and promptly filed it into one of those rarely used filing cabinets in the back of my brain. Little did I know that I would need to call on special VFR on a sunny summer morning.

The skies above my home in southern Illinois are a VFR pilot's dream right now. The fall and winter months provide the perfect combination of high ceilings, smooth air and just a touch of wind to keep things interesting. Unfortunately, during the remainder of the year those same skies are plagued by thunderstorms, turbulence, temperature inversions and just plain uncomfortable heat and humidity. The best time to fly during those difficult spring and summer months is early in the morning before the air grows unstable and begins to play its tricks. Consequently, last summer my husband (who is also a newly minted pilot) and I routinely rousted ourselves out of bed and into our rented Warriors at 5:30 a.m., a good hour and a half before the tower opened. We usually flew until around eight o'clock and then headed off to work.

My husband and I are fortunate to train at a Class D airport with a tower staffed by kind controllers. These long suffering individuals are all remarkably patient and understanding as the student pilots struggle to master radio communications as well as their airplanes. There is one controller, in particular, however, who not only tolerates us but who goes out of his way to teach us.

This controller is a private pilot himself, so he understands the importance of learning proper communication and flying habits early. He takes the extra time to help us learn because he knows that such techniques not only enable us to become better pilots but might even save our lives. If he isn't too busy, he offers to let us come up to the tower for a debriefing of our flying performance of the day. If the airwaves aren't too crowded, he provides suggestions for the proper way to communicate. If we are a bit far out on our patterns he sometimes challenges us to try to come in for a power-off landing, just to show us that we wouldn't have made it back to the runway in a true emergency. One of the reasons that my husband and I like to fly in the early morning is that our friend the controller is often the one who opens the tower.

One day last summer, when my husband/flying buddy was out of town, I headed to the airport at the usual time, routinely checked my airplane and the AWOS and took off. It felt like a normal soggy summer morning, the air dense and uncomfortable even before the sunrise. After fooling around over the practice field for about an hour, I heard my friend the controller open the tower at 7:00 a.m. with the usual information about airport procedures. This time, however, the routine I had come to expect varied dramatically; instead of advising the aircraft in the area of the current weather conditions, he announced that the field was IFR.

Yikes! It sure didn't look like the weather had deteriorated out in the practice field. I knew that I was well within the VFR minimums where I was. There was not a cloud in the sky, and although there was a distinct layer of haze well below, I could easily see through it to a large lake that I knew lay over 10 miles away.

I reasoned that fog must have moved in around the AWOS, tuned my radio over to its frequency and listened. While the ceiling was indeed well above 1,000 feet, the visibility at the airport had deteriorated to only one statute mile. I continued practicing, listening for the magic three statute miles visibility that would allow me to return to the airport. When the conditions still hadn't improved by 7:50 a.m., I knew I was in trouble, and that I would have to call in to my friend and explain my dilemma.

I didn't even try to bluff my way home. I tuned the radio back to tower, listened to make sure I wasn't embarrassing myself in front of too many other pilots, and announced myself and my position, adding, "I have AWOS, and I'm not sure what to do about the IFR conditions."

Silence, then a chuckle came back, "The field is indeed IFR; what are your intentions?"

I abandoned aviation speak. "Well, until now my intentions were to fly around out here until the conditions at the field changed, but I've got to get the airplane home. Any suggestions?"

Again silence, and then, "I can't make a suggestion, but think back on your training. Is there anything you want to request?"

I was so busy thinking back on my training, that I almost missed the clue. Suddenly I realized that I did have something special to request—special VFR. I radioed my request, it was granted, again with a chuckle, and I sailed back to my home base. To my surprise there was no fog, only the thick haze I had noted from above. I landed easily and, as I cleared the runway, requested permission to come up to the tower for a debriefing.

My friend was ready for me. He had the FARs open to the section on special VFR, and after I read through them, he explained that he had only given me a clue because controllers can't actually suggest special VFR since they wouldn't want to get a VFR pilot into a situation he couldn't handle. I, in turn, explained that I had viewed special VFR only as a tool to use in an emergency, and we discussed the fact that it was actually a fairly routine procedure. I learned that if the AWOS reported visibility of less than three statute miles but more than one and I could remain clear of clouds, not only could I contact the tower, or, if it wasn't open, the closest ARTCC, and request special VFR clearance to land, I could even request special VFR clearance from the ground, take off in IFR conditions like the haze we had that day, and hightail it to the obvious VFR conditions beyond the airport.

A week later, I was hanging out in the right seat enjoying the sunrise while my husband shot off touch-and-goes. The airport was rather busy that morning. Not only had somebody claimed the Warrior I usually flew, there were two other aircraft out in the practice field by the time the tower opened at 7:00 a.m. We were on short final when we heard it open. Once again, the controller, not my friend this time, announced that the field was IFR. The haze had snuck up on us again, this time while we were in the pattern. It sure didn't look like less than three statute miles visibility.

My husband and I looked at each other and said in unison, "special VFR." He picked up the microphone, reported our position and requested special VFR and clearance for landing. The controller didn't seem surprised by our request. It is, after all, a routine procedure. Clearance was given, and we landed without incident.

As we taxied off the runway, we heard the other pilots one by one announce their positions and request special VFR clearance for landing. From the sound of their voices, it was evident that they did not have the least idea what they were requesting, but, hey, since it had worked for us, it was worth a shot. If, like me, they had indeed filed special VFR away and forgotten it, I hope they went home and checked out the FARs.

We are all very lucky at our little Class D field. Thanks to our kind controllers, and one in particular who routinely takes the time to teach, at least five young pilots one hazy summer morning learned about flying from that.

Waiting to Exhale

A **POPULAR SONG FROM SEVERAL YEARS AGO** cited the roaring winds of November as an ingredient in the *Wreck of The Edmund Fitzgerald*. But aviators know wind is weather even when it stops. I explored the truth of this simple axiom my first winter as a rookie emergency helicopter pilot flying an AStar AS-350.

Late November. Hazy. Temp-dew point spread three degrees. Wind diminishing. At 11 p.m. the "bat phone" rang in my quarters at the hospital: twenty miles away a heart attack victim needed our services.

"It's not far," I said. "We can respond if we go right away and don't spend much time on the ground." I walked around the aircraft checking cowls, fluid levels, removing tie-downs—routine pre-launch activity. I glanced at the wind sock; it barely moved in the gentle breeze. We boarded, and minutes later were en route to the victim's farmhouse.

The crew asked for more cabin heat, so I reached down to twist the floor-mounted knob. A hand-fashioned sign adjacent to it advised that the knob be left cracked open at all times. With some difficulty it creaked open.

Immediately a rush of warm air flowed into the cabin and splashed against the windscreen. Below, I noticed small orbs of haze around each farm light. I alerted the crew to the potential problem, and reminded them of the need for minimal ground time with the patient.

A tall radio tower passed off our left a mile away. Lights of emergency vehicles on the ground directed me to the victim's home. A wisp of smoke rose from the chimney and I gauged my approach direction using it. I landed, shut down, glanced nervously at the wet sky and waited for the crew to get our patient stabilized and ready to travel.

A lengthy stabilization time usually means the patient is not doing well. What seemed like hours later the crew came back huffing and perspiring, carrying the loaded cot, CPR in progress. In a rush we shoved the cot on board, and I cranked up the engine.

The chimney smoke was now straight up; a perfect column disappearing into the inky sky. I brought the engine up to max enthusiasm, lifted off, and pointed the nose toward home. At one hundred feet my worst fear was confirmed: fog. Visibility all but disappeared. I gained enough altitude to clear known obstacles, careened from farm light to farm light, forcing the helicopter forward. As I debated over landing or pressing on, the airspeed needle bounced on fifty, then forty knots. A little voice fairly screamed at me, "Can't hover out here or you're lost. Keep your airspeed!" I glanced at our patient clinging to life, and kept going.

Things got worse. With the moisture in the cabin from the hard-working medical team, and the relative humidity outside, every window—and a few of the gauges—suddenly fogged over. To clear the windscreen I reached for the heater control, but it was stuck! Somehow in the process of loading the patient cot, we had jammed and overtightened the knob. It would not budge.

With a dying man beside me, a medical team trying desperately to prevent his demise, and all four of us stuck in nighttime IMC aboard a VMC-only aircraft, things were getting tense (and my old, ploddingly boring job as a corporate pilot was looking appealing).

For long stretches no lights appeared on the ground below. I crab-flew sideways, peering through the side vent, hoping to see something, anything that might appear on the midnight landscape.

While not given to conversing with myself under ordinary circumstances, I was now chattering away, discussing my options. "Where is that radio tower?" I asked myself out loud.

I knew it was between me and the hospital somewhere, but where? Approach control radar was closed for the night. Center would help—if we climbed to five thousand.

Just as I concurred with that plan the blessed lights of town burnished the horizon.

I exhaled.

I landed.

After that flight any kind of landing would have been uneventful.

The old saw goes: If it's bad on the ground, it only gets worse in the air. I pretty much proved that theory the night a long patient stabilization, a stuck de-mister knob, high humidity and the winds of November left me bound up in fog.

The Door Blew Off

A FEW YEARS AGO on a quiet Sunday in April I took our Aztec (N4647P, which would ever after be known as Forty-seven Doorpopper) and flew to Detroit City with plans to fly later to Flint and then back to Pontiac. The weather en route and at both ends was reported to be 2,200 feet broken, 3,500 feet overcast with four miles visibility in light rain and drizzle, so I departed Detroit City VFR, planning to fly at 2,700 feet to Flint. The minimum vectoring altitude along the route is 2,700 feet, so I knew I would clear obstructions.

After liftoff from Runway 33 at Detroit City, I climbed straight out (right on course to Flint) and leveled off at 2,700. I called Detroit Metro Approach (the radar facility for the area) and requested VFR advisories. After a very few minutes I noticed wisps of cloud forming beneath me, so I called Metro and advised the controller that I was IFR-rated and the airplane properly equipped and requested an IFR clearance to fly "present position direct Flint."

I was cleared as requested, given a new squawk code and told to climb and maintain 3,000. As I reached 3,000, I was solid on the gauges, and I began to encounter turbulence. I don't mean light chop, or even moderate turbulence: I was getting the kind of jolts in which you bump your head on the ceiling (hard) even with the seat belt cinched up tight. I asked the controller if he had his scope on circular polarization, which reduces weather returns on the display to eliminate clutter, or was he painting any weather, and he replied, "Both!" This was my clue that I was in or near a thunderstorm, as if I didn't already know. It also told me that I ought to be somewhere else. I called the controller and advised him that I wanted to amend my destination to Pontiac instead of Flint.

I was about eight miles northeast of the Pontiac airport, which, at the time, had two IFR approaches, one for each end of the 5,000-plus-foot east-west runway, both VOR approaches. The controller told me to turn right (away from the airport) heading 180 to permit me to intercept the final for the VOR 27 approach outside the final fix (Keego Intersection). As I started the turn, all hell broke loose. It was just like driving into a brick wall.

The door was ripped from the aircraft, leaving a circle of jagged aluminum around the receptacle where the upper door pin is supposed to secure the door, and blank spaces where the hinges used to be. The airplane was pitched inverted, plastering the microphone, which I had released, against the headliner. We were being violently tossed about. Because of the unbelievable pressure changes, the airspeed indicator was rapidly going from zero to 200 miles per hour, and the altimeter was showing 1,000 feet and spinning around to 6,000 in nothing flat. The airplane was equipped with an instantaneous vertical speed indicator and it was registering a climb of 2,000 feet per minute up and within a matter of a second or so 2,000 feet per minute down. About then the baggage door departed the airplane as well.

I had no idea what our altitude was. All the gyroscopic instruments had tumbled, and the magnetic compass was bobbing around like a cork in the ocean. More by instinct than thought process I retarded the throttles, and since I was being shoved against the belt to my right, I stomped on the left rudder. The first thought that flashed through my mind was, "That door has plunged through the roof of a house and killed a baby sleeping in a crib." I next came close to allowing the infamous hazardous attitude of resignation to take over. I was thinking that after 35 years and well over 20,000 hours of flying I was finally about to buy the farm. These two thoughts must have flashed by incredibly fast, because I then recall telling myself, "Okay, you dummy, if you settle down and do what you know how to do, you just might survive."

While I was struggling to regain some semblance of control over the airplane, the approach controller was reading me Pontiac weather, which he said was 1,000 and 3. I grabbed the mic and advised him that our door was off, not just open as sometimes happens. He asked if I wished to declare an emergency. Now, I'm not one of those pilots who are concerned about the potential paperwork associated with declaring an emergency, but I do know that the controllers' manual by which they have to live requires that they elicit a bunch of information when a pilot declares an emergency, including the amount of fuel aboard, number of passenger, etc. Since I had my hands full of an airplane and no time to bother with answering that stuff, I replied, "Negative. Cancel IFR." I was still IMC, but I couldn't be concerned with further communications at that time.

With the power reduced, I applied approach flaps. I was still holding full left rudder to keep the wings what I believed to be level. When the controller said that the ceiling at Pontiac was 1,000 feet, I gained a little confidence, because Pontiac's field elevation is 980 feet, so I thought I'd break out soon and be about 1,000 feet above the ground. No such luck. I continued to descend until I saw the ground, at which time I was only a couple of hundred feet above the surface. Now, with a horizon, I could at least keep the wings level, although I was still having a great deal of control difficulty.

I looked around and spotted a large water tank. Believing it to be the one located five miles southeast of the Pontiac airport, I started flying northwest, orienting myself by the section lines on the ground. (The mag compass was still useless and wobbling so as to be unreadable, much less reliable, and who knows where the directional gyro had ended up.) I switched over to the tower and reported, "Waterford tank inbound."

The tower controller advised me of the wind (300 degrees at some value or other), asked me if I wanted to declare an emergency (he had been advised of our plight by Metro), and cleared me to land on Runway 27. I again turned down the offer of declaring an emergency (this time because I thought I knew where I was), and I kept going. Long after I should have reached the airport (it must have been five or six minutes) I spotted a trans-mitter antenna tower straight ahead. Its top was in the cloud, higher than I was! I did a quick one-eighty. I then knew where I really was, about a dozen miles north of the airport. I called the tower and reported that I was now north and headed back toward the field.

When I was just off the northeast boundary, the local controller advised me, "We've had a wind shift. The wind is now 360 degrees at 38 knots, gusting in the forties. Runway 36 is favored, but you may have 27 if you like."

I looked out that great big hole in the side of the airplane where there used to be a door, and there was that gorgeous Runway 27, over 6,000 feet long and 150 feet wide. 36 is the shortest runway at the airport, being only 1,865 feet long and 48 feet wide, but it has a long overrun at the north end before you run into the fence. I opted to land into the wind on 36.

I extended the landing gear and flaps and made one of the best, smoothest landings of my long career. I had retarded the power on short final, and just as I started to flare, I added throttle. The left engine responded and the right engine ground to a halt. I don't know just when I lost my right engine, but I'm sure that loss contributed to my control problems.

The tower controller said I could make a one-eighty on the runway and taxi back to my office, "and by the way, it appears that a piece of that door is stuck in your tail." I told him that if it was all the same to him, I'd just sit where I was for a few minutes while my heart stopped racing and my breathing returned to normal. My passenger leaned out the opening on his right and looked back toward the tail, and he fainted.

When I got the airplane parked, I looked at the empennage, and I, too, almost fainted. The entire vertical stabilizer forward of the main spar was totally demolished, and the mangled remains of the door (all of it) was stuck in the tail. The baggage door was never found. The airplane had approximately one-eighth to one-quarter inch of ice all over it.

I went up to the tower to file a report and thank both the local controller and the approach controller, and I listened to the tapes of my communications with both. I'm proud to say my voice was perfectly calm throughout. After the initial moment of terror, I had applied my training and experience to survive. I was also lucky; about 10 minutes after I landed, Pontiac went to zero/zero. And the approach controller told me that when he turned off his circular polarization, the echo where I was had a hook at the bottom end which is indicative of a tornado.

Three days later a young lady whom I had never met, and who I haven't seen since, stopped by my office at the Pontiac airport and graciously presented me with three photos her husband had taken right after I parked the airplane. Her husband was a freelance flight instructor and they lived a few blocks from the airport. He had been listening to his airband radio and heard the entire episode. As soon as he knew I was safely on the ground, he rushed over and photographed the airplane with the door stuck in the tail.

None of the terrible weather that descended on the area that day was forecast. It was all unexpected. The lesson to be learned from this adventure is if you keep your cool and apply your training and experience, there's almost nothing that can happen in light aircraft that isn't survivable.

Personally, I have never since that day been in cloud where there is the potential for embedded thunderstorms without some sort of weather avoidance equipment aboard. I mean on-board weather radar, Strikefinder or Stormscope. They can show where the chop is, and that's what I want to know—and avoid.

ALONG FOR THE RIDE

Barry Ross

WITH FEW EXCEPTIONS, jets are flown by crews. There's a good reason for that. Crews are trained to do everything a really good single pilot can do and more, with built-in checks and backups. But then again, crews need frequent procedures training to make sure that every member knows exactly what their role is, as well as what it isn't, so the crewmember doesn't screw things up further in the process of trying to help out.

Almost every one of these stories involves sharing piloting responsibility with someone whose flying skills and/or judgment are an unknown quantity or who either causes trouble in remarkable unanticipated ways or reacts to a cockpit emergency badly. In one story, a trio of flight instructors on cross-country flight get into trouble and no one does a thing about it, until it's almost too late. In another, a pilot hitches a ride from a flying acquaintance with terrifying results. In yet another, a pilot takes a demo ride in a Lance with a pilot who seems to care more about his bucket of fried chicken than whether or not they'll survive the flight, which they almost didn't.

The fact is, the presence of an extra person in the airplane is a wildcard, and there's no telling what help, or hindrance, they might be when things start going bad. In fact, that other pilot might well be the one factor that puts the flight into jeopardy in the first place, and you might not even know there's a problem until it's almost too late to fix it.

Along for the Ride

AS PILOTS WE ALL KNOW THE RISKS OF FLYING, but in the 16 years I've been flying there was only once I really thought I was going to die.

I work in an air traffic control tower in South Texas. One day a controller from a neighboring city, let's call him Pete, called the tower. I had known Pete for about seven years and was happy to see him take flying lessons. Pete had recently got a private license and an instrument rating and was working on his commercial ticket. Pete was going flying one day to practice commercial maneuvers and asked the tower if someone wanted to go for a ride. Since I was the only one not working a position, I got to go along. I climbed in the right seat of the Cessna 182RG and we took off.

After the climb to altitude and a clearing turn, Pete tried a chandelle. The chandelle was fair at best. As I watched, I noticed that Pete was mainly concentrating on the instruments and not looking too much outside the aircraft. Pete then tried a lazy eight, and again I noticed he was concentrating on the instruments and not looking out the windows much. Because of this he was chasing needles and did not have very good control of his airspeed. The way he was letting his airspeed get away from him bothered me, and I thought that being an instrument-rated pilot he should have better situational awareness. I also noticed that his recoveries when the airspeed started to get away from him were not as prescribed in the pilot handbook. I told him that he needed to keep better control of his airspeed and if he had to break out of the maneuver to keep airspeed control, then that's what he should do. I also reminded him of the correct way to recover if it was getting away from him. I even showed him how I was taught to do these maneuvers and gave him a few other pointers, and then let him try again. He did much better and was in good control of his airspeed. He was even ending his maneuvers close to numbers.

Pete tried a couple more, and these too turned out very well. By this time Pete was feeling pleased with himself, and I too was pleased. Pete noticed the hour was almost up and asked if I was ready to head back. I said that he was PIC and that it was fine by me. It was at this point that all hell broke loose.

I think Pete wanted to impress me with a steep turn towards the airport. While looking over at me and grinning, he gave the controls a good hard yank to the left. Since Pete was looking at me and not looking outside, he didn't notice that the plane started to go into what I would call a half-wing-over, half-split-S. I quickly asked if he was trying to do a split-S, and then Pete quickly looked out the front to see nothing but ground coming up at us very fast. I quickly pulled the power all the way back and the carb heat on and told him to watch his airspeed, and waited for him to start a recovery. At this point I'm not sure if he froze or just wasn't reacting fast enough, but when it looked like Pete was not going to do anything, I decided that I had to stop this dive or we were going to die. I almost waited too long.

The first thing to do was level the wings. By the time I did this the airspeed was rapidly nearing the yellow arc and climbing fast. It's amazing but at this point all that popped into my head was my own flight instruction some 16 years ago. I remembered what my instructor Ron Ussery drilled into me: only smooth control movements in the yellow arc or you could overstress the aircraft. Right! Only smooth movements, but this sucker was starting to scream and I knew that I had to slow it down. I thought, lower the gear, there is a lot of drag when you first put the gear down in a Cessna. I looked at the airspeed indicator and knew that I was nearing the max gear extension speed and that if the gear ripped off and damaged the tail, it would be a long fall from 5,000 feet. All I could do was ride it out.

So I smoothly pulled back on the controls until I had a level attitude and watched the airspeed. By this time it had reached redline and was still climbing. It was at this point that I thought that I might die, that the plane might break apart. Hold her steady, I told myself, and I watched—five knots past VNE, 10 knots past VNE, 15 knots; then as it neared 20 knots past VNE the airspeed stopped climbing and started to go back down. Time stands still when you're waiting for the speed to get back below redline. Finally redline, then yellow arc, then green arc.

As I reached cruise speed I added power and started the turn toward home. I also quickly proceeded to chew the royal backside out of Pete. A dozen questions were thrown at him all at once. What the hell are you doing? What the hell happened? You trying to get us killed? I just told you how to correct for that. Do you know what VNE means? and so on. I looked at Pete and he was whiter than a ghost; it had scared him more than me. I asked if he was okay, gave the controls back to him, and we headed home.

I'm not sure if Pete knew what happened, but trying to make something positive out of this, I asked him the age-old question: "Did you learn anything from this?" Pete and I talked about what happened and he seemed to understand what his mistakes were. He made a good landing and his color was returning to him when I got out and went back to work.

Now, I didn't want to embarrass Pete, but I had to call his instructor, for two reasons: One, the plane had to be checked out before the next flight; no rivets popped or anything like that, but I had to be sure. I was grateful for that extra 50 percent G tolerance built into the certification standards. Two, it bothered me that it got away from Pete and I had to take over. I asked his instructor, "What if I hadn't been there? Would Peter have pulled out?" True, he probably would not have gotten into this situation in the first place, since he would not have been trying to impress me. But what if he got vertigo in a cloud, would he have known how to get out? I think he knows now. Later on it occurred to me that, had we crashed, the blame more than likely would fall on me. I was not PIC, and he wasn't my student; I was not instructing; I was just a passenger. But I was an instructor in the right seat, the more experienced pilot with more flight time. I got sloppy, I missed the signs, I was slow to react. I should have been ready. I should have been a little leery of a newly IFR-rated pilot, especially since he had already shown problems controlling the airspeed, but I thought he would recover because I'd just showed him how.

I'd been complacent, thinking that since I wasn't PIC, it wasn't my fault. "It wasn't my fault"—they nearly wrote that on my gravestone.

Hitching A Ride

I WAS NOT HAVING A GOOD MONTH. First, my Mooney M20C had developed a small fuel leak in the left tank. There it was, staining the bottom of the wing with its persistent drip, drip, drip. What started out as a minor inconvenience had become a nuisance and, lately, an expense. A "fix" to the tune of $400 had only lasted four months. The real fix, I found out, was to have the fuel tanks totally stripped and resealed—a costly but necessary solution. In the meantime I had learned to fly the airplane with less than full fuel in the left tank so as not to allow a high-pressure head to cause all my fuel (and fuel dollars) to disappear while the airplane sat on the ground. Whenever possible we left the tank empty for the same reason. A typical flight would call for the offending tank to be topped and burned entirely before selecting the right tank. It was while using this scenario that I found myself in Rutland, Vermont, with an empty left tank, a partially filled right tank, and an FBO having fuel problems of his own. I estimated that I didn't have enough fuel to make my return safely, and elected to leave the airplane and take ground transportation home.

When it came time to go back for my airplane, since it was one-way transportation I was looking for, I naturally scouted all my pilot acquaintances for the favor. I was in luck; I discovered that an acquaintance who had a Cherokee would make the flight for fuel expenses. On the appointed day we arranged to meet at the airport in the morning. It turned out to be a beautiful VFR day in the Boston area and I was looking forward to an uneventful ride as copilot and talking partner for the flight up. It turned out that I was as wrong as wrong can be.

In New England, they say that if you don't like the weather, wait a minute and it will change—a prophetic phrase, in retrospect. The climb out from the airport was spectacular with promises of even better viewing once we reached the Vermont mountains. We settled into a cruising altitude of about 5,500 feet for the flight up. Slowly but steadily a cloud layer began developing below us that at first did not give rise for concern. My "friend" was instrument-rated—newly minted, but rated nonetheless. Heck, I was instrument-rated also, so there was no need to be concerned over a little developing undercast, was there? I waited for my friend to make the first move. He said something like "we may need to contact ATC and receive a clearance to get us down through this stuff." That sounded like proper judgment to me. Complacently I assumed that he had the situation in hand and accepted the role of passive, albeit interested, observer.

Awkwardly my friend made contact with the local approach radar in an attempt to obtain a clearance, giving only his N number. When I prompted him that that wouldn't be enough to file a flight plan, he responded, "Oh, they have all my data in the central computer in Washington." Oh really, I thought to myself; this ride is going to bear close scrutiny. We somehow got inserted into the ATC system and continued our northbound trek on a hard clearance. As expected, the weather closed down as we approached our destination, Rutland's state airport—from crystal-clear VFR conditions to solid IMC in less than an hour and 100 miles. I now found myself over-flying mountainous terrain in an unfamiliar airplane with a brand-new instrument pilot I'd never had the pleasure of flying with before.

As we approached our destination, Boston Center abruptly cleared us for the approach with the stock phrase "Cherokee November thus-and-such is cleared for the LDA 19 approach at Rutland, report back on fre-quency for missed approach or your cancellation on this frequency." Hey, wait a minute, aren't they supposed to vector you onto final around these parts? I'm somewhat of a novice instrument pilot myself, but I at least know this much. My friend, however, was panicked. "What does he mean by that? Am I supposed to descend now? What direction is the airport from here? We're not even near the final approach fix! What are we going to do?" The pitch of his voice rose exponentially. But the real question that ran through my mind was, What am I going to do? Here I was stuck in this bucket of flying bolts with a seeming incompetent flying on instruments in the mountains. Thank God the temperature is above freezing, I thought, checking the outside air temperature, and we droned on, my pilot forget-ting the number one rule: Fly the airplane. We were now careening all over the sky, unwilling or unable to hold either heading or altitude.

"Look, we need to continue on and fly the full procedure," I explained as we sped on, uncomfortably unaware of our position over the mountain peaks. "From our present position, we just fly to the final approach fix, then take up an outbound heading and do a procedure turn just like it shows on the approach plate," I said, none too sure myself.

"But I've never had to do that," my partner bemoaned. Of course not; this kept getting better by the minute. We jointly discussed how the proce-dure should be flown: Maintain present altitude to the approach fix; then take up an outbound heading of 004 degrees, fly a normal procedure turn until intercepting the LDA inbound, then begin a descent to 4,100 feet until the final approach fix, timing the descent to the missed approach point.

Sounds simple, right? Wrong! It seemed I was explaining all this to a non-believer. It was becoming increasingly obvious that my friend was losing what little concentration he had as we bounced around in the clouds trying to keep the airplane upright and on course. And I was feeling grossly uncomfortable acting as his instrument instructor, which was what I felt like at this point. I had no previous experience flying from the right seat, so scratch the idea of offering to fly the approach. No, I decided to let Bozo continue flying his airplane and I would monitor his every move. I could always scream "missed approach" if I felt things were getting out of hand.

We got the radios set up. Final approach fix tuned to the NDB beacon, LDA tuned and identified. We hit the final approach fix and turned outbound while configuring the aircraft for the approach. "Go slowly now," I cautioned. As we came up on the beacon outbound my pilot again became disoriented seeing the movement of the needle on the number two VOR, tuned to a cross radial from the Montpelier VOR. I notice his scan stop, becoming fixed on the number two VOR. Slowly the airplane began to drift off course. "Watch your heading," I said. "That doesn't make any sense," he said. "We aren't where we are supposed to be. I don't understand why the needle is behaving that way!" "Just fly the approach," I said, not knowing what all the confusion was about. "That cross radial isn't telling us anything useful." Somehow he didn't seem to understand, still fixating his gaze. We were now down to 5,000 feet as depicted on the approach plate, and from experience, I knew we were over the valley that defines the approach corridor to Runway 19—in other words, close to the level of mountain peaks on either side of us, "precipitous terrain" as they like to say on the approach plates. I prayed that my friend was capable of executing a precise course reversal. Somehow we managed to get established on an intercept for LDA. Once again a VOR needle began its slide toward the center of the instrument. He made no movement to capture the needle, apparently mesmerized once again.

"Turn towards the localizer," I screamed to myself. Instead I said, "You're supposed to track inbound towards the final approach fix. Track the localizer." By now we had flown through the final course, and to add insult to injury (hopefully not mine) he began his descent with localizer needle fully deflected.

"What are you doing?" I shouted. "I'm just following the procedure. It says here we need to descend to 4,100 feet," he said, his eyes glued to the approach plate while mine were glued to the needle, still hard against the case. I was conscious of sweat pouring down my collar as he wrestled with a wind correction heading trying to put some life back into the localizer. After what seemed like an eternity, and with me adding to the control input, we finally slid back onto the localizer. Thankfully we passed the final approach fix NDB on course and began our descent. "How much time until missed approach?" I asked. "I don't know," came the reply, "I forgot to set the timer." Luckily, the missed approach point is collocated at the second NDB. I tuned in the MAP fix to give us some fixed distance information. I reasoned that since it is at the missed approach point, we could safely descend to the beacon before executing the missed approach. Luckily we broke out well before that and believe me, the sight of a runway never looked so good.

We landed under relatively good visibility and wind conditions. The overcast looked to be about 500 to 700 feet above minimums. Hey, nice approach, I thought as I thankfully pulled myself out of the airplane. You know what they say about landings: Any one that you can walk away from is a good one. On the spot I made a pledge never again to fly with him or anyone else whose judgment I find suspect, or know nothing about. But this case was more than just poor judgment; this fellow really did not have a hint about what was going on up there. I watched him climb back into his airplane and depart, once again IFR, oblivious of the danger from which we had just extricated ourselves. Some people are not meant to fly airplanes, but I wish him luck. He'll need it.

I'll Never Do That Again

IT WAS 1981 OR POSSIBLY 1982. I was a new major assigned to the 613 Tactical Fighter Squadron at Torrejon AB near Madrid, Spain. We were flying the F-4D at the time. I was sent out to fly a single ship training sortie with my weapon system officer (WSO).

We were holding in the number one position for takeoff in the hot summer sun. Tower cleared us on the runway to hold for approximately a five-minute delay due to the civilian airline traffic at Barajas, the international airport at Madrid, a few miles off the end of the runway.

We taxied into position and began waiting for takeoff clearance with our canopies open due to the 100° heat. Then the tower advised us to expect takeoff clearance in one minute. We then closed our canopies in anticipation of our takeoff clearance.

When my canopy came down I noticed that my master caution light stayed on, and the canopy locking indicator stripes were not aligned. I leaned over to look at the locking mechanism and could tell that it was indeed not locked. Additionally, I could see daylight under both sides of the canopy.

It was at this point that I decided to give the canopy a little tug to help it over the overcentering mechanism. I reached up with both hands to grab the canopy bow, but my fingers went instead between the canopy bow and windshield rim. Now the canopy decided to lock, trapping my fingers. I began to scream in pain but this wasn't being heard because I had my mask off and was on cold mic.

Then the tower said, "Holding in takeoff position, you are cleared for takeoff." All I could do was look at the microphone button and try to figure a way to get to it. A glance in the mirror revealed my WSO to be busy with other matters, and was unaware of my predicament in the front seat. I tried to raise my knee enough to get to the microphone button but it was no use. Then I tried shifting my hips over enough in the seat to mash the mic button but that was also no use. I could only stare at the mic button and try to think of a way to call for help.

Since we hadn't started our takeoff, the tower repeated its takeoff clearance, "In takeoff position, cleared for takeoff, acknowledge." Additionally, my WSO came over the intercom and said, "OK, Rocky, we are ready to go."

Then I began to think at about 1,000 miles an hour: "No one has a clue that there is anything wrong, and I have no way of telling anyone. Without being able to use the nose-gear steering button I can't taxi off the runway or back to the parking area. I am going to have to sit here, blocking the runway, in a cockpit that must be 160¡ by now, until someone comes to rescue me. That may be a long time. In the meantime, no one else can use the runway to take off or land. The engines can't be shut down from the backseat, and if someone from the outside came to rescue me they couldn't come up to the cockpit for fear of getting sucked into the intake. There is no way anyone can help me. I am going to be sitting here until I run out of gas, but I will probably be dead from heat stroke before that."

Then I decided, "Fingers or not I have to save myself." So I closed both eyes, gritted my teeth and jerked both hands back as hard as possible, not knowing if I would be leaving my fingers behind or not. Luckily my fingers came free and the canopy closed and locked.

My thumbs had not been caught, so I was able to use the mic button to acknowledge the takeoff clearance now. All my fingers still worked, but the tips were bruised so badly I couldn't bear to touch anything. Fearing the razzing I would get from the guys in the squadron for an abort under such embarrassing circumstances, I decided to go ahead and fly the sortie. I was able to get the throttles into afterburner without gripping them with my fingers, but the nosegear steering button was another matter. I couldn't bear to touch it. So I decided not to use it. Luckily, I didn't need it.

After an hour or so I was able to use my fingers again. For the next few weeks I had to keep my hands out of sight because my nails were black and my fingertips black and blue from the incident. All this had happened in a few seconds but to me it seemed forever.

Needless to say, I kept quiet about the incident, never mentioning it to a soul for five or six years. That is something you would never be able to outlive in a fighter squadron. Then one night after some drinks I related this story to several guys at the officers club. Evidently, it has gotten around in the Air Force because a few years later, I heard the same story from someone who had no idea he was telling it to the very pilot who did it.

Twenty years have passed now. I am quite a bit older and hopefully a bit wiser, but I will never forget the hot summer day in Spain when an F-4 delayed its takeoff roll for a few seconds.

Three Stooges

THE SAYING GOES, "There is nothing more dangerous than two flight instructors in the cockpit during a flight." Have any similar warnings been written for three instructors on board?

Supposedly, it was to be a pleasant trip south for three very experienced pilots, all of whom happened to be CFIs, looking to escape the winter doldrums of New England with a leisurely flight to Florida. The morning of departure from Norwood Airport near Boston was uneventful weatherwise, yet full of a sense of adventure for the three of us. Since the airplane, a 1962 Mooney M20C, belonged to me, and since I'd made the trip countless times in the past, I decided to let the two "junior" pilots do the bulk of the flying. It would allow me the luxury of sightseeing and critiquing their performance. Little did I realize the one most in need of critiquing would be me.

One friend elected to fly leg number one, an IFR stretch over Long Island and New York City, landing uneventfully at Norfolk (VA) International Airport. Since Norfolk would have been my choice for a fuel stop, the seeds of complacency were quietly sown. For leg number two, my other friend chose as his fuel stop Jacksonville, at a total airway distance of 382 nautical miles. At a true airspeed of 130 knots which with I usually flightplan the Mooney, this seemed to be well within the realm of flight on this particular day. I did think, however, that if it were me flying the leg I would choose Grand Strand as my fuel stop. My reason was that we were approximately four hours from our destination—Orlando, Florida— and Strand was about half that distance. My previous experience with this route was that since it was usually impractical to fly nonstop from Norfolk to ORL, it was more comfortable to fly two two-hour legs rather than one three-hour leg and one one-hour leg. This was strictly preference on my part, so I kept my mouth shut when my friend announced with confidence that our fuel destination would be JAX. It would not be the last time that day I kept my opinions to myself.

In order not to intimidate the flying pilot, I chose to take the back seat—literally, further removing me from the inflight decision-making.

The stage was now set. A cold front in the vicinity of Norfolk was responsible for the winds aloft forecast being inaccurate. In addition, a longer-than-expected climb was necessary in order to stay out of those iceladen clouds. Groundspeeds for the Mooney hovered in the high double digits for a good portion of the flight. In an effort to shorten the distance flown, a decision was made to continue along Victor 1 where it passes over water east of Savannah. Thanks to the intercom, I was privy to all the inflight discussions of the two flying pilots, but said nothing, complacent that all this flying experience added a safety factor to the proceedings. I watched as airport after airport passed off the right wing. Heck, I could always say something if I felt things were getting out of hand. By this time we were three and a half hours into the mission and well east of the coastline. Darkness had fallen and the urge to speak my mind was causing me to squirm uncomfortably in my seat. But hey, weren't these two experienced instructors up front? Didn't we have onboard loran to pinpoint our position and provide us with a constant update of our groundspeed and distance to go? Red flags were going off all over in my mind, but still I said nothing, respecting the sovereignty of pilot-in-command.

The fuel gauges read almost empty. They couldn't be right, I rationalized. I fumbled through mental calculations relative to our long-ago departure. It quickly became apparent to me about this time that we were in a race to the finish. If we had enough fuel to reach the airport, we surely wouldn't have the luxury of a leisurely approach or a go-around if needed. What if we couldn't spot the airport immediately? Or were issued a delay by the control tower? All these thoughts were in my mind as we finally made landfall. By this time we could see the rotating beacon for JAX. The loran said 15 minutes to destination. With a little luck we should have it made.

Suddenly we were flying over a rotating beacon of an airport right below us. I wanted to yell, "Let's land here right now, I insist!" but instead kept my tongue. JAX looked so close in the darkness. We were all three silent now, mesmerized by the situation—or stupefied by it. Without warning the airplane suddenly banked left as the pilot-in-command decided on his own to land. My faith in his judgment was restored.

The airport was St. Mary's, Georgia. As we taxied in, my mind alternated between terror of what could have been our fate and joy that we would live to fly again, despite our collective stupidity. As the lineboy attended to the aircraft, the three of us engaged in the false bravado that belies such a situation—until the lineboy handed me the bill for the fuel. Under the "quantity" column the total read 46.2 gallons. My Mooney can hold precisely 48 gallons (it is not one of the later models that carries 52 gallons.)

Now I was furious, mostly with myself for allowing the situation to develop without so much as a word to two people who couldn't know as much about this airplane as I do. I took the last leg, a 45-minute hop into Orlando Executive, and we flew in silence, all of us aware of how close we came to disaster that night—all because no one wanted to play the instructor and ask the hard questions.

Let's Play Chicken

I **WAS A 200-HOUR PILOT** with a fresh IFR ticket when a local businessman offered to sell me a partnership in his Lance. I met with the pilot (I'll call him Bill) and quickly determined the plane was out of my price range.

But Bill was persistent, calling again a few days later and inviting me to go along on a flight from our home base of Florence, South Carolina, to Evansville, Indiana, and back. I reluctantly agreed, and met Bill at the airport later that day after we'd both finished work.

A fast-moving cold front had turned Florence into solid IMC as we departed into the fading daylight, and a light chop greeted us the instant we left the runway. Almost as quickly, I began to notice what a sloppy pilot I was flying with.

At about 2,000 feet into our climb, Bill released the yoke of the poorly trimmed airplane and reached behind his seat for a takeout bucket of chicken. The plane rolled to the left and started losing altitude before Bill returned his attention to the instruments and regained control without so much as a comment. As he began to devour his evening meal, I glanced at the landing-gear lights and noticed that Bill had yet to retract the wheels.

"Can I get the gear for you?" I asked, trying to be polite. Bill snatched off a bite of chicken and jerked at the gear handle. "Oops," was all he said.

A few seconds later ATC inquired about our flight conditions. "Solid

IMC," Bill responded, and I could hardly believe my ears. We were between layers, with at least 3,000 feet of clear air above us. I was really beginning to get a bad feeling about the guy.

When we reached our cruise altitude, Bill turned on the autopilot and went back to his fried chicken. About five minutes later the plane snapped into a steep left bank and started a rapid descent.

Bill grabbed the yoke. "Gotta watch this autopilot," he mumbled. "Likes to run away from you once in a while." Great, I thought. Not only is the pilot inept, but the plane is, too.

An hour later, we were on the back side of the cold front and flying in the crystal-clear nighttime skies over Tennessee. Bill hadn't done anything stupid for a while, so I was beginning to become a little more comfortable.

We landed in Evansville without further incident, and Bill concluded his business in a matter of minutes. When he offered me the left seat for the three-hour return leg, I hesitated for a moment. I had never flown a complex airplane before, the night IFR conditions over the Carolinas were well beyond my personal minimums, and Bill was a rotten pilot in the left seat, so I knew I couldn't count on him in the right seat. But I climbed into the pilot's chair anyway, figuring my inexperience would still be better than Bill's inattention.

For two hours the night VFR conditions made for spectacular flying. I had almost forgotten how uncomfortable I'd been earlier, when suddenly we entered instrument conditions and heavy rain near Charlotte, about 100 miles from home. Flying the complex plane—at night and on the gauges—proved to be a real challenge, and the center frequencies were busy with everyone asking for higher altitudes to escape the turbulence. Bill was no help at all.

Twenty miles from Florence and already behind the airplane, I heard an overnight express flight break off its ILS approach because it had encountered severe turbulence. I glanced at Bill, but he didn't seem concerned. A moment later I asked him to go over the ILS power settings and airspeeds with me. I had studied about flying a retractable plane with a constant-speed prop, but had only done it once—in an instrument simulator.

I was chasing the localizer a second later when I saw the airspeed drop suddenly to zero. In the bouncing aircraft, my mind went numb. I was in way over my head and I'd just lost an important instrument. I pointed at the useless gauge and asked Bill what to do. The outside air was plenty warm, so I knew the pitot hadn't iced up.

"Oh, there it goes again," Bill said with a knowing nod. "Just watch your power and pitch . . . you'll be fine." If I'd had a spare hand I would have slapped the guy, just to bring him into reality. But I was busy chasing the localizer again, and there was this persistent beeping coming from the overhead speaker. Those beeps . . . the outer marker!

I'd read somewhere that this was a good place to drop the gear, and I reached out and pulled the handle (still slippery from Bill's chicken grease). We were bouncing like crazy. I wasn't thinking about flying a pretty ILS anymore; I wasn't really even thinking about landing. I just wanted to survive. Bill as usual didn't seem concerned and offered absolutely no help. Jacksonville Center was monitoring our approach and vectoring the overnight express flight for another ILS. They asked about the ride, and I told them it was very bumpy and not getting any better.

I had nearly full down deflection on the glideslope and was about to miss the approach when we hit the sharpest turbulence I'd ever experienced. Bill's chicken bones flew from the back seat onto my approach plates, and I tossed them aside as I shoved the throttle full forward. I was about to pull up the gear handle when I saw lights coming up out of the rain and fog. We were breaking out of the clouds—thankfully!

By now I had full-scale deflection on both ILS needles, but I was still well above decision height. The lights below looked nothing like the airport, and my heart sank as I considered climbing back into the soup before I flew into something. A few seconds later, though, I saw the approach lights about a half-mile ahead and to my right. I slipped the plane hard toward the centerline, yanked on the flap handle, and somehow managed to cross the numbers and get safely onto the ground.

A few minutes later Bill stood by, eating potato chips as I tied down his airplane. He acted as if it had been just another routine night of flying. It was all I could do to control myself.

I stayed at the airport well after Bill had gotten into his car and driven off into the rain. It was past two in the morning, I was dog-tired and soaking wet, but I wanted to wait until the overnight express plane landed before I left. And I wanted to spend some time alone thinking about what had just happened.

Standing there in the rain, I realized how close I'd come to becoming a statistic, the front-page story in tomorrow's paper. "Pilot error," someone would be quoted as saying, and they'd be right.

I'd erred by flying a plane that had a history of maintenance problems. (No wonder Bill wanted a partner). I'd erred by flying a plane I was not qualified to operate, in weather that was well beyond my capabilities. I'd erred by making the exhausting six-hour round-trip after a full day at work. But most of all, I'd erred by climbing into an airplane with Bill, the kind of pilot who gives general aviation a bad reputation.

Bill may have been a lousy pilot, and his plane may have been in poor condition, but they both taught me a lot that night about how not to conduct myself. And even now, six years later, I still can't stand the smell of fried chicken.

A New Spin On Skydiving

ONE OF THE SKYLANES that I occasionally fly is owned by a local skydiving club. They call me in as a backup pilot on busy days when they need two airplanes. I was fully checked out by their flight instructor on procedures several years ago and have flown three or four times a year for them ever since.

When the call came to fly on this particular Sunday, I could hardly wait to get to the airport. It was a day made for pilots—CAVU and an eight-knot wind right down the 2,000-foot grass runway. What more could I ask for except a nice airplane to fly? I had that, too. I would be flying one of two Skylanes scheduled for that day. My trusted friend, Mark, a top-notch pilot, would be flying the other.

A front was expected to move through later that day so the jumpers were in a hurry to get into the air and make as many jumps as possible before the winds picked up. As I preflighted the airplane, I had a nervous feeling about the rush, so I took my time and did a particularly good job. I didn't want my passengers' impatience to affect my preflight judgment. I had only flown this particular airplane once before and it had just come back from the shop after having its engine removed for motor mount replacement and other maintenance. I satisfied myself that all of the vital fluids and functions of the machine were in order and that the mechanics had completed the job.

My mission changed at the last minute when a group of first-time jumpers arrived and boarded the Skylane I had just preflighted. Since Mark had more experience flying for this group, I ended up climbing into the Skylane he had just preflighted. The full rush was on and as I applied power for takeoff, I felt uneasy about not having preflighted the aircraft myself. At the same time, I realized that in our haste to depart, everyone in the aircraft knew what the jump plan called for except me.

Competing with the screaming engine, I shouted to the jump master, "What's the plan?" The answer came back in some skydiver acronym that I did not understand, but which ended with the words "one pass at 11,500 feet." So I took off and climbed to 11,500 feet, totally clueless about what would happen next. My biggest, and nearly fatal, mistake was allowing my passengers to decide on the plan, without my knowledge or input. At the time, I felt confident that the jump master would provide me with directions and I was certain I would have no problem with the airplane.

The first pass was perfect but had to be called off because of traffic below us. The second pass was rushed, like most of the flight. We were suddenly over the spot again. Still unaware that anything unusual was planned, I opened the door when the jump master called for it. Nothing I could have done that day would have ever prepared me for what would happen over the next few seconds.

Instructing me to "hold it at 70," the skydiver in charge of photography exited the aircraft and hung onto the sides of the aircraft, back besides the trailing edge of the flap. Another skydiver climbed into the door preparing to jump. I held the speed steady at 70 mph following the one and only instruction I had. Suddenly and without warning, the smooth air that had been my welcome friend was interrupted by one sharp jolt of turbulence. Boom! I watched in terror as the airspeed indicator went from a perfectly proud 70 mph to nearly 0. All the wind noise suddenly stopped, replaced by an eerie, blank kind of silence. The aircraft stalled sharply. The right wing started to drop towards the cameraman. Unless I somehow made the airplane turn left instead of right, I knew the airplane would hit the cameraman. A spin was most likely to follow from such a deep and sudden stall with all that weight on the wing. Nevertheless, I pushed full left rudder to move the tail and avoid hitting the cameraman. I succeeded, but my intentional kick of the rudder had put the airplane into a full spin to the left. Even though I knew it was bound to happen, I couldn't believe it. The next thing I saw was the ground spinning at us in a way that reminded me of a special flying lesson I once had from a bright, young flight instructor, Steve Boyer, during my private training.

Over the jump master's screams from the back of the spinning aircraft, I heard Steve Boyer calmly reciting the procedure that would save us from disaster: Power off. Full opposite rudder and coordinate ailerons. Stop the rotation. Apply mild back pressure and fly out of the dive *slowly*. If it does not work, you forgot something. Do it over until it works.

Once. Still spinning, Twice. Still spinning. The third time was the charm. Almost as suddenly as the spin started, I was at 4,500 feet in level flight. I slowly descended to pattern altitude to cool the engine and myself, thankful that the story had a happy ending.

I still don't know why my airspeed dropped so sharply that day. Clear air turbulence? Stuck indicator? Did the cameraman disrupt airflow over the top of the wings? I'll probably never really know for sure.

What did I learn about flying from that? First, never let anything happen to or in an aircraft you command that might affect its flight characteristics, unless you are fully prepared for and aware of all the potential consequences. Second, never let a passenger's rush turn into your emergency; protect passengers from themselves. Third, if you don't have a flight instructor as astute as Steve Boyer, find one with an aerobatic airplane and learn spin recovery properly. Thanks, Steve, wherever you are!

Switching On a Fuel Leak

THE RENO POLICE DEPARTMENT owns two Cessna aircraft, a 1979 Cessna 210 Centurion II and a 1977 Cessna 172 Skyhawk. Both aircraft have been turned over to the Police Department through the United States Drug and Customs Enforcement Units locally. The Department uses the airplanes mainly for prisoner transport. Our T210 was in the hangar for its annual inspection, and we had been renting airplanes from around Reno for a couple of weeks.

On July 7, 1994, we had scheduled a flight up to Grants Pass, Oregon, to pick up a medium-risk prisoner, and bring him back to Reno to stand trial. Since the prisoner was not a large person, and the distance was only a little less than two hours away, I decided to take the department's 172 rather than rent. The weather was just beautiful. We had been getting good VFR weather conditions for quite a while. My partner, Flight Officer Jack Wilsey, and I left early in the morning in an attempt to avoid the bumps that are almost always present during the afternoon hours around this part of the country. The flight up to Grants Pass was pleasant, and we remarked on how smooth it was, and how rare that the high pressure had remained for so long in the Pacific West. Mounts Lassen and Shasta in California are beautiful this time of the year with the tops still covered with snow.

We landed at Grants Pass at about 10:30 a.m. and refueled for the trip home. The Sheriff's Department delivered our prisoner to us at the airport, and by 11:30 a.m. we were airborne again headed for Reno.

We had noticed that it was a lot warmer than when we had come in, and the 172 didn't perform as well as we had hoped. I was glad that we hadn't completely topped off the gas tanks. We finally got to 9,500 feet msl, and before long were cruising happily on our way to Reno.

The return trip was taking a little longer than the first leg with the slight headwind that we were encountering. I was talking with Seattle Center who was providing us with flight following. I use this service whenever I can get it. You never know when you will encounter other traffic in your path, and I just like the idea of knowing that there is someone on the ground looking out for my best interests. Things were going smoothly and I began doing systems checks in the cockpit. I reached up on the pilot-side doorpost and turned on the map light switch. The light itself is also located on the doorpost on most Cessna 172 models. I noticed that nothing happened. I also heard a "snap." I couldn't see the light illuminate, and immediately turned it off. I commented to my partner, "a lot of good this light is, it doesn't even work." A few minutes later I began to smell a strong odor of aviation fuel. Then I noticed that there was a steady stream of liquid flowing from the switch area and down the doorpost. The odor of gas fumes was increasing and becoming almost unbearable. The prisoner commented, "Hey, I smell gas." I said, "Yeah, I know, we smell it too." I told myself, "We're in big trouble." I knew that we needed to do two things: one, land—now—and the other, turn off the master power switch. I really hated not being in contact with Center as I knew that they were our only contact with civilization. We were over the most hostile part of our trip: nothing below us but tall timbers and no roads. Then I remembered that we still had the portable handheld radio in the glove box. I squawked 7700 (emergency), and called Seattle Center. I told the Center operator that we had an emergency and that we needed to know where the closest airport was. He relayed that Fall River Mills was at our 12 o'clock at 15 miles. Then he asked what the problem was. We told him that we had fuel pouring in the cockpit and that we were going off radio and needed him to notify Fall River Mills to have fire equipment waiting for us. Our ETA was 15 minutes. He acknowledged. I felt a little better knowing that fire and ambulance personnel would be waiting just in case we needed it. Then the toughest decision: time to turn off the master switch. All I could think about was the small spark you get when you turn off the light switch at home. Would this be the spark that blows us into millions of pieces? I looked at Jack. Jack said, "I think we gotta to do it." "I know, but I don't want to," I said. I turned the master switch off . . . we were still there!

The next 10 minutes seemed like an hour. I had Jack get out the sectional chart and find the airport. There is a lot to be said for carrying a current sectional with you in your aircraft. Next step was to go over the emergency landing procedures. Although the Emergency Landing Checklist tells us to land with full flaps and as slow as possible, we now had no electrical power to run the flaps, so a no-flap landing was our plan.

As we approached the area of Fall River Mills, we used the sectional to pinpoint the exact location of the field. A short time later we had the field in sight, and began a slow descent to final. We used the handheld radio on the unicom frequency to contact the airport and advise them that we were on a base leg for Runway 20. I decreased the power, and was able to be at pattern altitude on the base leg. Turning final I noticed that the windsock was favoring the opposite runway. I pulled the power to idle, and slowed to final approach speed. I told my partner to unlock his door, and we both opened the doors just in case we needed to make a speedy exit. I looked up to the middle of the runway and saw the fire and ambulance rigs waiting midfield.

I was a bit concerned with the amount of fuel that was flowing down the door panel and onto the floor at my feet. I knew that it had to be going somewhere. It was either under the floor boards in the belly of the plane, or dripping out of the bottom onto the landing gear. No brakes, I thought, I don't want to heat them up and start a fire. Because of the slight tailwind I was a little fast. I knew that the 3,600-foot-long runway would give me plenty of room to get stopped without them. I touched down on the numbers, and rolled to a stop at the end. "Let's get out of here," Jack and I said at the same time. We unstrapped the prisoner, and pulled him out of the back seat. By then the fire truck had come up to our plane, and the firemen were pulling out their hoses. From a distance of 100 feet we could see the fuel pouring out the bottom of the plane's belly. We were standing there thanking God that we were not a fireball, when Robert Swarm approached us. Mr. Swarm told us that he was a mechanic, and that he heard our "mayday" over his scanner. He wanted to know if he could help. Mr. Swarm has been said to be one of the best aviation mechanics in this part of the country. We welcomed his assistance and advice. He checked the plane and looked at the panel that holds the light switch. He dismantled it, and then turned and looked at me. Then he looked at the firemen, who were standing in awe. The light switch had literally torched a hole through the fuel line that runs down the post from the left fuel tank. He said, "There's no reason that I can see why you guys are still here. You should have been a fireball when you hit that switch." He said that he had heard of this same thing occurring in the past, but no one was around to explain it. Then one of the firemen said, "There must have been four people on board your plane."

With the help of all the good people at Fall River Mills Airport, and Sgt. Rick Phay of the Shasta County Sheriff's Office, we were able to get our man back to Reno safely.

If you own, or fly, a late-model Cessna 172, and your map light switch has not been checked, I would encourage you to do so. You just never know when little things like what happened to us can make your day!

No Good Deed Goes Unpunished

I CONSIDER MYSELF A CONSERVATIVE, WELL-PREPARED PILOT and flight instructor. I'm not perfect, however, and I learned that I'm capable of making major mistakes in judgment. One beautiful clear day, I walked into my FBO/flight school where I was employed as a part-time instructor and former Part 135 pilot. The chief flight instructor and the owner of the FBO were talking and when I walked in, they both seemed excited and happy to see me. It seems that they needed someone qualified to make a trip as a right seat pilot with one of their best customers, an older gentleman who owned a Cessna 414.

Having just completed King Air C-90 training, I felt more than qualified to accompany this pilot on his trip. After all, I had an ATP rating and a multiengine flight instructor certificate. Who's better qualified than me? The fact that I had never been inside a C-414 didn't seem to enter the equation at all. I was told that I just had to sit in the right seat and help out the older pilot with the radios and navigation. It would be a 121 nautical mile trip from Islip, New York, to Albany, New York, with a short stay in Albany. The fact that the weather was severe clear helped to keep my mind at ease during the decision-making process.

After being introduced to the pilot/owner of the aircraft, we were walking out to the ramp and I had my first negative thought: "I have no weather briefing." I quickly rationalized it by assuming the chief flight instructor would never send me out without some knowledge of the weather himself. Besides, the pilot was an experienced aircraft owner; he would never fly into any dangerous weather. I put those thoughts aside, looked up at the clear blue sky and decided to involve myself in the preflight and get the show on the road.

My first surprise came immediately after takeoff. We were about 100 feet agl when the owner retracted the gear and said, "Your airplane." I took the controls and flew the airplane while asking a few pertinent questions: "What's Vy? What are the proper power settings?" Although things were going fine, I immediately felt one of those annoying knots in my gut. I don't like surprises, and this was a surprise. There was nothing mentioned in our brief discussions that I would be needed to actually fly this cabin-class twin. As soon as I had the airplane in a stabilized climb, the gentleman asked, "How was my takeoff?" I thought that was an unusual query from an experienced owner/pilot.

I was just starting to enjoy the flying aspect of this trip when I decided to call ahead and check the weather in Albany. Great news: ceiling 200 feet, sky obscured, visibility one-half mile in fog. Oh boy! As I wrote down the ATIS on my lapboard, I glanced over at the owner, and he seemed to be completely oblivious to the situation we were about to encounter. Secretly, I wished the ceiling and/or the visibility would deteriorate so that I didn't have to attempt the approach. I asked for and received the appropriate approach plates and made myself busy preparing for the inevitable ILS ahead. I still had no idea if he was planning on flying the approach or if he intended to have the autopilot coupled to the ILS or... if he wanted me to fly it.

As if he were a mind reader, he asked me if I was up to flying the ILS into Albany's Runway 1. I told him that I could handle it if he assisted me with the appropriate power settings on the huge turbocharged piston engines. Albany Approach proceeded to give us vectors for the approach, and I dutifully followed all instructions. I intercepted the localizer and the glideslope and started following both toward the runway. As I got below 1,000 feet agl, I started to drift slightly off the localizer and the glideslope. I asked the owner to look out the window and tell me when (if) he saw the runway environment. I reached decision height, he did not have the runway in sight and I immediately went to a missed approach.

We both decided that we would shoot the approach another time and see if it went any better. I was hoping that the ceiling would lift just 100 feet. I suggested that we couple the approach with the autopilot and allow the computer to fly the airplane more accurately than we could. This time I was looking out the window, and at decision height I saw approach lights; we disconnected the autopilot and I landed the airplane on the runway.

As we taxied to the ramp, I noticed that my body was shaking and I had perspired quite a bit. I knew that I just completed a dangerous and careless trip. I had been completely unprepared for this type of flying. The owner was happy to be in Albany, excused himself to conduct some business and left me alone to be with my thoughts for the next hour or two. As I replayed the whole scenario in my mind, I realized that I was almost a statistic. I have read enough NTSB reports to know how this would have played out if we had been just a little sloppier with the approach. The report would have read: "ATP pilot, multiengine flight instructor with zero hours in type, no preflight weather briefing," and it would have been unclear to the FAA and NTSB as to who was actually flying the "accident" airplane. I could not believe my own thoughts and actions. I have never flown out of the immediate area without a weather briefing. I chastised myself for getting into this airplane without asking the owner exactly what my role would be in this flight. I was really frightened that I allowed myself to be in this precarious position.

After beating myself up a bit, I spent the rest of the waiting time talking on the phone with flight service, preparing for the trip home. I told the owner that we needed a definite plan before we took off as to who would be flying and who would be communicating with ATC. Having settled that, the trip home was basically a non-event. I now have over 4,200 hours flight time logged, and this particular trip was one of my most memorable and certainly a turning point in my aviation experience.

The Devil is in the Details

ONE MEMORABLE FLIGHT that still makes me shudder when I think about it took place when I was a high-time student. I had bought an old Cessna 150 so I could get more practice at less cost. The Cessna provided that beautifully. Fuel was only 35 cents a gallon then, and I'd cruise at about 40 percent power, so I could fly for a dollar an hour. I wasn't going anywhere, so why hurry? Talk about cheap fun. I managed to log hundreds of hours before I got around to getting my license. The Cessna was well used: the paint was flaking off, the brakes were almost useless even after installing new brake pads three times a year. The gyros were fine for flying around the pea patch, but any serious instrument work really would be serious. And the radio... well, it didn't matter. I flew mostly from grass strips anyway. But what the airplane did, it did well. It flew almost by itself and cost less than my car to operate. But I was a fair-weather pilot. Any overcast would keep me on the ground, and thunderstorms made me hide altogether.

Then one day I had to go to Columbia, South Carolina, for a short business meeting. From my home base in Ohio it would be a one-day trip by Cessna. Being a student pilot, I told a friend of mine about it and he offered to ride shotgun with me—he held an instructor's rating and he'd go along just for pleasure. Before making the trip, I decided to have some work done on the airplane. I had the gyros looked at and had the always-marginal radio overhauled. Oh yes, new brake pads, too.

On departure day, the weather was gorgeous. The forecast called for "clear and unlimited" for the entire weekend, all the way to South Carolina. We took off and pointed south, following a VFR course I had plotted. It surprised me that I had no problems keeping precisely on course right to my destination. The last few miles, though, got my attention. A high wall of clouds stood right over Columbia! Only 10 miles from our airport I had to duck below clouds that were probably too low for legal flying. I could see the airport on the edge of fog, so I headed straight in, sort of, ignoring winds and any kind of pattern approach. The advancing cloud front pushed in tighter and lower, forcing a roundabout final—I approached flying low over the river and around a stadium to get to the runway. We were flying below building tops to get in, and when we landed fog moved across the airport before we could taxi to the tie-down area.

From that point on, things went downhill. The business meeting was a failure. The fog thickened until you could walk on it, so we found a motel and tried to sleep it off. The next morning, the fog thinned enough to see a few buildings around the airport, but the sky didn't deserve its name.

Finally, the clouds lifted to a minimum level, so we took off. But instead of the weather clearing to the north, it got worse. The weather report said 50 miles to clear skies, but after about 40 miles we found the ceiling lowering again. "Ten miles," we thought. "Only 10 miles to clear skies..." The ceiling had lowered only a few hundred feet in the first 40 miles, so we pressed on. But the ground was rising, too. We were approaching the Smoky Mountains.

At 50 miles, there was no sign of clearing. The ceiling wasn't down to just uncomfortable levels, it was down to illegal and extremely dangerous levels. The terrain kept rising, and we were down to 100 feet above ground level while skimming through a few tufts of cloud from the overcast. Suddenly, I saw a power line flash past about 10 feet below our wheels. That did it; I cranked the wheel over and yelled to my instructor buddy, "I'm going back." Unfortunately, when I banked the airplane around to the left, it put my buddy up on the right side looking up into solid white. It scared him and he commanded, "Let me have it."

"OK," I said. He took the wheel, but it headed us right back into the descending overcast. In seconds we were whited out completely and somewhere only a few feet below us a power line threatened.

My instructor panicked. "What do we do now?" he blurted rhetorically.

He pulled it up and I watched the airspeed go down to 70, 60, 50 and into the 40s. I looked at him and he was frozen on the control wheel, staring straight ahead at the blank windshield.

I yelled at him, but he didn't respond. Then I pounded his shoulder and pointed at the airspeed. He mechanically shoved the wheel forward but his mask didn't change. In a half minute, I noticed the speed building—120, 130, 140. But the weary old Cessna normally cruised at about 90! I pounded his shoulder again and pointed at the airspeed.

He responded woodenly, but he did pull it up—slowly. Then he pulled some more and the airspeed slid downward. Slowly, everything got away from him completely. He went too far each direction, and vertigo displaced any animal instinct he might have had. We porpoised through the fog, and the gyro horizon began falling off on one side then the other. I couldn't get the controls from him, but he couldn't fly either in that state of terror.

I shouted and I pounded on him and I pointed. He couldn't hear me, so I waved my hands back and forth, pointing at the horizon and the airspeed. It took 20 minutes of that waving and pounding to coax him up to a safe altitude. We finally broke out at 7,000 feet into deep blue skies and bright sunlight. Twenty-five miles ahead a lone hump of cloud rose from the rippled white sea below us. After 15 minutes, he calmed enough that I could take the controls from him.

Our VFR flight planning was a lost cause because we didn't have the slightest idea where we were and the world, for us, had disappeared. I flew a magnetic course of 335 degrees while our gyro compass wandered out west somewhere. It couldn't hold any setting more than a few minutes. The navcom radio never was very good; that's why I had it repaired before the flight. But now that I needed it, it was completely useless for nav or com. Why had I neglected to test it after the repairs? The airplane didn't have any such thing as an ADF, and GPS hadn't been invented yet. This was a 1950s airplane. People flew those things by the seat of their pants.

At least we had a magnetic compass and enough fuel to reach Ohio, if not our base airport. After four hours, we spotted an opening in the clouds, and I spiraled down through it. After lining up a few railroads and rivers, we found our position in northern Kentucky then quickly located an airport. Surprisingly, we were almost exactly on the course we planned. After a quick fill up we took off again and flew below the overcast at 1,500 feet all the way to our home base.

I never flew with my buddy again, and I never forgot the series of mistakes that led to the problems we had. What a place to get vertigo—just a few feet above the wires and approaching the Smoky Mountains, trying to sneak under an impossible overcastÉwith a panel that rated only slightly better than junk. If we had been smart we never would have landed at Columbia at the beginning. We'd have turned around and landed at another airport and bummed a ride to Columbia.

If we had been really smart, we wouldn't have made the flight at all. I had the radio repaired for that trip, but I took off without testing it. The gyros never were very good and they remained that way. In fact, the whole airplane was like a leaky rowboat.

Now I want everything to be perfect. And thinking of what happened to my buddy, I've become a strong believer in all the warning we hear about trusting the gauges. He was a good pilot with lots of experience and ratings, but he panicked and his mind switched off while his senses had a party. So I've tried to program myself to react automatically when an emergency strikes: the rules, the gauges, the routine!

Barry Ross

OUR OWN
WORST
ENEMIES

EVEN AFTER ALL THESE YEARS, I'm still a little surprised that pilots would use *I Learned About Flying From That* as a forum to confess what amount to some pretty boneheaded moves. Of course, it's easy to say that when you're not the one under the microscope. I mean, who among us hasn't done some boneheaded thing as a pilot, like leaving a baggage door open, trying to take off on one mag or taxiing out with a tie-down chain still attached? I won't say which ones I've done.

Although we pilots don't typically like to admit our blunders, it's important that we do, so other pilots can learn from our mistakes. So while it might be embarrassing to us personally, there's a public good to be gained by sharing our mistakes with our fellow aviators. There's also a selfish motive. Only when we're really honest with ourselves about the errors of our ways can we hope to mend them and stand a better chance of avoiding future mistakes. (You also might get published in *Flying*.)

One of the most humbling aspects of flying is that there's no seeming limit to the kinds of serious mistakes we might make. One reader tells the tale of going out for a spin in a Zlin and nearly buying the farm because he didn't know one simple fact about the airplane. Another tells the tale of coming in too low to a high desert airport at night, with nearly disastrous consequences. And yet another lucky contributor tells of getting behind a fast new airplane and "bungling" what should have been a routine instrument approach.

Two common denominators: Every one of these incidents could have been avoided if the pilots had known their airplanes better or had simply practiced a little more left-seat common sense.

But there's a more positive and perhaps more important message here too: Every one of the pilots demonstrated that even when things start going south in a hurry, quick, calm and methodical action can still save the day.

This is the longest chapter in the book, a fitting testament to the enduring position of poor pre-flight and in-flight decision making as one of the leading causes of accidents and, as we can see here, close calls.

Out For A Spin

FUNNY HOW AIRPLANES JUST SEEM TO KNOW when a pilot is feeling a little bit too comfortable . . . a bit too confident in his or her abilities. It is then that complacency sets in and an airplane is most likely to inflict a painful bite. In this particular case the bite was very nearly fatal.

I had been giving an aircraft familiarization flight to a new pilot with just a few hours of aerobatic experience. He seemed to be enjoying flying the new Zlin Z-242L immensely, and after a little instruction, was willing to try his hand at rolls, loops, hammerheads and spins. He commented more than once about the great control response in the airplane.

We had departed Palomar Airport for the aerobatic training area just northeast of San Diego Wild Animal Park, a flat, barren plateau overlooking the city of Escondido. After going over the normal spins, I decided to demonstrate an accelerated spin, which in this airplane is entered with full rudder and just enough back elevator to activate the stall horn. The result is a greatly increased rate of rotation and, in certain cases, the necessity for a non-standard recovery procedure.

On the previous day, while with another student, this same maneuver was demonstrated without incident. Today, however, the existing conditions weren't quite the same.

In order to safely demonstrate the accelerated spin, I felt it prudent to put some more air between my airplane and the earth, so I trimmed the elevator and rudder for a 75 KIAS climb to 7,500 msl. In my eagerness to get on with the demonstration of my "complete mastery" of the aircraft, an item on the "Before Aerobatic Flight" checklist was overlooked—"TRIM-Neutral." I was about to receive a terrifying lesson from the airplane about the importance of checklists and of being familiar with its flight manual.

We cleared the area of traffic around us and especially below us, and the airplane was pulled up slowly until, at the sound of the stall horn, the right rudder was applied. The nose came down smartly as the rotation began, slowly for the first revolution or so, and then rapidly building up to a rate significantly greater than that of a conventional spin.

My student sat there in the left seat silent and relaxed, the picture of composure. Apparently he was under the mistaken impression, as was I, that I had everything under control. By this time the earth was really spinning around and I decided he had gotten the full effect. So, after four revolutions, I initiated the standard recovery procedure: full rudder opposite direction of spin followed immediately by elevators full forward until the rotation stops, at which point controls are neutralized and the airplane is pulled out of the resulting dive. Had I bothered to read what the airplane flight manual said about "Delays in Spin Recovery," I would have know that this procedure was not going to get it done.

While waiting for the rotation to stop, it slowly dawned on me—the rotation has not stopped! I'm holding full spin recovery control inputs and nothing is happening! My companion continued to say nothing, just observing as I neutralized the controls and made second and third attempts at a normal spin recovery, each with no effect.

In the midst of my rising sense of terror I happened to look forward over the nose of the airplane to notice that the earth, although still whirling around in somewhat of a blur, had gotten a whole lot closer and bigger. Time and altitude were both running out.

There to the right, aft of the instrument panel, was the red handle which would, if pulled, release the canopy should the need arise to exit the airplane before landing. As I was reaching up to grab it, the thought occurred to me: Why not try pulling back on the stick? What the heck. . . I figured, "At this point, what do I have to lose?" Immediately I yanked back on the stick and stomped the rudder in the direction of the spin, and held them. In an instant, the rotation slowed and the nose came up just a bit. Out of desperation and for the fourth time, I initiated the normal spin recovery procedure. The airplane, as if to say "What were you waiting for?" popped out of the spin and we were once again back in the realm of controlled flight.

The airplane recovered at about 3,500 feet msl with no more than 1,500 feet between us and the ground, having lost more than 4,000 feet and having completed no less than 12 spin rotations. In retrospect I'm glad we didn't jump, because a beautiful airplane would have been lost, but mainly because I had waited too long and we were much too low. I think the military refers to it as "outside the safe ejection envelope."

A call to the Zlin factory in Canada confirmed my errors. A factory test pilot informed me that, prior to spin entry, the elevator and rudder trim must be neutral. This particular spin was entered to the right, in the same direction as the rudder trim, with the elevator still trimmed for a 75-knot climb. Had the trim been set properly, as it had on the previous day's flight, the elevator and rudder would have had more authority to overcome the accelerated spin rotation.

As it turned out, my nearly-too-late application of full back elevator to slow the spin was precisely what was called for. An exact quote from the Zlin Z-242L flight manual reads as follows for delays in spin recovery: "Return the elevator and rudder control to the position corresponding to the spin entry."

So, through the process of elimination and at almost the last possible moment, I more or less blindly stumbled onto the correct procedure to save myself, my student, and my airplane from my own ignorance. If I had only taken the time to read the airplane flight manual more closely, an otherwise enjoyable flight would not have ended in near-catastrophe.

Pay Attention to How Autopilots Work

J. MAC MCCLELLAN, editor-in-chief of *Flying* magazine wrote in his May, 2003 editorial, ". . . most new instructors come out of a system that teaches them in the cheapest-to-fly, thus least-well-equipped, airplanes, so they don't have a chance to learn to use complex avionics, much less teach others." I found out he was right, the hard way.

On a recent Saturday night I took off with my CFI-I from Palm Springs (KPSP) toward Thermal (KTRM) to practice a VOR holding pattern. On the way out, my instructor asked if he could turn on and use the autopilot. The flight school has several Cessna 172 airplanes but only this one was equipped with a two-axis autopilot. I responded, "No, don't use it." "OK," he said, dejectedly.

After completing the lesson and on the way back to KPSP, while still under the hood and beginning the descent, I noticed in my peripheral vision that the instructor was fiddling with the avionics at the bottom of the radio stack. About 10 or 20 seconds later there were several loud beeps, then the airplane rapidly pitched up and decelerated.

At first I thought the instructor was pulling his yoke. I looked over and he wasn't touching it. I then saw the trim wheel rolling by itself until it stopped at full nose-up position. I pushed as hard as I could on my yoke and immediately applied full throttle and full-rich mixture. I glanced at the airspeed indicator, which read 80 knots and falling. I yelled, "Turn it off, TURN IT OFF!" "I'm trying," he replied.

I pressed the little button on my yoke that was right behind the electric trim rocker switch (not the push-to-talk switch, of course), but nothing seemed to happen. "Where's the autopilot circuit breaker," I asked while I began looking down at the row of white buttons. The labels were all so small, the lighting so dim, and I was pushing extremely hard with both arms on my yoke. I couldn't read any of the labels. Neither of his hands was on his yoke. As I removed one hand from my yoke and reached for the master switch, the Cessna's nose-high pitch increased even more. As I was about to push the master switch off, he said he had just turned off the autopilot. Next I noticed he was manually rolling the trim wheel forward.

My yoke was now easier to push, and we began to level off and gain airspeed. I never heard the stall warning horn, so I suppose the airspeed was at least a few knots greater than the stall warning horn airspeed, but not by much I'm certain. The entire sequence of events transpired in perhaps 10 to 15 seconds. While on final, my now ex-instructor commented that he would not charge me for this lesson.

I now know that the CFI-I had engaged the autopilot without advising me. He may have selected altitude hold mode, but that wasn't the source of the problem. The loud beeps sounded after I began my descent and was 200 feet below the preselected altitude. As I pushed forward on the wheel to descend, the autopilot then did what it was supposed to: It interpreted my control inputs as a need for nose-up trim and began to roll the trim in that direction until it commanded full nose-up trim. Pressing the disconnect button on my yoke indeed disengaged the autopilot, but by that time the airplane's trim was already positioned maximum nose up, and the airplane's attitude followed. Hunting for the circuit breaker was unnecessary at that point, as would have been turning off the master or avionics master switch because the autopilot pitch servo has very little power and I could have easily pushed against its maximum force. But the trim tab has lots of authority, and it took my best efforts to overcome its forces pushing the trailing edge of the elevator up. The real recovery came only after the CFI-I began to manually roll the trim wheel forward.

I have now learned that any time an autopilot with pitch axis control is engaged—that is turned on—the automatic pitch trim will run opposite any force applied to the elevator controls. In order to fly the airplane with the comparatively little strength available from the pitch servo, the autopilot must keep the airplane in trim. But the autopilot has no way of knowing if normal air loads are applying the force on the elevator controls or if the human pilot is pushing or pulling. The rule is that only one pilot—the automatic one or the human—can fly the airplane at the same time. Whenever a two-axis autopilot is engaged, don't push or pull on the control wheel or you will end up fighting a big trim force that keeps on increasing until the trim system reaches its limits.

Ironically this maximum out-of-trim event was an excellent learning experience. Unless a pilot takes immediate action to correct the out-of-trim condition (regardless of the cause), loss of control may quickly ensue. I later learned that I should have immediately pushed and held the autopilot disconnect switch on the wheel to stop the automatic trim from running. I also could have reached over and stopped the trim wheel from moving because it, too, has a slip clutch between the servo and the cables, and it's easy to overpower the clutch. With my thumb on the disconnect/trim interrupt button on the wheel I could have rolled the trim back nose-down and the forces on the control yoke would have gone away. Adding full power was instinctive but unnecessary and even added a little to my workload because a power increase naturally lifts the nose when I wanted it to stay down. And, finally, I could have banked the airplane because any airplane's nose naturally falls in a turn and that would have helped relieve the push forces on the wheel.

My instructor knew none of this, because if he had, he wouldn't have engaged the autopilot while I was hand flying. I learned that understanding how autopilots work is as important as mastering all other phases of flight on my way to becoming a proficient instrument pilot.

Stalls Can Lead to a Spin Surprise

BEFORE I TOOK MY PRIVATE CHECK RIDE, my instructor gave me spin training in a Cessna 172 over Lake Tahoe. The Skyhawk was very difficult to spin—it took several tries to find the right combination of accelerated stall and hard rudder to kick it over. We did three spins. My only other spin training had been many years earlier, when an instructor had shown me spin recovery in a glider.

Now I had 275 hours in my log and hadn't done a stall in over a year. I took a Cessna 182 out over the Sierra Valley for some brush-up proficiency flying. I did some touch-and-goes at Sierraville, a short narrow strip with hills at both ends, then climbed to 8,500 feet (about 4,500 agl) for some stalls.

I set up an approach configuration, 20 inches at 2,000 rpm, and trimmed for 90 knots, basically what I'd use for the turn to downwind. Holding level altitude, I did a gradual, slow stall, keeping the ball centered and the wings level. The break was clean, slow and straight, and the plane actually gained altitude, returning to straight-and-level, on the original heading, about 200 feet above the original cruise.

That was pretty benign, I thought. Now what would happen if distraction or a near-midair in the pattern caused me to pull up more quickly?

I tried it, pulling back the yoke more briskly. The nose pointed up. It took some heavy right rudder to keep the ball centered and the wings level. The airspeed indicator dropped off the scale before the stall horn sounded, but the nose kept going up. When the wing finally stopped flying, it dropped off sharply to the left and into a nose-down left spin.

"This is a spin," I said out loud, in some surprise. At the same time, I found myself doing a bunch of things pretty much automatically: I pulled the throttle back, then neutralized the ailerons, pushed the yoke forward and applied right rudder. The spin stopped after about half a turn. I was still flying, but diving. The wings were level, so I eased the yoke back and leveled out at 7,500 feet, 3,500 agl, heading due south. I put in 24 inches of throttle and there we were, cruising at 135 knots, nice as can be.

I had lost 1,000 feet in half a turn. If I'd been at pattern altitude, I'd be dead. I stared at the placard on the panel: NO SPINS, it said. Sweating, I flew back to Truckee, landed smoothly enough, and hangared the airplane. A walk around showed no wrinkles or bends in the skin.

I called my instructor to tell him about the inadvertent spin. "The deck angle was so high it felt almost like a hammerhead stall," I said. "I had the impression the airplane was almost spin-proof."

"You did an accelerated stall with the nose high. It's a good thing you had altitude," he said.

It was an attitude I would certainly never approach in "normal" flight, nor will I simply haul back on the yoke again, in any airplane, with the power instruments pointed to green arcs—unless I'm with an aerobatic instructor and wearing a chute.

I'm glad I knew what to do when the spin started. I'm glad I had the sense to climb before practicing stalls. I'm glad I was in a tough airplane. And I was glad to back the plane into its hangar none the worse for the lesson.

The other plane I fly regularly is a Grumman Tiger, a short-coupled sports car with a reputation for terminal behavior in spins. I've stalled the Tiger (it mushes smoothly, straight ahead), but I'll never yank it by the tail.

Displaced Confidence

I **HAVE BEEN FLYING FOR 22 YEARS,** and pride myself on being an outstanding pilot with an unblemished record. I hate having to tell this story.

My wife, three children and I wanted to visit Santa Fe, to visit some old friends who had named a son for me. We knew that our friends would be leaving the next day, so it was important to arrive Wednesday evening to be able to have dinner with them.

All I had scheduled that morning was to accompany a client to a Planning Commission hearing, and we were the first item at 9:30 a.m. That would allow enough time to leave by 1:00 p.m., completing the flight in daylight. But the Commission took another matter first, and we did not finish until about 2:30 p.m. I packed quickly and left for the airport. During the day, I had called our mechanic to remind him that we continued to have an intermittent, occasional alternator-out indication. He had left a cheerful message with my secretary that it was no problem, just don't fly at night. Now, the whole trip was to be at night. I considered doing the flight with minimum electrical devices on. After all, I'd be out over the desert most of the time, and wouldn't need many lights.

But past flying experiences helped me make a good decision. Even though I knew it could force me to scrub the trip, I had him remove the alternator to check the alternator clutch. As it happened, the clutch was not the problem, and eventually, one and a half hours later, we found a frayed alternator wire that had been troubling us for months. At 6:30 p.m. we took off from Santa Barbara, California. I have about 350 nighttime hours, and was very comfortable with night flight.

We picked up our son in Upland, took off immediately, and flew under the overcast through the Banning Pass to Palm Springs. Turning northwest, we climbed in the clear toward Twenty-Nine Palms and the open desert. The hours passed quickly as the family napped in the rear, and I chatted with my son in the copilot's seat about his college options.

The trip to Santa Fe flight planned at just about the total fuel my Bonanza A36 carried. With the nice tailwind I had, I thought I would be able to make it with the fuel on board. But I made the prudent decision to stop for fuel and thought we'd grab a bite to eat at the same time. Winslow, Arizona, was directly en route and had been our planned daytime stop.

Ten minutes before touchdown I called Prescott Radio, and obtained the Winslow wind and altimeter. Wind was out of the southwest, and favored Runway 22. I took a quick look at the airport diagram, and planned—as I always like to do at an unfamiliar airport—a standard downwind, base and final approach. I always shoot right for the numbers, feeling that a good, short landing shows control over the plane. I feel I am being sloppy if I land long or hot, float down the runway, and touch down thousands of feet past the threshold. It shows no skill. What if I ever need to land short and have no practice?

Abeam of the numbers, I was 1,500 above the runway—a little high because I was trying to avoid shock-cooling the engine by too-rapid power reduction. But I figured if I put on full flaps and dropped the gear, we would descend in time. I broadcast my position to the nonexistent nighttime traffic as I entered downwind, turned base and final. On final, chatting with my son, I flipped on the landing light, and adjusted the intensity of the PCL runway lights by clicking the mic.

About five seconds before touchdown I saw treetops below me in the landing light. "What are trees doing in the approach path?" I thought. They were some 20 feet below, but much too close for night flying. I raised the nose a bit and started to add a touch of power.

Suddenly, we hit something. I was stunned! I couldn't believe that I'd hit the tops of the trees; they were definitely below. How could it be? I'd already been applying power; now I hit full throttle, tried to stabilize the yawing aircraft, maintained control, carefully underreacting. As I flew down the runway, I made sure the wings were level, that I was climbing, that the plane was flyable. I raised the flaps, and remember consciously checking the artificial horizon as I flew into the desert blackness with no horizontal reference, and thinking, "I'm glad I'm instrument-rated. This is where a lot of pilots might lose it."

Stable and climbing, I raised the gear to improve rate of climb. Warning horns went off, and the three green lights continued to glow. The gear was jammed! I must be dragging a branch. "Is it bad?" my son asked. "This is very serious," I told him.

I gradually circled back to prepare for landing, only to encounter a new problem. I couldn't find the airport! I had learned how hard it is to see airports at night from directly above, and figured that I had just overflown it to the point at which it was difficult to see the runway. So I circled again, taking a wider radius, and again attempted to enter downwind. But I still couldn't find the airport! Although I thought I was completely calm, I wondered out loud if I was so rattled that I couldn't see the obvious. I knew where it was in relation to the town, and the RNAV was set for the airport. But it wasn't there. What was happening? What would I do if I couldn't find the airport? For the first time, I started to get nervous.

As I flew directly above what I thought should be the approach end, I saw three or four flashing red lights. With shock, I realized that I hadn't hit the trees at all. I had struck power lines—as I later learned, 12,400-volt main transmission lines—taking out all the airport lights and about one-third of the lights of Winslow. The emergency trucks were looking for us on the ground.

With this revelation, I realized that I could see the runway in the dark, and briefly considered landing without runway lights. Again, I made a good decision. I put on the autopilot, verified that it was flying the plane correctly, asked my son to watch for traffic, and got out maps. Flagstaff was only 44 nm away—only 20 minutes. Even though I hated to continue to fly a possibly disabled aircraft, the plane was climbing nicely, I had well over an hour of fuel, and I thought Flagstaff would have lighting and emergency vehicles. After many unanswered radio calls, I finally reached Prescott Radio, told them the problem, my intentions, my name, and the identity of my four family members on board. That scared my son, listening on the intercom.

As we neared Flagstaff I handed my son the fire extinguisher, and showed him how to use it. I also reviewed the door opening procedure, and briefed my wife and twins in the back on opening the rear door. My wife had the presence of mind to have everyone in the rear put their shoes and warm jackets back on. As I switched to the CTAF, the crash trucks called to say that they were ready for us, and added that they had the capability of checking the landing gear on a fly-by. I declined; I didn't want to fly the damaged plane any more than necessary, and I figured that there was nothing that would change the plan. No matter what they told me, I would still land.

I decided to fly over the runway at a little higher speed than normal, to see if I was dragging a cable. Then if everything seemed normal, I'd slow down and land. The approach was fine; I took comfort in the three green glowing lights. The plane handled fine at 90 knots, so I slowed to 80, 75, and lowered gently. The left wheel touched down, the nosewheel, and then a loud, scraping noise as the right wing dropped low. Something was wrong with the right gear.

The plane began to slide to the right side of the runway, but I found that with just a little braking on the left main I could keep it on the runway. I decided to use the minimum braking possible, allowing the plane to drift all the way to the right edge of the runway as it slowed down, to avoid overbraking and possibly spinning or cartwheeling the aircraft.

My family was calm and ready, and within five seconds we had opened the doors and jumped out, as the crash trucks circled us and sprayed foam and water. But there was no need. The landing, in the end, had been smooth and controlled.

Examining the plane in the headlights of the emergency trucks, we saw the problem. We had lost a wheel at Winslow. But we were amazed to see that with the exception of the missing gear and damaged gear door, which showed the arc of an electrical cable, the plane had no apparent damage. We had landed on the left main, nose gear and right strut. As the plane came to a final stop, and the tail lowered, the passenger step prevented the tail from touching. There was no skin damage. Though close to the ground, neither the wings nor the tail had touched. In the glow of the truck lights, the mechanic speculated that we might be able to replace the right main and be flying within a few days.

But he was wrong. Examining the plane next morning in the good light of the hangar, we could see a very small crimp in the right aileron, and a very subtle buckling of the thin skin leading from the wheel, back to the right rear aileron. The stress of the wire strike or the abrasion of the landing stressed the wing enough to deform the skin.

The next day, returning to Winslow by car, we met the airport manager, who was carrying our wheel in his pick-up. The wires had struck the scissor joint just below the upper hinge, snapping it. The compression in the strut then forced the unrestrained wheel assembly out, leaving it apparently undamaged in the approach path.

The wires we struck stretched between two telephone poles directly in the approach path. They were unlighted, and uncharted. I was shocked to see how relatively low they were. But when I examined the airport diagram in my Jepp book the picture came clear. Runway 22 has a displaced threshold of about 1,000 yards. I have landed at a number of airports with displaced thresholds, and have noticed that the pre-threshold portion of the runway is often rougher and less well maintained. I always just assumed that the threshold was displaced either for noise abatement reasons, or because it was not surfaced as well. But looking at Winslow I realized there is a third reason. A displaced threshold is used when the airport does not have normal clearance in the approach zone leading to the beginning of the paved runway. Rather than clear the approach zone, the airport declares the beginning to be farther down the runway.

When I first called the airport the next morning, I told the young man who answered that I was the pilot who had come in the night before. "Yeah," he said. "I found out about it in my hot tub at home when the lights went out." But he also told me that the airport had been having trouble with the VASI, and that it had been inoperable that night. I later confirmed that the VASI has a separate receiver for mic clicks, and that it had failed during the night. It had not been reported until the following morning.

As with so many incidents I have read about on this page, the lessons are manifold. I tried to land at Winslow because it was right on my route, avoiding what I assumed would be a delay of flying to a bigger airport, slightly off course. But in reality, Flagstaff would have saved time, because unlike Winslow, it was attended at that hour. We could have fueled and had dinner quickly.

Approaching an unfamiliar, 5,000-foot-high airport at night, I should have avoided all conversation, and been more concerned about danger. Desert airports don't seem high, because there are no high mountains around them. I underestimated the sink rate from my high downwind, started at 7,500 feet. Of course, I should have used a nice, steep approach. There was plenty of runway, and what you can't see can hurt you. And I should have been more knowledgeable about airport lighting. There was so much information on the chart that I did not see or understand—the small displaced threshold symbol; footnote 2, after "MIRL" under Runway 22, stating "Southwest 6240' only."

But I did some things right as well. I had learned the importance of a careful preflight inspection. Despite my very strong desire to get to Santa Fe to have dinner with our friends, I did not leave until the electrical system was repaired. The plane was otherwise in perfect working order, I was current on IFR and night flights. We had called our friends and told them to forget about dinner, so we would not feel pressed. As a result, when it was most important, I was calm and relaxed. I was able to calmly choose to land at Flagstaff, and had plenty of fuel to go around or circle if necessary. The approach at Winslow was too low, of course, but the aircraft was otherwise in perfect landing configuration.

Twenty-two years ago, when the Flight Examiner handed me my pilot's license, he looked at me sternly and told me that he was handing me a license to learn. I take some comfort in the thought that good pilots are not those who never err, but those who keep learning.

Unacquainted with the Autopilot

FIFTEEN YEARS AGO, I was asked to fly an old Queen Air from Florida to Puerto Rico for a friend. When I arrived in Florida the day before the trip I thought that I should give the old bird a short hop around the patch to check it out. I had limited experience with autopilots. A friend of mine asked to ride along, which was okay with me.

As we taxied out and went through the runup, things were fine. I ignored the autopilot as always. The takeoff went well and the old bird performed as expected. We climbed out to about 5,000 feet and played with props and power settings. I gave the Queen Air a good checkout, and the old bird checked out as I was told it would. So, after about an hour I headed for home port. For some reason as we were flying back I had the urge to turn the autopilot on. Which I did (first mistake). At first the autopilot worked perfectly. First a left bank, then right, then I set the heading bug for dead ahead to the airport and we settled into a little idle conversation. With no warning the Queen Air nosed over. I had not touched anything.

So I took hold of the yoke and applied back pressure. The more I applied, the more nose-over we became. By now my passenger (who is a pilot also) was pulling on the yoke too, trying to help, to no avail. I had no idea about how the autopilot system worked. All I knew was that I was in trouble and needed to do something fast. My airspeed was climbing and I was looking at a part of Florida that I would rather be looking at out the side window.

How and just why I'll never know, but I caught a glimpse of the trim running wild nose-down. I told my now-copilot to disconnect the autopilot as I reached for the trim to try and stop it. The autopilot was turned off but the trim was still trying to run. Not until my friend unplugged the monster and I re-trimmed by hand did we gain control of the airplane. When we finally leveled off, we were only about 500 feet above terra firma. I'm sure I don't need to tell you just what had been scared out of me and my friend.

The rest of the trip back was uneventful. When we were back on the ground I inquired about the autopilot. Not a soul knew how it worked or anything about it. But I didn't give up. I found an old salt who knew autopilot systems inside and out and got a very well-needed ground school. I learned that the pitch trim is the most powerful force an autopilot can muster and that if you pull or push the control wheel against the movements of the autopilot the trim will run in the opposite direction. The autopilot itself can't overpower the weakest pilot, but if allowed to run away, the pitch trim can't be overcome by the strongest pilot.

I was very lucky; had my friend not been with me that day, I don't think that I would be here now. I bet there are a lot of pilots who don't have a clue about the real workings of autopilots, let alone how to preflight one or to identify a trim runaway. Now I make sure that I understand everything there is to know about the autopilot I am flying.

Fast Mooney Leaves Its Pilot Behind

IWAS LOOKING FORWARD TO THE FLIGHT. After an afternoon of ice fishing with my family on Lake Of The Woods, I looked out of the ice shack at the salmon-colored sunset. Far in the distance, the snow-track vehicle trundled around ice heaves and snowdrifts to pick us up. It might as well have been a half-track on the surface of the Sahara desert. We'd caught enough jumbo perch for a nice gourmet meal.

I called for my briefing one hour prior to the flight, which would go from Baudette Airport to Anoka County. The route would take us over the desolate bogs and heavily wooded areas of northern Minnesota, ending under the Class B air space of Minneapolis. The briefer told me it would be a good flight with a terminal forecast in the Minneapolis area of 25,000 thin overcast, visibility eight to 10 with light and variable surface winds. There was a chance of six miles visibility with occasional ceilings of 6,500. I was assured of a tailwind up high. I filed an IFR plan.

My new Mooney TLS was waiting on the Baudette ramp, fueled and with the Tannis heater plugged in for the –20° surface temps. I planned one hour for the 222-nm flight with a 30-knot tailwind, figuring a true airspeed of 190 knots at 9,000 feet. I had flown the TLS about 40 hours and I was becoming comfortable with its sophisticated navigation features and complex flight systems. I ordered the plane with almost every conceivable avionics option since I enjoyed instrument flying. The plane it replaced was also a complex IFR platform, but cruised 50 knots slower.

Level at 9,000 feet, my airspeed was 195 knots true, the GPS showing 227 knots groundspeed. My face was frozen in a grin as I gazed over the jewel-like lights of the panel. The boys fell asleep in the back seat.

About 60 miles out, the vertical guidance in the GPS suggested descending. I received a 4,000-foot clearance from ATC. Monitoring ATIS at Minneapolis Crystal, I was still told 25,000 thin broken, 10 miles visibility. As we rocketed into the Minneapolis area, the bright orange glow of the metro area was completely absent. I was still certain of a visual approach but suddenly the aircraft was in a black cocoon of solid night IMC. Only 30 miles out, I was not set up for an approach. The GPS showed nine minutes estimated time en route remaining. I fumbled to get out the approach plates.

By now I had backed the manifold pressure gradually from 34 to 24 inches, but the high-powered Mooney was still indicating 160 knots and chewing up ground at nearly 200 knots. Quickly I dialed the initial approach fix Aadco in the RNAV computer for the RNAV 17 approach. I had done this approach several times before, but never in true night IMC. I received vectors to Aadco from Minneapolis Approach and indication that much of the Twin Cities was IMC. Temperatures and dew points were close together. I was held up at 4,000 feet due to traffic. Seven miles from Aadco I was cleared for the approach and 3,000 feet. Switching the RNAV computer to the approach mode I simultaneously deployed the speedbrakes. I backed the manifold pressure down to 20 inches, set the autopilot heading bug for intercept and engaged the approach capture mode. I was doing four things at once. I now made the mistake of twisting the inbound course on the HSI arrow to 165 degrees instead of 175. I was just beginning my pre-landing check.

Suddenly the approach controller told me I was beyond Aadco and to verify my position. Dumbfounded, I glanced at the RNAV distance indication and noted .6 miles but counting *up*!

The fast-moving airplane had quickly gotten ahead of me. It is amazing how rattled you get when something goes wrong. I disconnected the autopilot and turned inbound. The controller verified that I was coming back onto course and offered to take me around again or vector me to the VOR 8 approach at my discretion. Instead, I tried salvaging the approach. I punched in the "direct to" function on the GPS, something I should have set up well in advance. I found myself doing a lot of staring at the attitude indicator due to my overcontrolling. With my nervousness I pulled the throttle back to 10 inches, and to add to the confusion the gear warning horn started blaring. The course-deviation needle on the HSI went full-scale. I had blown it.

Suddenly we were out of the clouds in VFR conditions with some haze. When you become visual it is easy to forget you are flying an instrument approach, and technically a missed approach. My wife thought she saw the airport and I instinctively turned the aircraft where she pointed. Glancing back at the navaids we were now nearly 20 degrees off course and only three miles out. ATC called back wondering why I was performing all the S-turns and if I was truly visual with the airport. It is amazing how invisible an airport is at night when you are off course. Finally, I did have the runway-end identifier strobes in sight. ATC told me to cancel on the ground. Frustrated and embarrassed, I kicked the rudder in a base-to-final turn and felt the plane mush and shudder a little. If it wasn't for my 100-knot airspeed, I would have been a typical pattern stall statistic. I dropped gear and flaps and the airplane slowed quickly, the gentle landing belying the horrible approach.

After canceling on the ground, I thanked the controller and explained my bungling. Shaken, I went over the checklist and found that we had landed with speedbrakes up and no landing lights!

No matter how sophisticated and wonderful an airplane is, it is only as good as its pilot. Instrument situations certainly call for a high degree of both mental and mechanical preparation. Weather can deteriorate rapidly and a fast, sophisticated airplane can bite you squarely in the butt. As if to underscore the night's events, the next day's news told of four people who died in a crash south of the Minneapolis area in the same sudden IMC conditions that I encountered.

Stealth Bonanza

I WAS WORKING AS A NEW FLIGHT INSTRUCTOR at what was then Orange County Airport in southern California. With five months of instructing and a grand total of 800 hours, I considered myself a real pilot. And as a real pilot, I should be able to hop into any airplane and know how to fly it the very first time. After all, that's how it was done in the movies.

It was a beautiful November afternoon when the boss asked me to take a couple of employees to LAX to catch an airline flight. He generously told me to take the Baron, a prospect that positively set me to drooling. However, I made the one good decision of the day when I confessed that I had never flown a Baron and I had a grand total of 10 hours multiengine time from when I did the rating last year. My boss was very understanding and suggested I take the Bonanza instead. I had never flown a Bonanza, but how hard could it be? It only had one engine and one set of systems to worry about and it was only a 10-minute flight. And I didn't want to turn down my boss a second time.

This airplane was on the sales line and had been sitting for some time. As a result, the battery was dead. While the battery was being recharged, I looked for the operator's manual and a checklist and couldn't find either one in the cockpit or the office. I decided to go anyway. Jim, one of the FBO's employees who was building time and working on his commercial license, decided to come along. We loaded our two passengers into the back, Jim in the left front seat and I on the right for an uneventful ride to LAX.

LAX is shaped like the letter "H" with two sets of parallel east-west runways and a north-south taxiway connecting the two across the middle. Back in those days, a large mobile home type building served as the commuter terminal and was located on that taxiway. Jim and I dropped off our passengers there and did a quick preflight for the trip home. The battery was dead again. There was a start cart available from one of the commuter airlines, but the lineman had to work a flight first and we had to wait. By the time the commuter taxied out and we got a jump from the start cart it was dark. I got our clearance and, as we taxied out, started getting all the radios set up, interior and exterior lights on and turned on the landing light. The airplane went completely dark as the electrical system failed on us. I cursed the fact that I didn't have a flashlight with me and started recycling circuit breakers in the dark. With some luck, I restored the electrical system. This time I left the landing lights off and used only one radio to minimize the load on the system.

We were quickly cleared for takeoff and launched midfield from the south complex. I selected gear up and the lights dimmed momentarily then went dark as the electrical system failed again. We were now in the middle of the world's busiest airspace with no lights, transponder or radios and the landing gear in the halfway retracted position.

First things first. Our clearance was to maintain runway heading to the coastline, then a left turn to exit the TCA. We flew our clearance and continued south, staying just off the coast to avoid traffic over Torrance and Long Beach. While Jim flew, I searched the floor around our seats for the gear handle and finally found it behind my seat. With the gear halfway up, I couldn't tell which way to crank to put the gear down. The handle moved just as easily in both directions, so I took a guess and started cranking it clockwise. It was very awkward to crank a handle that was behind my seat so I took the controls and Jim cranked the gear clockwise to the limit. It was a dark night but there was enough glow from the city lights off our left wing to dimly illuminate some of the gauges. After cranking the gear, Jim and I were concerned that we had cranked it up because we did not see a decrease in airspeed.

It was my habit to have charts and approach plates on my lap, with a clipboard and other papers sandwiched between my hip and the door. These promptly exited the airplane when my door popped open. Fortunately, we did not need to depend on charts since it was VFR and we were flying to my home airport. I started recycling circuit breakers again and restored the electrical system once more. This time, the only piece of equipment we powered was one radio. I left the lights and transponder off and I definitely was not going to touch the gear handle.

Crossing the coast at Huntington Beach, I contacted the tower and asked for a flyby so they could confirm the landing gear was in the down position. This was approved and they confirmed the gear was in fact retracted. We headed back out over the coast again as we cranked the gear down. I'll never forget; it took 54 turns *counterclockwise* to lower the gear. We reentered the pattern and made an uneventful landing. As we turned off the runway fire trucks with lights flashing formed a conga line and followed us all the way to the FBO. The final insult of the evening was that I could not open the door that had popped open in flight. Struggling with the handle in the dark and totally flustered at this point, we had to be freed by my boss.

Every accident and near accident has a chain of events leading up to it. The first link in this debacle was my attitude. It was unrealistic to expect that I could fly any airplane without any familiarization. The next link was my decision to take the Bonanza, an airplane I was totally unfamiliar with. I should have insisted on taking an aircraft I was experienced and current in. I compounded the stupidity of this decision by going without any operational information, manual or checklist. The next link in the chain was my reluctance to turn down my boss twice in a row. Refusing the Baron was my only smart decision of the afternoon; I should have taken the initiative and suggested another airplane to him. Finally, I learned to always carry a flashlight. I was expecting to complete this trip in daylight and did not bring one. If we had one, we would have seen the mechanical gear indicator flag on the floor at the base of the console and known whether the gear was up or down. Now I always carry a flashlight, day or night, and fly only airplanes I've been checked out in.

I Was Just Plane Lucky

I **WAS AN F-18 INSTRUCTOR PILOT** when I became friends with a fellow officer who owned an S1S Pitts Special. We became good friends and he asked me if I would be interested in forming a partnership in the little acrobatic biplane. I had never flown a Pitts (or any taildragger) and welcomed the opportunity to fly it.

The first thing I needed was a checkout in a taildragger. With a little asking around, I located an older gentleman who owned a Stearman and had taught crop dusting for many years. I recall a thorough briefing on the finer points of handling a taildragger and then getting into the backseat. It was quite a contrast to what I was flying professionally. There wasn't much in the way of instruments and it had no intercom system. He passed notes to me. It was pretty humbling trying to land without seeing anything but sky and the top of the fellow's head in front of me.

We did 17 roll-and-goes, and toward the end I started to get the hang of it. Just full-stall landings, keeping the stick in your lap and the same amount of pavement on either side during the roll-out.

The next day I took the single-seat Pitts up. The principles were the same, although everything happened a lot faster. I spent the first few hops in the landing pattern getting used to the sight picture and trying to get the landing flare lower than the Stearman's. Once I felt okay with landing the Pitts I started doing acrobatics.

I really liked doing acrobatics. I had done all the basic maneuvers many times over in my military flying, but there was one maneuver I had never attempted: the outside loop, which became my immediate goal. I had seen *Waldo Pepper*, read some about the maneuver and wasn't married, so I didn't have a family to worry about.

I started working up to the outside loop by doing a series of English Bunts. It's a very simple maneuver. You tighten your harness until you think it is going to cut you in half, and then from level flight you push forward on the stick until you are inverted going in the opposite direction. It's basically the second half of the outside loop. They seemed simple enough, and although the negative Gs weren't much fun, I felt I had the hang of it.

Now it was time to put it all together and do a complete outside loop. My game plan was to roll inverted, push until level on top of the loop and then do the English Bunt portion.

At 2,500 feet, with the throttle wide open, I rolled inverted and started to push. I twisted my head back to pick up the opposite horizon while enduring those negative Gs. It was when the stick hit the stops and no horizon had appeared that things got ugly. The Pitts departed controlled flight.

The first thing I'd been taught with any loss of control situation is to neutralize the controls and let the airplane stabilize. The Pitts did stabilize and very rapidly went into an inverted flap spin! (I later found out in the Pitts that is 30 degrees nose up inverted spinning at 400 degrees a second.)

I had never been in an inverted, nose-high flat spin like this, and I felt the panic start. I knew that roll is opposite to yaw in an inverted spin and looked outside to try to determine the spin direction. I became immediately and totally disorientated. It was then that I recalled being taught that the turn needle never lies and always points in the direction of the spin. I looked into the cockpit for the turn needle and couldn't find it. I then realized the Pitts didn't have one! Oh boy! I though of bailing out but sensed I still had some time to do something. Rudder! I didn't know which rudder to apply, so I just stomped on one and the little biplane really wrapped up. Wrong rudder. I stomped on the other rudder, and right away the Pitts started to respond. It was then that I thought "power" and pulled the throttle to idle. The nose fell through, I neutralized the rudders and was flying again. WOW! I was at 900 feet and pretty shaken up. I returned to the airport and reflected on what I had just experienced.

I had known enough to get dual time in a taildragger before I flew one. It never occurred to me that I should have applied the same principle to aerobatics. I was over-confident in my abilities and just plane (intentionally misspelled) lucky to have survived. Trying to come up with a course of action while spinning inverted at low altitude for the first time is certainly less than ideal. Know your limits, recognize the difference between ability and ego and be properly prepared.

Cornfield Arrival

I'M A SALESMAN and had spent the entire day, a Friday, on the telephone working orders. It turned out to be my best sales day ever, and by five o'clock, I was ready to take the 172 out for a spin.

Seeing that there was still lots of daylight left on a beautiful early June Wisconsin day, my wife and I decided to take a trip to a small private grass strip where there's a restaurant you can taxi right up to. My wife had always loved flying with me, in part because she felt so confident in my abilities and experience. That day's flight would end her confidence in my flying skills forever.

Things started out just fine. We flew into the strip, as we had done many times before, and I proceeded to park the airplane. Then we went inside for one of Wisconsin's famous lake perch fish fries.

Before leaving the airplane, however, I did something that would prove fateful: I moved the fuel selector from "both" to "right." I have always done this because if the airplane is sitting with the left wing low, fuel could drain out of the overflow tube. It could even siphon fuel from the right tank as well.

My wife commented that during dinner I was doing a little daydreaming. What I was really doing was thinking about work and all the loose ends that still needed to be taken care of.

Done with dinner, we walked out to the airplane and jumped in. I was in a hurry to get home, and my wife commented that she was too. We raced out to the runway and back-taxied to the end where there is a runup area. I did my runup and never looked at the checklist. Mistake number two.

We went roaring down the runway and were successfully climbing out when I remembered the fuel selector. I proceeded to reach down and twist it into its "proper" position.

We were at about 400 or 500 feet when the engine suddenly quit. I was above the trees at the end of the runway, but beyond that there were big trees everywhere.

I caught a glimpse of a cornfield that lay ahead and to the left and turned toward it. For a moment I let the airspeed drop below the best angle of glide speed and I started to freeze. We've all read about this, but when an emergency happens, it's hard to snap your brain out of its shutdown mode. But I did and was able to nail the airspeed on best glide. I got the airplane lined up with the rows of corn and actually had to slip a little and extend full flaps. I didn't want to overshoot.

Instead, I almost undershot, clearing a line of oak trees by inches—I was surprised that I didn't hear the airplane hit them. The cornfield was made. A few seconds later, I pulled back and made a beautiful full stall landing. The tires met the soft, sandy soil and the airplane very quickly decelerated to a complete stop. Luckily, the corn had only reached a couple inches of height that early in June.

It was at the moment that the wheels touched that I realized what I had done wrong. I swear that had I been higher, I would have figured out my error before a forced landing had been necessary. In my rush to get home I had inadvertently reached down and turned the fuel selector to "off" instead of turning it to "both." The engine ran long enough for me to have forgotten what I had done.

The rest of the story would be humorous had it not been for the seriousness of the offense. Spectators showed up immediately. I surveyed the situation and thought for a moment that maybe I could just get back in and fly it out. It was apparent however, that the soil conditions were not going to allow that to happen. It was also apparent that there was no way the airplane was going anywhere without a bunch of hands pushing it.

So, I got back in, started the engine and roared over to where a small crowd had gathered at an exit point on the field. I shut down the engine and went looking for a couple of big guys.

In the meantime one of the county's finest had showed up. He and I made a quick assessment of the situation, and he agreed to help me clear the traffic so I could taxi my airplane under its own power back to the airport where this had all begun.

I gave instructions on where not to push, and the big guys helped me move the airplane out of the sandy soil onto the paved road. Other officers blocked off the roads all the way back to the airport.

The owner of the airport showed up, and I asked him if he'd ride in the airplane as I taxied it back. He saw that my face was beet red, and did me that favor. My wife chose to ride with the officer.

We taxied the side road down to the main highway, stopped at the stop sign and pulled out, making sure not to exceed the speed limit. I had to weave back and forth to avoid the signs along the way, but I eventually encountered a spot where signs were placed exactly on opposite sides of the highway, leaving only barely enough clearance—two inches at most—to pass. But we cleared them and made it all the way back to the airport.

I checked over the airplane—other than some erosion to the propeller tips, there was not a scratch on it—and thanked both the officer and the airport owner. Then my wife and I climbed into the airplane and taxied back out for takeoff. We flew home, uneventfully, never once speaking to one another.

The event was far from over, however. It would be weeks before I could sleep at night. I kept going over the event in my mind. Eventually, I just accepted that God placed that cornfield exactly where I needed it that night.

What did I learn? Let's just say lots.

Never go to the airport with too much on your mind. All I could think about before our unplanned landing was work. If you can't get it out of your mind on the way to the airport, then make a 180 and go home.

Also, I now religiously check the fuel selector when I get into the airplane, and I never take off without going through the checklist.

Thank goodness I had had it hammered into my head to never turn back to the airport after an engine failure on takeoff. I would never have made it.

There's one other thing I want everyone to think about. When you have a loved one in your airplane who enjoys flying as much as you do, make sure you do everything by the book so your flight comes off without a hitch. If you do screw up—even if you're as fortunate as I was—there will be residual effects. My wife no longer likes flying with me. I scared her silly that evening, and flying will never be the same for her. It's been several years since this happened and I make most of my trips to the airport alone. The few times she has joined me I could tell that she was very nervous, and she watched me like a hawk.

I took something fun away from her, and from us, and I will always regret it.

Overcoming Airsickness the Hard Way

WHEN I WAS 19, I was rejected from the U.S. Navy Pilot program because I had too much overbite. To this day, I don't know what the alignment of my teeth has to do with being a jet jockey but I wasn't about to give up my love of flying because the Navy thought I couldn't bite right. However, when I finally did find myself at the controls of a Cessna 150, 28 later, I discovered a physical handicap that threatened to put my aviation dreams to rest forever: I could not spend more than 15 minutes in the air without experiencing agonizing nausea.

My instructor was understanding above and beyond the call of duty. On one unforgettable smoggy, cloudy, hot, humid afternoon over Los Angeles, he demonstrated the use of the spin to drop through a hole in the overcast. Turning to me with a grin of smug satisfaction, he asked if I would now like to practice some stalls. My answer was my lunch, all over the cockpit. I have never seen anyone land a Cessna 150 and race to the FBO faster, before or since.

"Your problem is an inner ear phenomenon," he always used to say. Being a physician, I tried to assure him that I was aware of the physiological complications of sailing through space in a small tin box better than most. But deep inside I knew I was lying. I knew that the thing that sank to the bottom of my stomach 5,500 feet over the San Fernando Valley was nothing more complicated than stark terror. Under the hood, I could recover from unusual attitudes all day long without so much as a twinge of heartburn. But take off the blinders, pull up the airplane's nose till it falls from the sky and then look face-down as you plummet toward the earth, and my intestines wanted to get up and head for the nearest exit. Inner ears? No, not really. Inner fears, maybe.

Still I persisted, determined to prove that the Navy missed its best chance for an ace fighter pilot. I soloed in 14 hours (15 minutes at a time) and was off to the practice area to hone my skills in a brightly painted Cessna 150, when I came face to face with my worst nightmare.

I leveled at 5,500 feet and pulled the throttle to idle. Sweaty palms strained at the yoke till I sensed the buffeting and I held on for the stall. There it was! Over the hill now like the peak of a roller coaster, then staring straight down at the dry crust a mile below and all my tension translated into the strain of my feet on the rudder, struggling to keep the nose straight. In spite of my best efforts, I could not keep the left wing from falling and suddenly I was in a spin. All I could think of was those movies where the ill-fated aircraft spins irreversibly to a fiery impact with the unforgiving earth. I'm not sure how long I sat there spinning out of control, helplessly resigned to the conviction that this was the end.

Suddenly I remembered my instructor's words. "When all else fails, let go of the controls and the plane will right itself." He was right! It stopped spinning; but now I was in a power dive. I slammed the yoke back against my chest and caught a glimpse of the altimeter just before the back of the seat gave way. At 2,000 feet I was flat on my back, waving my arms and legs like an upended cockroach. When I finally forced myself upright and gained control of the plane, my clammy arms and legs voted to take the rest of the day off, but my stubborn pride refused. I actually convinced myself that if I did not go back up and do a stall the right way, right then and there, I probably would never fly again. So up I went.

Every unfortunate move was duplicated. The stall, the spin, the power dive, the seatback release, the flailing legs and arms, all an agonizing instant replay of the first disastrous performance with one very important difference. Now I was not terrified; I was furious. I realized that the rumors of flashy paint jobs over poorly maintained airframes by the FBO who rented me this bird were probably true. To prove the point I returned to the field, got another 150 and performed three stalls without a hitch. But the best news of all was that I could now fly for hours and never feel a twinge of nausea!

I have read with interest the debates in flying magazines regarding the pros and cons of teaching spins as part of the private pilot instruction. My inadvertent lesson in spin recovery provided me with the confidence that I could recover from a worst possible scenario and in the process cured my fear-induced nausea. For me it was an invaluable lesson that permitted me to enjoy a romance with several airplanes over many years. And although I never realized my dream to become a naval fighter pilot, I have become one of the most dangerous objects in the sky: a doctor in a V-tail Bonanza.

My Last Buzz Job

AS A 17-YEAR-OLD STUDENT PILOT, I was exploring the newfound freedom of solo flight. How wonderful to be able to soar with eagles and also swoop down towards prey like a fighter pilot! Of course I knew from my instructor and the FAA regulations that I was never to fly below 500 feet agl except during takeoffs or landings.

But what possible harm could come of a low pass or two over my Mom's house in sparsely populated rural Kentucky? Having set up a beautiful approach to fly between the television tower on the house and the large oak tree in the front yard, I proudly made a perfect run between the obstacles and pushed the throttle in to full power in the Cessna 150 trainer.

Having climbed skyward to perhaps 1,000 feet or so I decided one more run for good measure was in order. Besides, my Mom and younger brother had made their way out the front door to see what in the world was happening! I would make another perfect fighter-pilot-like pass and head for the airport.

Circling back around to set up my flyby, I watched my Mom and brother look up in amazement as they realized who had just blown the shingles from the house!

On this pass, I thought, I would pull the power back to idle on approach, extend the first notch of flaps, and ease past at only 50 feet off the ground. I would put on a show they would never forget.

Lined up and descending, I pulled off the power, let down the flaps, and as trained, reached for the carburetor heat to insure continued smooth operation of the precious engine at my low altitude. To my total shock the engine fell quiet and the sound of rushing air replaced the comforting sound of a well-tuned engine. What had happened? I looked in horror as the ground rushed up to meet me; contact with terra firma was certain to take place in seconds.

What had my instructor said to do in the event of engine failure? Scan the panel. As my eyes darted across the instruments and engine controls I saw the problem: I had mistakenly pulled the mixture to full lean instead of pulling out the carburetor heat. As fast as possible with only seconds left till ground contact I pushed in the mixture to full rich. Thankfully the now-windmilling prop bit into the air as the engine roared to life in the nick of time.

I had nearly bought the farm right in front of my loved ones. I realized at that moment why the FAA had written in the regulations buzzing is not allowed. It is neither cool nor smart. And I never have nor never will buzz again.

I can only hope some new pilot feeling his oats or an old pro out playing on a Sunday afternoon will read this and realize what can happen. No matter how much you might feel that my major screwup could never happen to you, I hope everyone thinks twice before they do a buzz job.

Mountain Adventure

IT WAS A HOT SUMMER DAY IN 1969 and I was living my dream. I was flying for an FBO in Salt Lake City, getting paid for it and loving every minute of it. Earlier that year I had received my CFI with 261 hours that had taken two-and-a-half years to accumulate, showing in my logbook and now here I was five months later with another 440 hours in my logbook. Most of that time was logged as instruction given, but occasionally a charter would come in that the more senior pilots weren't available for and it would be mine. Life was good.

An attorney had called that morning and asked if we could deliver a letter to Loa, Utah, that afternoon. I was between students and the only one available to take it, so it was my trip. The date in my logbook is August 27, 1969, 2.7 hours from Salt Lake City to Loa, Utah, and back in a nearly new Piper Arrow 180. We had two of them, and while they were new and in beautiful condition the 180 was underpowered for summertime flying in the mountain west.

According to the numbers on my July 10, 1969, Bryce Canyon WAC chart, the Wayne Wonderland Airport at Loa had 4,200 feet of paved runway at an elevation of 7,020 feet msl. That's enough to make you check the density altitude performance of the airplane, but it was only going to be me and one of the linemen who wanted to go along and log a little cross-country time for his private license. And Salt Lake City has an elevation of 4,220 feet; we were used to density altitude problems, so not to worry, we could handle it. If the density altitude is too high for takeoff when we get there we'll hang around until temperatures cool down. Good plan.

We usually kept all aircraft except the trainers fueled at something less than full to accommodate passengers and any luggage or gear for trips of two or three hours, and this time was no exception. With two guys, no baggage and roughly half fuel after we got there, we should have no trouble.

This was my first and, as it has since turned out, only trip to Loa. When we arrived it was about mid-afternoon and a thunderstorm that could still be seen in the distance had just passed across the airport from northwest to southeast. The runway was still wet but not a hint of a breeze in any direction; the wind sock was hanging straight down. The airport sits on the western slope of a mountain and the runway is east and west, sloping up considerably to the east. To the west of the airport the terrain slopes down gently and there are few obstructions—one small tree stands out in my mind. About 10 miles to the east is the 11,306-foot peak of a mountain. We landed upslope to the east easily in half the distance of the runway and taxied on up to the east end where there was a hangar, and the courier was waiting for the letter.

There had been some survey work going on around the airport so about 10 or 15 yards north of the runway were some stakes with orange ribbon tied to them. I had decided that I would take off downhill to the west and had picked out a survey stake about halfway down the runway. I had decided that if I wasn't very close to flying speed by that halfway point I'd shut it down and wait until the temperature cooled down. The Arrow has mechanical flaps that are operated by a handle between the front seats. The owner's manual recommends two notches of flaps for takeoff, but I had decided that I would leave them in the retracted position until we achieved flying speed and then extend them. I had also leaned the mixture for takeoff, both procedures commonly used in the mountains, especially in the summertime.

We began the takeoff roll and everything was normal. As we reached the halfway point of the runway we were still about four or five mph below stall speed but I thought that we could easily make that up in the second half of the takeoff roll, so I continued the takeoff. The problem was that the airplane didn't accelerate as well during the second half of the roll as it had during the first half and as we came to the end of the runway we were still just under the stall speed. I pulled back on the yoke and pulled (jerked it is probably a better word as I did it with some urgency) on two notches of flaps at the same time and we staggered into the air, stall warning horn blaring loudly. We were barely flying, not climbing, in ground effect. Thank goodness for the downward slope and no obstacles. As soon as the airplane began to stabilize, I brought the landing gear switch to the up position, but the Arrow fail safe landing gear wouldn't come up because we were still too slow. I grabbed the landing gear emergency override switch right next to the flap handle and the gear started coming up. As the gear was coming up, I looked at the throttle, and it appeared to have crept back a bit off of the stop, so I let go of the emergency override and made sure the throttle was all the way up. With the stall warning horn still blaring, the gear fell back down. This time when I grabbed the emergency override I told the very wide-eyed lineman to hold it up for me and I got back on the throttle and prop. At about this point I suddenly noticed that the little tree I had mentioned earlier was dead ahead and getting larger. We were still too low and slow to try banking, so I gently came on with some left rudder to miss it. As we went by the tree the stall warning horn was intermittent and soon thereafter stopped completely. As we milked the speed up a little more, we started climbing slowly and continued on an otherwise uneventful trip back to Salt Lake City.

When we got back to Salt Lake I checked the handbook and found that we had needed several hundred more feet of runway than had been available for the takeoff at Loa. I don't remember the exact numbers, but we had needed quite a few hundred more feet for a normal takeoff. That was the last time that I ever took anything for granted in an airplane.

Over the years I have often thought about that incident, which was a major turning point in my life. There are lots of lessons to be learned here, but the thing that really stuck with me was how close I had been to disaster and yet had escaped unscathed. In the years since that time, I have had the pleasure of operating a wide variety of fun, usually fast, machinery and each time I do I remind myself of the words of my first flight instructor on my very first lesson. Just as we were beginning the walk-around he stopped me and said, "Flying is great and this is a great airplane, but if you mistreat it, it will kill you." And though I still don't like admitting it, through my neglect I had mistreated and nearly killed that pretty little Arrow and myself in the process.

Airborne at Three Feet

AT A UNITED STATES AIR FORCE BASE some years ago, my F-15 squadron hosted an open house for the families of the squadron members. One of the activities was an F-15 taxi ride around the airfield for a family member, to include an actual takeoff through rotation, followed by an abort and taxi back. As the unit's most junior pilot, I drew the short stick as the taxi driver and bemoaned my fate to any fellow pilot who would listen. The big moment finally arrived, and I tried to act interested as I was introduced to a young woman, Cathy, who would be my passenger.

I briefed Cathy and her husband on the events of our upcoming "ride." I couldn't imagine a duller thing to do with an F-15, but I did my best to sound enthusiastic during the briefing. Cathy seemed nervous, so I concentrated on trying to ease her concerns with a detailed explanation of what we would be doing. Stepping out to the jet, I noted that Cathy was becoming even more anxious about our impending adventure—though for the life of me I couldn't imagine why, given the fact that we wouldn't even be leaving the ground.

I had, in fact, strict orders from the squadron's operations officer, Happy, not to get airborne. Happy—so called because he had a permanent scowl on his face—had cornered me prior to our leaving the squadron building.

"Do not, under any circumstances," he barked, "leave the ground!" Geez, I think I can handle it, I thought to myself. After strapping into the two-seat F-15D, I gave Cathy a running narrative on engine start and the preflight checklist events. She was sounding downright scared on the intercom, so I worked on distracting her by pointing out things for her to look at and comment on inside and outside the jet.

We taxied to the active runway, and I thought I heard whimpering from the back seat. I tried to calm Cathy down by having her raise and lower the speed brake in a greeting as we rolled past the tower. I was running out of distractions. She was somewhat amused by the end-of-runway flight control checks, and I started to have a glimmer of hope that our jaunt around the field wouldn't be so awful. We pulled onto the runway, and I ran up the engines.

My first indication that things were not normal was the fact that, with engine power at 80 percent, I couldn't stand on the brakes hard enough to keep the Eagle from inching forward. No sweat, I thought. I'll just release the brakes, push the throttle to full power, and we'll roll. However, we didn't roll—the jet jumped forward and we shot down the runway, our heads pinned to the seatbacks. About that time, I saw we were already at rotation speed, so I pulled back on the stick to establish takeoff attitude. I managed to quickly pop the nose through the 10-degree target and had to push over slightly. Then, two things happened: I determined that our over-rotation had allowed the airplane to get about three feet in the air. And I noticed a large blue van parked off the side of the runway. All the family members and a few squadron personnel were standing outside the van to watch our not-so-simulated takeoff. Sitting in the van's driver seat, scowling, was Happy. I could feel his eyes boring holes into me as we floated by.

I yanked the throttles back to idle, but the F-15 was in ground effect and wasn't ready to slow down. We eventually settled back to the concrete. "I'm doomed," I thought as I braked and rolled out to the end of the runway. I had violated a simple, direct order—don't take off. I had a new appreciation as to why Air Force pilot wings were issued on Velcro.

As I pulled off the runway, I figured out what important bit of information I had missed. Normally when we stepped out to fly, we walked up to a fully fueled aircraft. Today, since we weren't actually going flying, I'd been assigned a jet that hadn't been refueled after its previous mission. With the distraction of a nervous passenger and a poor attitude about the mission, I hadn't done the preflight check of the fuel gauge—a pretty basic error. So I didn't realize that instead of having over 15,000 pounds of fuel on board for takeoff, my fuel load had been less than 2,000—quite a bit lighter gross weight than normal, making for a much higher thrust-to-weight ratio on takeoff than I had been expecting. The light weight also explained why the nose had rotated so quickly, and why we had gotten airborne so easily.

While visions of Happy smirking and ripping off my Velcro wings danced through my head, Cathy had done a 180 of her own. She was whooping and hollering on the intercom, "Hey, let's do that again!" I didn't think I'd get the chance, at least not after the court-martial. I taxied in as slowly as possible. Might as well prolong my last few moments in the cock-pit. We pulled into parking, shut down and crawled out. I could hear Cathy joyfully describing the experience to her husband as I snuck into the back of the squadron building.

After doffing my flight gear, I crept down the hall to the operations desk, avoiding all eye contact. I nearly had the post-flight paperwork done when Happy barreled around the corner. I braced myself. He looked me over disdainfully. With his scowl marred by the faintest of smiles, Happy muttered, "That was hot s***!" He turned and stomped away.

I was stunned. I checked the Velcro on my flight suit—yup, the wings were still there. I stumbled down the hall, found the nearest empty brief-ing room, collapsed into a chair and contemplated what a lucky son of a gun I was.

Practice Emergency

MANY TRAGIC OR NEAR-TRAGIC TALES begin with actions that are either foolhardy or just plain dumb. This one is definitely the latter. In 1967, I was a brand new flight instructor eager to teach new students. On a particularly beautiful day for flying I took a potential customer up for an introductory flight lesson in a Beech Musketeer Sport. While airborne at 3,000 feet, he asked the typical question, "What happens if the engine should quit?" That prompted a complete discussion of what makes an engine run and what makes an airplane fly, and resulted in my turning off the mixture, mags and master switches. I even took the key out and laid it in my lap. That was the first and last time I ever did that.

The engine fell quiet as we began to glide gracefully toward earth. The glide time was taken up discussing the finer points of picking an emer-gency landing field and setting up the proper flight pattern to successfully accomplish a landing. With the propeller windmilling and my trying to concentrate on quality instruction concerning emergencies, I pushed the mixture back in so the engine would run when needed, but it somehow slipped my mind that I had completely shut down the engine by turning off the magneto switch with the key.

When the aircraft reached about 500 feet, I pushed the throttle forward for a go-around and climb back to a safer altitude. To my chagrin, the engine did not respond. Instantly realizing what had occurred, I began a search for the keys, which had slid back under my rear. We were fast approaching telephone wires and a real emergency landing if those keys could not be produced quickly. Too late! It was time to concentrate on the landing. Trying to maintain my flight instructor composure, I proceeded to explain to the student how to land. We touched down and rolled along in a soybean field as the propeller stopped. When the airplane came to a halt the student commented, "Cool!"

Good, he wasn't aware this was not normal. I started the engine, and decided to taxi back in the field and take off before the farmer appeared with a shotgun. The engine came to life and we proceeded toward the edge of the beans. Thankfully the beans were very short and the aircraft wheels fit perfectly into the spaces between the rows, so we didn't even damage the crop. I explained the technique for a soft-field-type takeoff, and away we went plodding toward the skies. Unfortunately trees loomed at the other end of the bean field. Part way through the takeoff it became painfully obvious to me that we were not going to clear the trees, so I aborted the takeoff, and we rolled to the edge of the field.

My guardian angel was still hard at work as I thought of other alternatives. The student was now beginning to realize that all was not normal. Our landing had been in the field of a farmer who was very neat and had removed his fences and cleaned up the hedgerows. I could easily taxi down the lane without hitting the wings on any posts, and get to the next field. The next field was clover about 6-8 inches deep. I considered it for a moment, but concluded it was not good for a takeoff because of the deep vegetation and potential holes that could damage the aircraft. Continue down the lane.

The next obstacle was a drainage ditch, but the farmer had quite usefully laid 2x12 boards across the ditch in order to get his tractor into the fields. What a guy! The boards and landing gear seemed to be in alignment. Go for it. We now found ourselves on a blacktopped country road with electric wire along only one side. This was much more hospitable terrain. I didn't take the time to instruct my now nervous student about the finer points of escaping into the air from a road. Turn down the road; check for cars coming; add power; move left after liftoff to stay away from the electric wire. At last we were once again free from the bonds of earthly travel to enjoy the experience of flight.

With a somewhat elevated heart rate, I continued the lesson as we headed back toward the airport, called the tower, landed normally, and proceeded to the tiedown area. After all, I didn't want to lose this potential student. As we walked toward the hangar, I noticed two State Highway Patrol Officers standing inside drinking cold drinks from our pop machine. It would only be a matter of time before jail was my new home. What would happen to my family? The officers weren't moving toward me, so I continued to the instructor's room, debriefed my student, signed him up for another lesson the next week, and sent him on his way with a new and different experience.

The tension was high and that elevated heart rate was back again as I walked out into the hangar, where the two policemen were still leisurely drinking their cold drinks. Why weren't they interested in my whereabouts? Expecting to be handcuffed any minute, I couldn't stand it. I strolled to the pop machine, got a bottle, opened it up, walked over to the two highway patrolmen and asked, "What brings you two fellow around?" One said, "We're flying that Cessna out there on turnpike traffic watch and we decided to stop here for a while. Nice day for flying, isn't it?" YES!!! It was a very nice day for flying, I thought as I slowly walked away, thoroughly enjoying my pop.

Oh, by the way, my student didn't keep his appointment the next week. I wonder why.

MECHANICAL

JAM

AIRPLANES are incredibly complicated machines. While every pilot should know that, those of us who own airplanes or work on them are all too well aware of it. So it's not too surprising when some mechanical part fails in flight. Things break. That's the nature of machinery. But when they break in an airplane there are complications that are unique to flying. First, flying commits you in a way that almost no other activity does. Once you've made the commitment to go flying, you've got to land somewhere, generally on an airport, and hopefully leaves the occupants in one piece.

Because of the nature of airplanes, there are also built-in barriers to troubleshooting. Although there are famous tales of aviators climbing out on a wing to make repairs, in the real world, in-flight grease monkeys have an extremely short lifespan. Generally, pilots who run into a serious mechanical problem in the air are forced to diagnose the problem from the cockpit, where, more often than not, there's limited information available to make the assessment. In cases like these, the pilots learn the nature of their airplane's woes only after landing and being able to take stock from outside the cockpit.

A pilot faced with a disabled bird is at a tremendous disadvantage from the get go: It's hard to tell what the problem is, and even if he knows, there's seldom anything that he can do about it. This is what happened to the pilot of an old Cessna 172 that had recently undergone maintenance. All he knew was that the airplane was almost impossible to control. Nor did the pilot of a Cessna 421 know what he was up against when he experienced a dual alternator failure over the Cascades and had to continue the flight using a handheld GPS. These pilots, and the others whose stories follow, tackled and overcame what has to be the biggest piloting challenge—troubleshooting a serious mechanical problem while keeping the airplane right side up and out of the rocks.

Shedding Light on a Total Electrical Failure

"**O**NE THREE SEVEN CHARLIE MIKE, MEMPHIS CENTER, we've lost your Mode C, say altitude." I've always had a temptation to say "altitude," but I've always managed to resist the temptation.

"Seven thousand five hundred, one three seven Charlie Mike."

"Seven Charlie Mike, do you plan on maintaining that altitude all the way to Tyson?"

"Affirmative, seven Charlie Mike."

"One three seven Charlie Mike, do you plan on maintaining seven thousand five hundred to Tyson?"

"Affirmative, seven Charlie Mike."

"November one three seven Charlie Mike, this is Memphis Center, how do you hear?"

By this time I realized that something was not right. My panel lights were beginning to dim rapidly. I reached for the transponder and squawked 7600 to indicate that I had lost the ability to communicate. Next I turned off the strobe light, the GPS and the number two navcom. The panel lights continued to dim.

When flying alone, I always keep my flight bag within easy reach behind the seat. I reached back and retrieved my flashlight and started checking circuit breakers and switches. Everything was in the correct position. Just moments earlier, I was sitting on top of the world.

My partners and I had flown from Knoxville, Tennessee, to Mena, Arkansas, to pick up our freshly painted Cessna 310L. We had recently put a new engine in it, had an Apollo GPS installed and had taken it to Mena for paint, new interior, new glass and VGs. We had made the 500-nm trip out in a Cessna Cardinal. Kim was working on her instrument rating and had used the trip out to satisfy her IFR cross-country requirement. Once we got to Mena, we found that the front two seats had not been completed, so there was going to be an hour or so delay. I told Kim and Mike to go ahead and start back, since the trip in the C177 would take considerably longer than the trip in the 310. I finally left Mena about 8:30 p.m. I usually file IFR even in VFR conditions, but by this time the FBO was closed and my cell phone was not in range of an appropriate cell tower, so I decided to wait until I was in the air to contact Memphis Center.

I climbed to 7,500 and contacted Memphis Center. I decided that, since the weather was so good, I would remain VFR but request flight following and clearance through Class B airspace. By the time I reached Memphis, it was a dark and moonless night.

As the lights on the panel started to dim, I realized it was decision time. Since I had just left the Memphis Class B airspace, did I try to land at an airport near Memphis or continue to my home base in Knoxville? I decided that I would go on to Knoxville, about two hours east of Memphis. I turned off the remaining electrical load and started assessing the situation. I had a flashlight, a handheld Garmin 195 GPS and a handheld transmitter. I also remembered that several years earlier someone had given me two light sticks, the kind that you activate by bending. This light stick gave off a uniform soft glow that did not have to be directed like a flashlight to be effective. I found that I could lay the stick in the seat beside me and see the panel instruments clearly. It also provided enough light to read the "Electrical System Emergency Procedures" section of the owner's manual.

I started reviewing my systems to determine which ones were affected by an electrical systems failure. Obviously, I had no communications or navigation radios, no transponder or lights. That meant that besides the handheld radio, I could not talk to anyone, nor could anyone see me either visually or with radar other than as a primary target. I decided to save the handheld radio until the landing phase of the trip because I did not know the status of the battery pack. The flaps of the 310 are electric, as is the gear extension motor.

I attached the Garmin 195 to the control yoke connected to the antenna and turned it on. I selected the "go to" function and entered TYS to take me directly to Knoxville. Shortly after turning it on, I got a low battery indication. Again I was thankful for the light stick, which provided hands-free light that helped me to change the batteries. I removed the GPS unit from its mount, removed the battery compartment, replaced the old batteries with new, reinstalled the battery compartment and remounted the unit. I turned the unit on only to receive the low-battery warning again. I went through the process one more time to find that in the semi-darkness I had placed one of the batteries in the compartment backwards. Once this problem was corrected, I was again headed directly to the Knoxville McGhee-Tyson Airport.

As I planned my arrival at Knoxville, the thought occurred to me that now that I had just installed a new engine on the right side and had a new paint job, there was a remote chance that the gear wouldn't lock down and I could ruin both the paint and the engine. In obtaining my complex endorsement and multiengine rating, I had never actually practiced cranking the landing gear down by hand. I decided at that moment that my students would get to actually experience the process. My plan was to maintain 7,500 feet until 50 miles from Knoxville, slow to gear extension speed, then lower the gear manually. At 20 miles out I would try to contact the Knoxville tower on the handheld transmitter.

I crossed Hinch Mountain, which is about 50 miles west of the Knoxville Airport, at 7,500 feet, then slowed the 310 to Vle. On the chance that I had managed to save some of the battery charge, I turned on the battery switch and moved the gear-extension lever to the "down" position. Nothing happened. I reached down and loosened the gear-extension handle. After the first couple of turns, nothing happened. As I tried to fight the sinking feeling, I continued to crank. After another half turn or so there was that comforting sound of the gear doors breaking into the air stream. I continued to crank until the crank wouldn't turn. There was no light to indicate that the gear was locked in the "down" position, but there was nothing else I could do.

By this time I was approaching the distance that I had planned to contact the tower. I descended to 3,500 feet. I removed the LightSpeed noise-attenuating headset and the engine noise was initially overwhelming. I wondered if I would even be able to hear the tower on the handheld. I rapidly adjusted to the new noise level and discovered it was not as bad as the initial impression. I punched in 121.2 for the tower frequency and called the tower. To my joy, they responded immediately. I explained to them that I had experienced a total electrical failure and had only a handheld transmitter for communication, had no lights and had manually put the gear down but had no cockpit indication that they were locked and in the "down" position. I was immediately cleared to land on Runway 23R and was requested to report turning right base for 23R.

The tower reported a United flight on a 12-mile final for the left side but stated that they would hold the United flight until I reported on the ground. The tower asked my position and altitude. I reported 12 miles and descending out of 3,500 feet. I reported turning right base for Runway 23R. With no flaps I was still faster than I needed to be because of the need to descend. Turning final, I had the airspeed under control, but the rate of descent was still a little high. I wanted to touch down a little nose high since I did not know the condition of the gear lock and assumed that the nose gear would be the most likely not to be locked.

The sound of the tires contacting the runway was music to my ears. I reported to the tower that I was on the runway. They cleared me to take the first left and to hold short of 23L for landing traffic and to report off the runway. Without taxi or landing lights it was difficult to see the runway turn-off markings. I taxied clear of the runway and held short of 23L. The tower cleared me across 23L after the landing traffic passed. They asked if I needed further assistance. I replied that I didn't and they agreed to contact Atlanta Center and Memphis Center to notify them that I had safely landed. The group that had installed the new interior had damaged the wiring at the circuit breaker panel.

Several things were reinforced that night. First, if you are alone in the cockpit, make sure that all your resources are within reach. A flight bag in the luggage area would have been no help. Make sure that you have fresh batteries for all your equipment, including flashlights, GPS, handheld transmitter, etc. Third, know your systems. Practice manual gear extension so that you will know what to expect. Stay calm. You can bet that I am going to get more chemical light sticks for my flight bag, and I'm going to recommend them to everyone I know.

Hit the Ground Running!

NOTHING SEEMED OUT OF THE ORDINARY on the beautiful spring day in California's northern Sierra Nevada Mountains where I give instruction and fly charters out of Quincy. My student, Coy, was taking his fourth lesson and it was time for demonstration and practice on the stall sequences as training for his private pilot license. Our reliable company trainer, a '57 model Cessna 172, had recently come out of maintenance for the usual 50-hour oil change and spark plug cleaning. Two Three Bravo ran up smooth as glass in preparation for the flight.

Coy had done a thorough walk-around and checked all the control surfaces for freedom of movement during both the preflight and again prior to run-up in the cockpit. Just before we taxied onto the runway, I glanced once again at the suction gauge, which had been moved and remounted in the panel during the 50-hour inspection. Everything appeared normal as we departed Runway 6 and climbed to 8,000 feet msl above American Valley to begin the lesson.

Once at altitude, we warmed up with a brief review of turns, flight at minimum controllable airspeed and then started practicing departure and approach to landing stalls. All went well as I finished the lesson by demonstrating a few accelerated stalls so Coy could see the effect an increased angle of bank had on stall speed. During the first stall to the left in a 50-degree bank, accompanied by brisk back pressure on the elevator, I felt a slight "bump" in the yoke as the nose was lowered during recovery. It was one of those feelings that was noticeable but not to the point of really grabbing my attention. During the second accelerated stall demonstration to the right, I learned a lesson about paying attention to anomalies in flight.

As the airplane stalled in the steep bank, I pushed forward on the yoke and leveled the wings with aileron, but the yoke was jammed in nearly the full back position! The act of unloading the wings was just enough to momentarily break the stall, but we were left nose up, power on, with no way to reduce the angle of attack. For a span of about 10 seconds, I realized we were eventually going to stall again and enter a spin, with no way to recover. Somehow, the thought of how that would unavoidably happen played out very logically, with an almost resigned acceptance in my mind. The next 30 seconds or so were filled with reactions of a more frantic nature, guided by the survival instinct and past training.

My first thought was we had to get the nose down to avoid the impending stall one way or another. Coy is a strong guy and I yelled at him to push forward on the yoke with me, in an attempt to overcome the obstruction. Believe me, two guys pushing and banging on dual controls in a 172 can apply a lot of force. This caused the elevator to react slightly as the control column moved in an inch or so; but still we were left in a nose-high attitude that would eventually lead to a stall. My next thought was to get Coy under the instrument panel to see if he could find what was blocking the yoke, but, although he tried to get his head under there, he really didn't know where or what to look for. Much to my relief, with his weight under the panel, the center of gravity had moved just far enough forward to bring the nose down a little more, and, for the first time, I felt we could avoid an imminent stall. Actually, by pounding the yoke forward and getting both seats forward and Coy under the panel, I had enough control to mush the airplane around without stalling.

I called my sister, Judy, on the unicom and told her we had a bad problem and to advise other traffic that I was going to attempt a landing with the yoke stuck. She also notified my boss, but, not knowing the nature of the problem, there wasn't much they could do. By now, I had tried everything to see how it affected pitch control, but each try seemed to make matters worse. Power only seemed to affect vertical velocity, and forward trim inexplicably caused the nose to pitch up even more. Adding flaps caused the airspeed to deteriorate as expected. The best flight regime for control was about 1,500 rpm, no flaps and neutral elevator trim. With this configuration, I was able to fly with the nose up at about 55 mph and maneuver in shallow turns. From here on, the main concern during the rest of the flight was knowing I couldn't go around if I was short or long on the approach.

Our descent rate was quite low and while maneuvering to downwind, a hilarious thing happened that inwardly made me laugh. Coy told me that if we were going to crash, he thought he could save himself by opening the door at the last moment and hitting the ground running. The approach and landing went fine, and, as we taxied up to the hangar, my very worried boss ran out to see what had gone wrong. As soon as we got our heads under the panel, it became clear what had happened. In the course of rerouting the copper line from the suction gauge to the directional gyro, the nuts had only been finger tightened to the instruments. The centrifugal force applied in the accelerated stall turns had swung the line down so it looped directly behind the yoke control column while in the full-back position. It had almost done it in the first turn and that was the bump I felt. In our attempts to dislodge the controls, we had actually stretched the copper line quite a bit and that, I believe, saved our lives. Maybe this is why most vacuum lines are now hoses that can easily be broken if they get hung up.

A lot of hangar flying was done after this incident, and it was finally agreed I could have helped matters by using the elevator trim in reverse. Since the elevator would not move, the reverse trim tab would have acted like a miniature elevator to help bring the nose forward. Although I've instructed for several thousand hours, that was the only really serious problem I've had with a student. As for Coy, he came back for one more lesson but decided his odds were better with stock car racing!

Out of a Jam

IT WAS A TYPICAL FALL DAY IN MICHIGAN, with a cold overcast and fairly low ceilings. My instructor and I decided not to go anywhere and just stay in the pattern and practice takeoffs and landings. Oakland/Troy Airport does not permit touch and goes, so doing this would burn up a fair amount of time. I did a full preflight while my instructor sat in his vehicle and looked on with his watchful eye.

I accumulated four hours into a five-hour check out in our flying club's 182. I had just joined this club hoping both to learn high performance and to earn an instrument rating all in one. High performance was totally new to me. All my previous time was in fixed-pitch low wingers. My instructor and I had been up several times trying to satisfy this insurance requirement and I was finally getting a "feel" for this airplane. It is a satisfying comfort that you gain with experience in an airplane.

We did the full checkout routine making sure we weren't cutting any corners as I wanted my money's worth. Stalls, slow flight, high bank turns, emergency procedures, takeoffs and landings in every possible configuration. We did four or five takeoffs and landings to a full stop and taxied back each time. I just knew a go-around missed approach would have to be coming up soon, so I was ready for it. We were on short final with 40 degrees of flaps when my instructor saw a deer on the runway and called for a go around. I had the checklist nailed; everything to the firewall and retract the flaps from 40 to 20 degrees, open the cowl flaps and get a positive rate of climb. I did all this and established a climb at Vy while my instructor reminded me to climb out to the right of the runway.

Clearing all obstructions I retracted the remaining 20 degrees of flaps and all was normal with the usual sound of the flap motor. When the flap motor stopped, I felt strong pressure on the control yoke. Trying to bank the airplane right, I grabbed the control with both hands and looked out my window and did not see anything unusual. I thought it may have been ice building up on the ailerons but the bank right force was unexplainable. I was fighting for aileron control. I don't think my instructor noticed me struggling with the control yoke so I yelled, "something is wrong!"

He grabbed the yoke and I let go for a moment so he could feel the force wanting to bank right. He looked out his window and with eyes as big as eggs he immediately grabbed the mic and said "5YG has got a problem." He told me the flap was down and distorted on his side.

We immediately leveled off and turned left onto the crosswind leg with both of us manhandling the control yoke, playing tug of war for aileron control and doing it with so much force we were concerned that the control cables might give out. With one flap down and the other up I knew we were experiencing asymmetrical drag, but I never imagined that so much force would have to be exerted on the yoke.

As we turned downwind in close to the runway, I wondered if we may have been fighting each other. So I asked my instructor if he could control the ailerons himself. He nodded yes. I let go of the yoke and he leaned forward to be able to exert more force.

Fortunately there was no one in the pattern at the moment as we were only several hundred feet agl. Our only thought was to land this thing ASAP. I keyed the mic and again announced "5YG got a problem with a flap" and I think someone acknowledged but I'm not quite sure. We were both so intensely concentrating on landing this airplane.

We decided to leave the flap switch right where it was because we weren't sure what had gone wrong. I did a landing checklist and other than intentionally landing a bit fast because of our known flap problem, it was uneventful. We taxied back to the hangar and got out to survey the damage. We were astounded at the total destruction of the right flap. The inboard roller had somehow caught itself on a guide and froze that end of the flap. The flap motor just kept pulling up the free end of the flap, literally ripping the sheet metal at the motor attach point and shoving the free outboard end of the flap in at angle. The flap was a total loss. Worse yet, the flap was shoved right into the aileron! The right aileron was jammed up in a slightly up position against the distorted flap. It would not move in any direction.

Throughout this entire landing we knew there was a problem and we really weren't scared. But when we saw this jammed aileron, we were shocked. It had been the cause of those heavy control forces, not the asymmetrical flaps! We were stretching the aileron cables which allowed enough movement in the left aileron to enable us to bank. It could have been a not-so-happy landing. Who knows what could have happened if the control cables broke or the flap fell off hitting the elevator!

An expert from Cessna came out to see the aircraft and stated he had never seen such a problem occur in a 182. He attributed the glitch to unusual wear on the flap guides. The only indication of this unusual wear was a tiny paint scrape where the flap had occasionally been rubbing against the guide. I have preflighted airplanes hundreds of times, and this preflight was no different from any other. Looking back, I do remember seeing the worn paint but at the time I didn't think it was anything unusual. After this incident, however, I make it a point to always take the extra time to really look and investigate on the preflights, rather than just going through the motions. Even if it means taking the time to get the advice of a mechanic, regardless of how minor the problem may seem.

Aviate, Navigate, Communicate

THERE ARE ITEMS ON MY AIRPLANE that I never touch, because I never need to. On a lovely day last month, I learned that these items need my attention anyway.

The airplane is a beautiful bright yellow open-cockpit Waco biplane, vintage 1999. We use it for providing scenic tours along the beaches in sunny South Florida. The Waco was down for five days for its 100-hour inspection, and I was there to pick it up and pay the bill.

The head mechanic went down the list methodically, explaining every fix they had made. One of the items he mentioned was the replacement of the turnbuckles in the tail assembly. These turnbuckles hold and control the tension of the "flying wires" so prevalent in a biplane. In spite of my efforts to keep them protected with a hard coating, the Florida salt spray had corroded the turnbuckles to the point that they needed replacement. The maintenance man told me that they had replaced the eight on the tail, effectively re-rigging the whole assembly. I made a mental note to check their work before flying off. Once the bill was squared away, I preflighted the Waco. One time two years ago, a mechanic had pulled my fuel flow handles to full cutoff position. Since I never touch these handles down under the control panel, I had not noticed, and the airplane started, sputtered and quit. I made it a point to take a look at the fuel cutoff handles this time. I wasn't going to go through that embarrassment again.

I also took a good look at the flying wires on the tail. I handled each of the turnbuckles and twanged each of the flying wires. Everything was fine. All other items checked out, and I was ready to go. Ground control cleared me to taxi, and soon the tower had placed me in "position and hold" on my takeoff runway. I was feeling great. It was a beautiful sunny day, the Waco was squeaky clean and rarin' to go. I hadn't flown all week and was missing my daily affirmation of life. I finally got the word from tower, and we were off and running. The takeoff drill in this hefty taildragger is to hold the stick full forward until the tail comes up, meanwhile dancing on the rudder pedals to keep the airplane pointed straight ahead. When lightly loaded as it was now, the tail comes up in a hurry and the rudder work takes all the attention. Once airborne, the drill is to shift to full hard right rudder and to adjust the stick to climb at 75 mph or so. Again, the rudder demands plenty of attention to keep the ball centered, and the stick work is more or less second nature. The airplane is equipped with a large trim wheel down to my left side, but I never touch it. The Waco's controls are balanced so wonderfully that trim just isn't needed.

With a pretty fair headwind, the Waco popped off the runway with enthusiasm, not uncommon for this bird that loves to fly. I rammed my right foot hard on the rudder and eased up on the forward stick force. Right away, I knew we had trouble. As I loosened my grip on the stick, the nose shot straight up and the airspeed dropped sickeningly. I quickly grabbed the stick with both hands and pushed forward with everything I had. The nose came back down grudgingly and I got the airspeed back to 75 mph. I'd managed to avert a stall, and the airplane was more or less under control, but what was the next step?

I'd asked for and received an intersection takeoff from the long runway, so I didn't have enough left to simply power down and land. With both hands pushing hard on the stick just to keep the airplane aloft, I wasn't interested in doing any steep turns and trying to get it landed. I could have called the tower, but there sure wasn't anything they could do for me at that point. *Aviate, navigate, communicate.* It was important for me to keep aviating at this point. It finally dawned on me that there was a trim wheel next to my leg. I had been told when I purchased the airplane that the wheel took a lot of turning to have any effect, another reason why I'd never used it. It was sure worth a try.

Locking my right arm firmly against the forward stick, I loosened my grip with my left hand and started turning the trim wheel forward. Cranking it vigorously, I very carefully eased up on the stick, and the nose shot up again. No effect! Without any other brilliant ideas, I just went back to cranking the trim wheel. Both arms were tiring from pushing and cranking when I started to detect just a bit of easing on the stick force. I continued to trim, and sure enough, it was working. With a bit more adjustment, I was able to release my death grip on the stick, and the airplane hummed along straight and level. I headed for home with a relieved grin and a sweat-drenched shirt.

Trim on the Waco is accomplished with a vertical jackscrew, plainly visible for inspection in the tail assembly. The threads on the screw are very narrow, thus the prodigious amount of turning needed in the cockpit. Apparently, when the tail was re-rigged, the jackscrew was positioned in the full nose-up position. During my ever-so-careful inspection of the tail, I completely ignored the jackscrew, as I have done since the day I bought the airplane. No more.

I re-learned two important lessons that day. Number one: Nothing, but nothing, goes uninspected after maintenance on the airplane. And number two: Keep on flying and keep on trying.

Thanks, Dad

THOSE OF US WHO HAVE HAD A PARENT as their flight instructor know how lucky we are. A parent is certainly the most demanding flight instructor you can have. And the one you most want to please.

My dad and I were once in a Super Cub floatplane a thousand feet above Michigan's Lake St. Claire. I was flying from the front seat, my dad was instructing from the back. I would be taking my private pilot flight test soon, and very much wanted to impress my dad.

Looking up at the gas gauge in the left wing root, I could see that the left tank was about to run dry. We commonly ran a tank dry before switching tanks, and I rehearsed the procedure in my mind: lower the nose to maintain airspeed, engine-out checklist, switch tanks, advance the throttle and away we would go.

Even when you are expecting the engine to quit, you cannot hold back the surge of adrenaline brought about by the sudden silence. Feigning nonchalance, I lowered the nose to establish best glide speed and switched tanks. Very professional. Advancing the throttle there was...silence. Silence!

As if he still had to shout to be heard over the roar of the engine, my dad was bellowing from the back seat, "What are you going to do now?"

"I guess we are going to land," I said feebly, still in disbelief that the engine hadn't started. My dad let a few seconds pass before delivering the verbal blow: "Finish your checklist!"

I suddenly felt very stupid. I realized what had happened. My dad had turned off the magnetos! I was so sure that the engine stoppage was from running the tank dry, that I never thought any further. I had been trapped by my own assumption. Had I completed the checklist, I would have seen that the mags were off. I flipped the mags back on, and the Lycoming came immediately to life. I was totally embarrassed. But this was a lesson that I would remember. And fortunately so.

Move the clock ahead 16 years or so. I was planning a canoe trip, and would take five friends along in my Cessna 206. We were going to fly from Palo Alto, California to Cloverdale in the morning, and return that same day. I had just had a bad magneto replaced on the engine, but had no time to test fly the plane before loading all the seats for this trip. I felt bad that I had not first test flown the plane with the new mag, but eased my guilt with an especially thorough run-up before departure.

The flight from Palo Alto to Cloverdale took us over the rolling vineyards of Napa Valley, through smooth morning air of Northern California. The engine ran perfectly. At Cloverdale we rented three canoes, and enjoyed a great day on the Russian River. My canoe was the only one to capsize, but I simply explained to my friends that I was practicing my barrel rolls. We paddled downstream to Healdsburg, and then caught a ride back to Cloverdale for the flight home.

On the return flight about 10 minutes from Palo Alto, I was thinking about how well the engine was running with the new mag. Then the engine quit. Damn! Something had to be wrong with mags! I fiddled with the key: Left mag, Right mag, Off, Both...Silence. No matter what I did with the mag switch, the engine was still dead. Then I heard my dad's voice from the past: "Finish your checklist!" Mixture rich, electric fuel pump on...and the engine came to life! There was nothing at all wrong with the mags; the mechanically-driven fuel pump had failed! A tiny electric fuel pump was now all that was supplying fuel to the thirsty engine.

Palo Alto Airport was busy. The Watsonville Airshow had just let out and droves of planes were returning to Palo Alto. With only the electric fuel pump keeping me aloft, there was no way I wanted to fly an extended pattern low over the San Francisco Bay.

"Palo Alto Tower, 124WN is having a little trouble with our fuel pump and would like to avoid an extended pattern."

"124WN, Roger. Request priority downwind if you have a problem."

So that's how it's done. You *request priority* shy of declaring an emergency.

"Palo Alto Tower, 124WN requesting a priority landing."

Tower responded immediately, "124WN cleared to land," and instructed planes on final to overfly the field at 1,200 feet.

Thank you, Tower! The ground never felt so good.

The next day my mechanic showed me what had happened. The square shaft that drives the fuel pump had worn almost completely round. Rather than drive the fuel pump, the rounded shaft was spinning futilely in a square hole. Thirteen years after this flight the FAA issued an Airworthiness Directive for the IO-520 engine requiring inspection of the fuel pump drive shaft. "If the fuel pump drive shaft disengages in flight, engine power will be lost, and this loss of power could be critical depending on the phase of flight." The AD was prompted by a fatal accident.

With 2,000 hours now in my logbook, this is the only engine failure that I've had. Thanks to my training, I knew how to handle it. Thanks, Dad.

We've Got A Problem!

THE PLEASANT MORNING BREEZE was not particularly welcome, I remember noting as I drove toward the airport that October morning. I knew that the stronger the winds, the harder it would be to make the "perfect maneuvers" required. Normally I would have welcomed it but this was not a normal day. I was on my way to meet with the examiner for my commercial check ride.

The FAA Designated Pilot Examiner that was going to ride with me that day was Clyde Shelton. Clyde had given me check rides for my private as well as my instrument ratings. I knew he was a stickler for details. I left the house earlier than needed so that I would have time to leisurely fill out the paperwork necessary to rent the Cessna 210. I also did not want to be rushed in the preflight of the plane, even though I had flown the aircraft twice in the last two days and several times over the previous three weeks. Today I certainly did not want to miss anything. I felt that a professional attitude and good planning would help me convince Clyde that I was qualified enough to pass the practical portion of the exam.

After a thorough preflight before meeting with Clyde, I felt like I was ready for the exam. We went through the required oral portion and I provided the proof that I had all the prerequisites and I filed a flight plan for the destinations I was given.

Clyde and I went to the airplane where he watched as I preflighted it again before we departed Madison County Executive Airport (M82), which is just north of Huntsville, Alabama. As we launched into the sky from Runway 18, I noted the breeze from the south was making the wind socks dance, but my attention was now turned towards impressing Clyde with the skills that I hoped I had recently acquired. The morning brought hazy skies and temperatures due to be in the eighties.

We spent the next hour and forty-five minutes maneuvering with Clyde asking questions that are normally simple, such as, "What will be your new course heading, distance and time en route to an unexpected destination?" I found myself wondering what phenomenon caused maps to be wonderful tools one moment and an embarrassing "unfoldable" pain in the lap the next. I recovered my composure after doing battle with the maps and we began the landing demonstrations with the complex aircraft. We moved on to engine out and short field landings. Then we began the required maneuvers that I had practiced during the last few weeks in the absence of wind.

I was setting up for the 8s around the pylons at 1,100 agl when a deafening silence slammed into the cockpit. I looked at Clyde as if to say, "Okay! What did you do?" He looked back at me with a firm expression that said, "I did not do anything!" I was not completely convinced that he had not put me in this predicament on purpose, so I checked mixture, fuel tanks, tank selector, mags, carb heat, throttle and fuel pump.

After I had finished checking, changing, adjusting and rechecking everything I could think of, I heard him say, "Have you ever done this before?" I looked at him and realized that this was not a test. I rather quietly replied, "No." Our attention was now turned toward the outside of the plane when he said, "Pick your landing spot."

I looked out at the farmland surrounding us and saw a farmer plowing his field. I decided to land as close to him as possible, so that we might be able to ask him for some assistance, hopefully nothing more than a ride. The gear was down and locked. There was no one to call on the radio because we were 20 miles from the nearest controlled airfield, and things seemed to be under control given the circumstances. I mean—isn't this what we practice for regularly?

We were about 700 feet agl when I looked over at Clyde and said, "We've got another problem." He looked back and asked "What now?"

"I have fuel running down my right shin and filling my sock and shoe," I told him. "Are you sure it's fuel?" he asked.

As surprised as I was with the engine quitting, I was pretty sure that it was the plane that was leaking, and not me. I responded that I was certain that at least most of it was fuel. He said "Just fly the plane."

With fuel on me and filling the cockpit I pictured the plane flipping over and catching on fire while trying to land in a plowed field. I then renewed my effort to restart the engine. I tried pushing, turning, and pulling every handle and switch that I could reach.

We were now at 200 feet agl and lining up to land very close to the tractor plowing the field when the engine coughed, sputtered and returned to life with a vengeance. The throttle was in the firewalled position and my mental picture of the 210 with its wheels in the air and wings in the dirt of the plowed field faded.

As we climbed to 3,000 feet agl, we turned toward the nearest airport which was eight miles away. We began our radio calls to the airport frequency requesting that all traffic clear the pattern due to our emergency.

The commercial pilot of a twin-engine aircraft that was on a 10-mile straight-in approach to the uncontrolled field in Fayetteville, Tennessee, responded by saying that he was still on straight-in final to Runway 20. We again broadcast our plight and asked that the traffic pattern be cleared.

The Cessna 210 was firewalled and we left it that way because of the fear that any changes might bring back that dreaded silence. The fuel was still running down my now saturated leg, socks, shoes and into the puddle on the floor. I looked over at Clyde and said again "Uh! We've got another problem!"

"What is it now?" he asked. "We have fuel coming out of the crack between the front engine cowl and spewing on to the outside windshield." This did not seem so bad at first, at least it wasn't getting on me, until I realized that it was getting on everything under the cowling, including the mags and exhaust manifold.

The idiot flying the small twin and its passengers wanted to know more about our emergency as he continued his approach. We repeated that we had a serious situation and requested that the traffic pattern be cleared.

We were approaching the airport from the southeast and could now see the twin on straight in Runway 20. Because of his landing to the south he cut off our option to land on the nearest end of the runway even if it would be landing with the wind.

We flew a modified downwind and turned base to final with the throttle still firewalled and fuel flowing freely inside as well as out. On short final, as the twin was still on the south end of the runway, I touched the throttle and the stampeding silence returned. The strong winds from the south that had originally concerned me earlier in the morning now caused me a problem that I had not expected. We were not going to make the runway.

I had expected the engine to just reduce the rmp, not stop. It was evident that we were going to hit the upsloping terrain short of the runway. Then Clyde used his years of experience and resources to try to restart the engine as I guided us to 40 feet agl. Just as I started a terribly uncomfortable flare over rising unfriendly terrain, Clyde's efforts paid off as the engine came to life briefly, just long enough to reach the runway, but then grew quiet again. When the wheels touched down we threw open the doors and coasted off the runway just in time to hear the pilot of the twin ask as he was taxiing what kind of problem were we having. I did not respond in a professional manner.

After we jumped out and looked back at the plane we could see fuel dripping out of the engine cowling, the floor panels and off of my leg.

The problem was a metal fuel line that runs from the top of the engine through the firewall and to the fuel flow meter in the dash. It had broken between the fitting and the fuel line on top of the engine.

We rode back to the north Huntsville airport in a car where we had originally taken off. During the trip back I was still hoping that I had passed the practical portion of the exam when Clyde said the phrase that I was beginning to hate. "Uh! We have a problem!"

I looked at him and asked what he was talking about.

He said that I had not completed all of the required maneuvers and therefore was not finished.

I looked at him in disbelief and asked if he was serious, which he let me know in no uncertain terms that he was. He told me to go find another plane so that we could finish.

We had arrived at the airport and I told him that I have never turned down an opportunity or excuse to fly or ride in an airplane but that I wasn't too sure that I should be testing fate again so soon. He continued to be adamant in his position and I am thankful for his professionalism and courage to fly with me as we finished what we had started earlier that morning.

Heart of Darkness

I FLY A CESSNA 421C for an architectural firm. My wife, Dianne, had come along on this trip to Oregon and we planned to spend a couple of days around Portland while my boss worked on a project in nearby Salem. The weather had been cold and rainy . . . but that's hardly surprising in Oregon in March. Now, though, as we taxied out to fly to Salem and pick up the boss before continuing to Cortez, Colorado, the left alternator refused to come on line.

Fortunately, the mechanics at Flightcraft hadn't yet left for the day. They determined that the alternator's field coil had burned out, and they had a spare alternator on the shelf. Because of the delay, my boss elected to drive back from Salem and meet us in Portland. The second preflight run-up had been entirely normal. As we'd taxied out, I'd told the boss, "If we had to lose an alternator, at least the best place to have it happen is on the ground, right in front of a major FBO. With the weather and ice we'll be going through on the way to Cortez, I wouldn't have considered flying with just one alternator." What hubris!

An hour later, we were cruising at FL 230. We'd picked up some ice during the climb-out over the Cascades, but the boots had worked fine. The heated pitot tube, windshield and props were keeping us ice free, although a haze of rime would still occasionally appear on the unheated copilot windshield as we slipped in and out of the tops.

Seattle Center had just handed us off to Salt Lake City when there was a momentary crackle in the radios, the panel light flickered and dimmed. . . and both alternator warning lights came on, together with the red LOW VOLTAGE annunicator. I immediately shed the biggest electrical loads—windshield and prop heat, the cabin heater and the radar and tried recycling both alternator field switches. No joy and even when I turned off the outside lights and all the remaining avionics except the number one comm, the transponder and the Bendix/King KLN 90B GPS, the ammeter was pegged on the discharge end of the scale.

I reached back to the awkward spot, at the extreme aft end of the big electrical panel, where Cessna put the alternator output circuit breakers. Both were tripped. The emergency alternator field switch is back there, too, but flipping it didn't change anything. The panel lights were already perceptibly dimmer than a moment before, and voltage was down below 20. Only my portable GPS (a Garmin GPS Map 195), mounted in the center of the yoke, continued to shine brightly on its own batteries.

I called Center at once and told them I needed clearance to the nearest VFR airport. "Burns, Oregon, is in your 1 o'clock position at about 40 miles," I was told. Weather there wasn't the greatest, as reported by the Burns ASOS and relayed by Center—visibility right at three miles and ceiling of around 1,500 feet in light snow and mist—but my options were dwindling with every passing minute. As I started to reply to Center that Burns was where I was going, the last comm radio went silent.

Cessna's checklist calls for resetting the alternator circuit breakers and trying to recycle the field switches again, but I had serious reservations. "We have the GPS to get us to the airport," I reasoned, "and a handheld radio to turn on the pilot-controlled runway lights when we get there.

The airplane is flying okay, even if we pick up some ice on the descent. I still have a good vacuum-powered gyro horizon, and there's a vacuum DG on the copilot side... Something has happened that was serious enough to trip two 100-amp breakers and discharge the battery in about five minutes, and I'm already busy enough without an electrical fire." I left the breakers out and gave up on the idea of getting any power back.

I also gave up on the idea of shooting the full instrument approach. On the last transmission we'd been able to receive, Center had cleared us down to 9,000 feet, adding that we could expect 7,500 once we'd passed the Wildhorse VOR, located right on the Burns airport.

I decided, instead, that I'd follow the GPS to the field, then use it to stay within two or three miles of the airport center while spiraling down to 5,000 feet. It was fortunate that I still had the NOS book of Oregon approach plates out: I knew from the GPS database that the field was at about 4,100 feet, and I had time to glance at the Burns VOR Runway 30 approach plate and see that circling minimums were about 600 feet and one mile of visibility. We were descending in solid clouds now; the windshield had iced over, and every couple of minutes there was a loud "thwack!" as ice shed from one prop or the other and hit the nose.

By now, the instrument lights had become so dim as to be useless. I handed the flashlight to Dianne to light the panel for me. Within a moment I had to hand her a second flashlight to illuminate the altimeter on her side of the panel: The electrically-powered servo altimeter on my side was unwinding at a clearly unrealistic rate and the barber pole had appeared across its counter window. Finally, in hope of saving enough power to operate the landing gear, I turned off the master switch and the last dim panel lights vanished. I pulled my handheld radio out of my flight bag, plugged my headset into its dangling adapter jacks and tried Center, but, with nothing but the little rubber ducky antenna inside the airplane, there was no answer.

The GPS map display was extremely helpful, and I simply kept the airplane on the line leading to the Burns airport. As we got closer, its handy auto-range feature kept decreasing the scale to the point that I could actually see the runway diagram. After what seemed like a long time, we arrived over the airport at 9,000 feet; I reduced power further, rolled into a 30-degree left bank, and we started down.

At around 5,500 feet I started seeing a few scattered lights on the ground. The GPS map showed the airport at our 7 o'clock position, a mile or so behind us. Tuning the handheld radio to the Burns unicom frequency, I held it up to the windshield and keyed the push-to-talk switch seven or eight times. As I continued the left descending turn I looked back over my shoulder. I've seen some lovely sights in my day—the Glen Canyon of the Colorado River before it was flooded by Lake Powell, or sunrise over the Himalayas—but they were no more beautiful than that row of runway lights, glimmering up through the mist.

I turned the master back on, held my breath and put the gear switch down. I needn't have bothered—the system was dead. I pulled the red T-handle below the panel; there was a loud hiss and the gear slammed down.

Burns, out in flat country several miles away from the town, is one of those "black hole" runways. With no flaps and an unknown amount of ice on the airplane, I kept about 120 KIAS and tried to hold 'red over just barely pink' on the VASI. We landed, turned off on a taxiway by the light of a flashlight held out the storm window and shut down in front of the FBO. As the gyros whined down to silence I could hear a dyspeptic gurgling from somewhere in the nose as the outraged hydraulic system tried to rid itself of the nitrogen from the emergency "blowdown" bottle.

We were lucky, of course, that we were close to Burns when we lost electric power and that the weather there was at least better than circling minimums. I think we were also lucky that I'm something of a gearhead "geek"—the term used charitably by my friends—and thus had the GPS Map 195 not only aboard but already mounted on the yoke and operating when the electrical system died. Similarly, we had a handheld radio in my flight bag, with its headset adapter already plugged in, and since I think of these gadgets as emergency backups, they both had their alkaline battery packs installed.

What I did right, as it turns out, was not to reset the alternator circuit breakers. Walt Sitz and Steve Hurlbert of Eagle Wings Aviation in Burns sacrificed much of their weekend to get us on our way again.

When we looked into the electrical panel, we found a charred mess. Over the years, the terminals on the two heavy wires from the 100-amp alternators had corroded, causing a high-resistance connection and a lot of heat—enough to melt a post right out of the big main bus terminal strip and allow the primary wiring to touch the airframe.

What might I have done differently? Perhaps I shouldn't have been in such a hurry to get the airplane on the ground. Apart from the pegged discharge indication on the battery and the precipitously dwindling voltage, there was no direct evidence of an electrical fire—no smells, no smoke. At the time of the failure, we were in and out of the tops at FL 230, and I knew there was VFR weather ahead if not at Boise, then certainly at Salt Lake City. I could have climbed to a "quasi-VFR" altitude above the weather—say, FL 245 or 255—at which I'd be unlikely to meet any other traffic (remember, no transponder and no lights), pressed on to VMC, and landed at a lighted airport.

I've since realized that one of the most important aids I could have used was some kind of "no hands" light source. The airplane has gone in for an annual inspection, and we're adding an extra comm antenna with its coax ending in the cockpit in case we need to use a handheld again.

The episode also brought home to me how easy it is to become complacent with modern electronic aids. In bygone years, I'd no doubt have worked out a complete flight log with leg distances, headings, times and so forth. Nowadays, I generally use a laptop computer with appropriate software to work out a flight plan and file it directly—after all, why bother to write all that stuff down when it pops up automatically on the screen of the panel-mounted GPS? Why, indeed—until the GPS goes dark. . .

Nothing against electronic aids, though! Ultimately, it was that Garmin portable GPS, and the handheld radio, that got us down safely, and if I've sometimes been cavalier in the past about taking them along, or keeping them charged, I certainly won't be in the future.

Barry Ross

CLOSE ENCOUNTERS WITH THE GROUND

PILOTS HAVE ALWAYS HAD a love/hate relationship with the ground. Leaving the earth behind is the defining characteristic of this activity we love so well; then the goal of every flight is to return safely to terra firma.

But it's the ground that is the bane of aviation safety. It is either on an ill-fated departure from the ground or on an unexpected return to it that nearly every aviation accident occurs.

Luckily, in true *I Learned About Flying From That* fashion, the stories here all end, if not happily, at least with no injuries, though each gave the pilots flying that day a good surge of adrenaline.

In one too close encounter tale, an admittedly overconfident pilot tells of his unannounced visit to a friend's private grass strip and how he wound up getting back out, if only by the barest of threads. In another, our own Russ Munson tells about his downwind landing at Sun Valley in his prized Super Cub. Another pilot, this one in a tiny Cessna 150, relates the story of getting stuck on the runway, immobilized by, of all things, an arresting cable, as a giant C-5B Galaxy bore down on him from above.

With small airplanes takeoff and landing accidents usually result in bent metal, damaged egos and little or no injury to the occupants of the airplanes involved. And if it's a good story, it might wind up in *Flying* in the form of a heartfelt *I Learned About Flying From That*.

CHAPTER FIVE

We'll Meet in the Middle

CRUISING AT 14,000 FEET in my P-Baron over rural Nebraska, I looked down with contentment at the farmland coming to life with early spring colors. I was flying the short route from Omaha to Atkinson, where I did a monthly orthopedics clinic at the local hospital. I was Associate Professor of Surgery at Creighton University and did the clinic purely for the personal pleasure of flying my airplane, getting out into the countryside, and spending time with the western Nebraska ranchers, who are a special breed of friendly folks.

Descending over the James Baker Municipal Airport at O'Neill, I cancelled IFR, called my position over the unicom, and flew the pattern into Atkinson's 4,000 foot gravel strip. When the nosewheel touched down, the Baron swerved right, then left before coming under control. Damn! After more than a decade in this airplane, I wheelbarrowed my landing. I was glad I didn't have my usual resident and medical student along. But the P-Baron is nose-heavy, particularly with no one in the back seats, and it's hard to avoid hitting the nosewheel first.

My clinic was brief that morning, and I was soon headed home, intent on doing a better job of holding the nosewheel off the ground.

"Intercept localizer one eight, track inbound," instructed the approach controller. Thirty miles out, and I was already locked onto final. I love big airports as well as small.

"Three-six-eight-nine November, cleared to land one eight, hold short of intersection one four right," said the tower.

"Eight-nine November, cleared to land," I answered.

"No sir, you must read back hold-short instructions."

"Eight-nine November, cleared to land one eight, hold short of intersection one four right," I answered.

The land-and-hold-short clearance was almost automatic. Usually, by the time you were landed, the conflicting traffic had cleared, and the tower instructed, "Cross intersection, turn left at Charley, taxi to parking." You seldom actually held short. The restriction often seemed to be given just to keep the controllers' options open.

I looked out the right window for the anticipated airline traffic on final for runway one four right. This time I could not see a conflict. Often an airliner appeared at the same altitude, with no relative motion, by definition a collision course. I always remembered the country tune, "I'll start walkin' your way. You start walkin' mine. We'll meet in the middle. . ." But apparently not today.

When flying the Baron VFR, I usually touch down on the first part of the runway, below the glideslope. I know you're not supposed to land under the visual path of the VASI, but then I don't have to vary technique for shorter runways. I concentrated on making a perfect approach. This time I was going to keep the nosewheel off, and I held 12 inches manifold pressure into the flare. On touchdown, the Baron swerved violently, right, then left. I fought for control and fought to keep the airplane on the runway.

"Eight-nine November, if you would stop at that hold line right ahead, it would be fine," the tower controller said with surprising calm.

I slammed the brakes and looked up to see the 737 racing through the intersection just ahead, nosewheel off the ground, just at liftoff speed.

Back at my desk, I was still shaking, still not comprehending how I had lost control, how I had forgotten the hold-short instruction. In front of me I noticed a pink telephone message from Gene Simpson. "Don't fly your airplane until you change the nose tire. It could explode on takeoff." The note was dated the previous day. This was the second Baron I had bought from Gene, and he remains a good friend. I phoned him.

"I passed through Elliott Aviation and saw your nose line was delaminating," Gene said. "It wasn't much, but I've seem them before. I couldn't get you on the phone, so I left a message with your office, and I told the line guys here to remind you." No one had passed on the message.

Had I collided with the 737, even my ATP rating would not have kept me from being labeled a careless doctor-pilot. I have always tried to be professional in my flying but also have assumed that I can make a mistake just as anyone. I was too quick to blame my flying technique for the initial landing problem in Atkinson when I should have blamed my pre-flight technique. But a tire defect can be hidden or subtle. In the Sundowner, the notorious crow-hop landing ends either in a go-around or in a crash. Any number of other events could happen suddenly without any major pilot error that would put the airplane through the intersection. Had I touched down on the IFR blocks 1,000 feet down the runway, I never would have stopped the Baron in the remaining 3,000 feet. And it would be easy to anticipate the routine "cross intersection, turn left at Charley" clearance.

There is considerable controversy about the simultaneous use of intersecting runways with land-and-hold-short clearances. The Omaha controller placed us on a collision course by the timing of his takeoff clearance for the 737. Certainly the tower controller also provided the safety margin on that day by his vigilance. They are friendly competent controllers in the Omaha tower, and I am not criticizing them.

Revised standards for LAHSO (land-and-hold-short operations) published by Jeppesen in May, 1999, specify that "air carrier aircraft shall not be issued a clearance to land or depart on a runway when a non-air carrier aircraft is landing to hold short of the air carrier runway." This change should comfort the traveling public. By the old procedure, it was most often the responsibility of the small airplane pilot to make the land-and-hold-short procedure work. When two airplanes are established on a collision course, it is amazing how difficult it is to break away and how close you actually come even when you spot the conflict early. I think the standards should require that no controller ever place two airplanes on a collision course and require a pilot to accomplish a maneuver so that they don't meet in the middle.

Tailwind Gamble

I'VE NEVER MUCH BELIEVED IN LUCK. Not that I have answers to life's unfathomable twists of fate that we sometimes attribute to luck, it's just that a lot of what we call luck, good or bad, seems to be of our own doing. Have you ever noticed, for example, that working hard often brings "good luck"? And that blindly slogging through the minefields of daily life provokes "bad luck"? And what about the times when you know that a certain act will involve needless risk but you do it anyway? Sooner or later you get caught. When you do it's not bad luck, it's stupid. That's what I was in the late morning of last August 18th.

Three friends and I took off at 7:30 a.m. that day from Friedman Memorial Airport in Hailey, Idaho, located in the beautiful mountain valley in which Ketchum and Sun Valley are also nestled. We were on a breakfast flight to Smiley Creek, a lovely grass strip 40 miles to the northwest. One friend flew with me in my Piper Super Cub, and the others flew a Piper Pacer and a Cessna 140; three taildraggers out to enjoy a beautiful morning. Our route meandered a bit in order to check out the extent of forest fire smoke that was choking parts of Idaho last summer, but we soon slid over Galena Pass and down to land on the long, smooth turf at Smiley Creek. After parking wingtip to wingtip we took a few photographs of these three veteran aircraft that seemed so at home in the grass with their noses pointed skyward. Just a few months earlier mine had been completely rebuilt, and her fresh Cub Yellow finish fairly glowed in the morning sun.

Directly across the highway from the Smiley Creek strip is a rustic roadside cafe that is a favorite with pilots. My friends and I hadn't seen each other for several months, so there was a lot of lying to catch up on over a leisurely breakfast.

It was about 11 a.m. by the time we neared Hailey on our return flight. At five miles out the tower said the wind was calm and Runway 31 was the active. Then three miles out the tower reported the wind from 180 degrees at five knots and cleared us to land on 31 as a flight of three. Hailey Airport has a single, paved 6,602-foot strip, Runway 31/13, and the town is immediately off the departure end of 31. To avoid overflying the town for noise-abatement reasons, the airport authority prefers traffic to land on 31 and take off on 13, even with some tailwind component. There is also a slight upgrade on 31. My own guideline at Hailey is to request the opposite runway if the active has a tailwind component over five knots, and the tower controllers have always been willing to oblige. I didn't this time. My finger rested on the mike switch, but I didn't press it.

I was number two behind the Pacer, which landed well down on 31 without a problem. The wind was now reported as 180 degrees at six knots, and I was wary of landing with the quartering left tailwind. Was the wind increasing or was it a mild gust that would soon diminish? Turning final, I considered abandoning the approach and requesting Runway 13. It is far better to land with a quartering headwind than tailwind, especially in a taildragger. But the air was smooth, the windsock at the end of 31, although indicating the tailwind, drooped benignly; my friend in the Pacer had rolled out fine, I was tracking the centerline with negligible crosswind correction, and I didn't want to disrupt the traffic pattern needlessly. I decided to continue the approach and make a wheel landing so that if I didn't like the first few seconds of the roll-out I could make an immediate go-around while the tail was still up.

Planting the main gear on the runway just beyond the numbers, I retracted the flaps, and held forward stick to keep maximum weight on the wheels in case braking was needed. The roll-out was straight and easy for about 100 feet, not the least bit squirrely. I was relieved. Aside from the faster groundspeed, the landing seemed normal. Then, suddenly, even before the tail started to settle, the wind increased considerably. I applied right brake and full right rudder as the airplane veered sharply to the left. My actions had no apparent effect against the strength of the wind. The airplane wasn't slowing, and continued to swerve even more quickly to the left. Was the brake functioning, I thought? Yes, I could hear the screeching of rubber from the right tire. This couldn't be happening. An instant later we were off the runway, and the tail was swinging around to the right with the vicious momentum of a full-blown groundloop. Further braking at this point would only aggravate the situation. My beloved Super Cub which I have owned for 26 years without putting a scratch on it, this graceful, adventurous machine that had taken me many times across the United States, was now skidding awkwardly sideways through the rough. I thought we might just slide to a stop without damage when the right gear, digging into a depression in the dirt, collapsed and folded under the fuselage. As it did, the right wingtip slammed into the ground and bent the spars upward outboard of the strut attach points. Amid the dust and sounds of rumbling and structure-bending the little airplane heaved to a stop, having turned more than 180 degrees.

Switch off, master off, fuel off: The emergency procedure was automatic. My passenger and I crawled out and stood up. My first thought after feeling thankful that neither one of us was injured, was that the southerly ground-swell of a breeze hitting my face was in excess of 10 knots, which was confirmed by the now-billowing windsock. Whatever it was at its peak, the wind had exerted a force greater than the airplane and I could handle. I looked at the runway and saw the track of the right tire. Under heavy braking it had left a graceful, arcing skid mark from the middle of the asphalt to the edge, then bushwhacked a trail through the grass and dirt and stones that widened and deepened as the aircraft careened to the point where the gear failed. Then I looked at my airplane heeled over on a crumpled wing, and I felt like I had kicked a friend. The old saying came to mind: There are two kinds of taildragger pilots, those who have groundlooped, and those who will. It was no consolation. I waved to the tower signaling that we were okay. Moments later the crash truck arrived, but there were no ruptured fuel tanks or lines.

With the generous help of the Friedman airport manager and crew, and the expertise of Sun Valley Aviation's superb maintenance staff, we soon had the airplane in a hangar. Fortunately, the prop didn't strike the ground. Damage was confined to the right gear, right wing, right tailfeathers, and the lower rear longerons where the tailwheel attached. After reporting the accident by phone to the FAA office in Boise and calling my insurance company, there was nothing more to do at the moment other than to analyze what happened.

Let's take a close look at the conditions that morning. Hailey lies in a valley that rises to the northwest. Usually, the early-morning surface wind is from the northwest because the cooler, heavier air from the higher terrain flows down the valley. When we took off at 7:30, for example, the wind was five knots almost straight down Runway 31. By late morning on a summer day the air has heated up enough for the winds to begin to shift and flow up the valley. We landed during this cranky transition period. Also, as at many mountain airports, the wind at Hailey can be quite different from one end of the runway to the other as its flow is influenced by the interaction of the prevailing weather system with nearby hills, airport buildings and canyons, which can create a venturi effect funneling a fast blast of wind toward portions of the airport. Wind direction and velocity as measured at the tower, therefore, is not necessarily accurate for the touchdown zone. That's why Friedman Memorial has three windsocks. Wind in the mountains can be trickier than a politician in heat.

Speaking of heat, what about density altitude? Was it a factor here? It sure did not help. We learned as student pilots that true airspeed increases with the thinner air at altitude. At a high-density-altitude airport, therefore, you land and take off at a higher groundspeed even though your indicated airspeed is the same as at sea level. The two main forces in a groundloop, kinetic energy and centrifugal force, both increase as the square of the groundspeed. The faster you go, the more damage you do when kinetic energy, the energy of a body in motion, is brought to a sudden stop, and the quicker your taildragger plays crack-the-whip once centrifugal force is triggered by a swerve.

The temperature that morning was about 75° F, so the density altitude at the 5,315-foot elevation airport was 7,200 feet. My indicated airspeed at touchdown was probably 45 knots. Using the rule of thumb that true airspeed increases by two percent for each thousand feet above sea level, my groundspeed at touchdown, disregarding wind, was some six knots faster than it would have been at my sea-level home airport on Long Island. Tossing in a tailwind component of about five knots (before the gust) brings the groundspeed up to an 11-knot increase over sea level. Putting it all together, my groundspeed at touchdown on Runway 31 was about 56 knots. In a Super Cub that's moving. It would have been 46 knots on Runway 13, a big difference for a little airplane.

What of luck and what-ifs? Was it bad luck, as someone said, that the wind increased just after I touched down? Was it bad luck, therefore, that caused the groundloop? Accidents usually result from more than one factor. When I succumbed to the herd mentality by accepting Runway 31 I took on additional risk. My neck was out. The wind merely wielded the ax. What if I had rammed in full throttle the second the aircraft started to swerve? Could I have become airborne before hitting the hefty runway marker immediately beyond the place where I left the runway? Maybe, although torque and P-factor at full power would initially tend to pull the nose farther to the left and I already had full opposite controls. Applying power can often get you out of trouble, but in this case any opportunity to do so would have been extremely brief. After that, power would have only increased the damage. What if I had landed three-point? Would I have been down before the wind picked up? And if so, would the tailwheel on the asphalt have prevented the loss of control? Possibly. The groundspeed would have been at least five knots slower, too. In hindsight this would have been a better choice.

There is a reason why we never see birds landing downwind. The only sure way to have prevented the groundloop would have been to land on Runway 13. Shoulda, coulda, woulda. The fact is I didn't, and I got caught. Luck had nothing to do with it.

Got Hung Up

AN AIRCRAFT CARRIER is a massive ship: 80,000 tons, 1,000 feet long, and drafting nearly 40 feet. The Thimble Shoals channel in Chesapeake Bay is just about deep enough to let such a ship into the U.S. Navy's largest base, Naval Air Station Norfolk, Virginia. When the carrier is loaded, it drafts even more. Since scraping the bottom is bad, carriers get "unloaded" before coming in. Off with the F-14 Tomcats, off with the Sea King helos and off with the E-2 Hawkeyes. Do airplanes really weigh that much? In the government they do. Each F-14 is 72,000 pounds, each A-7 is about 40,000, each SH-3 Sea King is 20,000, each A-6 another 60,000 and so on. When a carrier is normally loaded with over a hundred airplanes, unloading before coming into port makes a big difference in draft.

Now, carrier pilots are supposed to be the best in the world, right? (I know, I know; Alaskan bush pilots rate right up there.) So what I can't figure out is why such great pilots can't land on a normal runway without their annoying arresting gear. For all of my research, I cannot figure out why an F-14 can't stop using brakes alone on a mile-long field.

I was a member of the Norfolk Navy Flying Club a few years ago. It was a small club, with only two Cessna 150s and a 206. We had a maintenance trailer and a small clubhouse trailer on the field at N.A.S. Norfolk. It was a fun club to be a part of, because of the F-14/A-6 flight test center, the Sea Stallion wing, and all of the big military planes that went in and out every day.

There was one drawback, however. Since N.A.S. Norfolk is where carrier planes routinely land, there's an arresting cable strung across the runway. It made for a challenging obstacle for a plane with tiny tires, like a 150.

The arresting cable itself is braided steel line about an inch thick with large rubber bands on the ends, strung tight, and suspended about five inches off the runway by 10-inch-diameter rubber discs. The trick with a small plane was not to take off over it, or land and then hit it, but to carefully taxi up to it, and then "bump" over it, or in landing, to land just beyond it.

One fine day a friend and I had decided to go flying. After the usual pre-flight routine, taxiing and run-up, we were at the threshold and ready for takeoff. The tower granted permission and asked me to expedite because of landing traffic. Naturally, I looked out to the final leg and saw what looked like a fairly large airplane quite a ways off. No problem. I had plenty of time to taxi out and carefully deal with the cable, and then let 'er rip.

I acknowledged the tower and taxied out. As always, I slowed down just before the cable, made sure I had full rise on the elevator, and with about five feet to go, gave a little blast of the throttle to "jump" the nose gear over (the most delicate part). Usually, having just cleared the nose gear, the mains will clear on momentum alone. This time I ran into trouble. The five inches of cable height is almost halfway up the mains, and I didn't have enough speed for them to clear.

It was like a miniature carrier landing. Suddenly we were jerked to a halt, and even went backwards for about a foot. On a small scale, we were forced forward against our shoulder straps. That's when the brilliant thought came to mind: Whoa! We're stuck on the cable. Three seconds later a more interesting thought came to mind: Landing traffic.

I looked back and around the rudder to see how close the traffic was. In the 20 seconds that had passed, it had gotten significantly closer, was on short final, and was close enough to clearly identify. It was a plane I had seen many times on the ramp, a massive ship with a very distinct appearance—a large round nose, enormous wings backswept and with negative dihedral, four massive smoking engines, and a huge T tail. Unmistakably, the landing traffic was a C-5B Galaxy.

I was suddenly very focused on getting out of the way. I don't think I was worried about getting hit. My biggest concern was the thousands of dollars it would cost the taxpayers if the C-5 pilot had to do a go-around. Either way it was a heated moment. "GET OUT AND PUSH!" My poor passenger was unable to push us over the cable, even if I went to full throttle.

He was standing in the door trying to push against the door frame and step on the cable at the same time. No joy. Now what? Should we crouch down in the road like a helpless rabbit trapped by someone's headlights? Should we pull the mixture and run? No combination of throttle and control input was getting us anywhere. The radio was alive with concern. I had one more idea: We would both get out and push.

I know what you're thinking: A plane taking off under full power with the pilot and passenger left behind tangled in some wire, right? No way. I thought the same thing. We did both get out, and with the throttle at idle, pushed the plane back until the nose gear was again touching the cable. Was it safe? How should I know? Drastic times call for drastic measures. I actually got halfway out, so I still had one leg in the cockpit, and my former friend was already outside and we desperately pushed the plane back. Then he got in. Before he could even close his door, I went to full down elevator (hoping for the wheel-barrel effect) and full power. In a convulsive lunge, the poor little 150 tripped clumsily over the cable and then in the normal, underpowered fashion, slowly came up to rotation speed and took off. The landing traffic, though concerned, landed normally without further incident.

I must have spent 10 minutes trying to figure out the best way to word it in my logbook. I eventually just wrote "Got hung up on arresting gear during takeoff roll," with no mention of any landing traffic. I guess next time I'm told to expedite, I'll sooner sit on the ramp and wait. It's always fun to watch landing traffic, anyway.

Summer Float Flying: Beware of Hot, Humid Weather

THE TASK SOUNDED SIMPLE: fly five adults to Devils Lake for a day of fishing. Pick them up before dark with their day's catch and bring them back to base. Yet of all the flying I have done (at last count my logbook showed more than 5,000 hours and 12 different aircraft types, including everything from Cessna 152s to F-18s), this is my story of "I Learned About Flying From That."

I was flying a C-185 floatplane in Barry's Bay Ontario, in 1985. Devils Lake was our favorite fishing hole. It was the roundest and smallest of all the lakes we took our customers to, but it had the best fishing. Landing there was never easy; it was always glassy water, and a pilot had absolutely no room to land long. Taking off was worse; you had to taxi into the weeds to give yourself enough room to get airborne and clear the 40-foot spruce trees at the end of the lake. Did I mention the winds, how about calm winds... all the time.

My passengers that day were an ex-World War II bomber pilot, his wife, son, daughter and her husband. I took them in two groups due to weight concerns. The bomber pilot was very large and had to hold his stomach in with his hands so that I could have full use of the yoke/elevators. Needless to say, he sat up front for weight and balance considerations.

The morning trips in to Devils Lake were uneventful. The weather was perfect but rather hot and humid, with light winds. The light winds resulted in glassy water landings, but I was well practiced at these.

At approximately 4 p.m. I flew back to Devils Lake to pick up my passengers. My first load consisted of the bomber pilot, his daughter and her husband, a collapsible boat, a small outboard motor and some fish. My first takeoff was aborted as I could tell that the aircraft was not getting on the step quickly enough to get airborne in time. Despite leaving the boat behind, I had to abort my second takeoff for the same reason, not stepping up quickly enough, as we like to say in the business.

Attempt number three was going to be the one in my mind. I left behind the outboard motor and the fish; I pumped out the floats to bone dry and took only the three passengers. I taxied into the shallowest of water to give myself every possible inch of lake to take off from. As I turned toward the middle of the lake, I went full power so that the instant I was aligned for takeoff the engine would be operating at maximum horsepower. The acceleration felt good, and I was quickly planing. I lifted one float out of the water to reduce all possible drag. We were now committed to take off or crash, as the decision to go or not to go had to be made as soon as you were on the step.

Airborne! Even if only in ground effect, we were airborne in plenty of time to clear all obstacles. Then the unthinkable happened; as soon as I tried to climb out of ground effect, we sank back on to the lake! There was no doubt in my mind; we were going to crash! I immediately cut off the engine, dropped the water rudders and dropped full flap. With the water rudders down, I tried to do some fishtailing. I had to make the airplane come off the step to slow our collision with the shore and the trees.

Then I saw it. I had seen it before but never considered it usable. A shallow creek fed into the lake and it was coming up fast. Was it deep enough? I had no idea. I was not even sure if my wings would clear the trees on either side at the mouth of the creek. Before I completed that thought we were past the trees and going up the winding creek like a rocket.

Only the laws of physics and aerodynamics were going to stop this floatplane, or, wouldn't you know it, a beaver dam! As we came around a bend in the creek a beaver dam appeared dead ahead, blocking the entire creek. We were going to ram it. All of my schooling, flying, effort and luck was about to end due to the handiwork of a family of eager beavers.

God must have been smiling or possibly laughing at this point and decided enough was enough, because 30 feet before impact the floatplane came off the step. Once a floatplane stops planing it will come to a complete stop in a matter of feet, and it did. No crash, no smash, no damage and, most important, nobody hurt. I simply looked over at the wide-eyed bomber pilot still holding his stomach in and said, "Sorry." He never responded, and, in fact, I don't recall him talking to me again, ever.

I jumped into the waist deep creek to pivot the aircraft around, as it was not wide enough to taxi turn. Once pointed in the other direction, I tried to start the engine, which, with three aborted takeoffs, was overheating. I eventually started the engine and taxied all passengers back to shore to await sunset, cooler temperatures and better takeoff conditions.

Sunset arrived and it was decided that I would fly out only the daughter and her husband. The others would have to spend the night in a makeshift cabin, but they had plenty of provisions, including beer.

I was certain I had only enough battery power to try one more start. With that in mind I decided to paddle the floatplane to the middle of the lake. The son had volunteered to bring his sister and her husband to the airplane by boat. I noticed he had been drinking but thought nothing of it at the time.

There we were, the daughter, her husband and I, ready for takeoff. I had all the switches set and was waiting and watching the son drive the boat back to shore. I noticed he was steering from the wrong side and had a beer in his other hand. He was well clear of us when I started the floatplane, but I then noticed the boat starting a sharp turn. The son had lost control of the boat and had lost his balance. The boat had suddenly turned 180 degrees and was headed straight toward us. I desperately tried to turn but could not avoid the oncoming boat. I had no choice but to shut down the engine.

What I saw next sent a chill down my spine. The son was going between my floats with his arms up trying to protect his body and head from my turning propeller. I quickly opened my door, dreading what I might see. Miraculously, the son was unhurt. He had leaned over the back end of the boat and avoided the propeller by one foot. Now what to do? My battery was essentially dead. My base would surely think I had crashed, as had happened a few summers ago to another pilot. We all headed back to shore to spend the night. I opened my VFR supplement and built a signal fire for the arrival of the Search and Rescue (SAR) helicopter. I decided to sleep in the floatplane to welcome our rescuers. All others slept in the cabin.

Around midnight I was dreaming and hearing these words "Peter, Peter." As I came to I realized the words weren't "Peter, Peter," but, "They're here, they're here." There, hovering 200 feet away at an altitude of 100 feet, in the blackest of nights with a billion stars shining as a backdrop, was a SAR helicopter from the Canadian Forces. Its turbine exhaust was spewing forth a blue flame, the rotor wash rocked my floatplane and its search-light was blinding. I was unable to contact them on the radio to tell them I needed another battery. So they lowered a SAR technician down on a winch to find out if all was OK. I notified the SAR technician nobody was hurt and passed on my request for another battery.

The next morning another floatplane flew in with an extra battery. The weather had cooled and the takeoff was a non-issue. All passengers were delivered safely back to base, albeit a day late.

So what did I learn? Number one: Takeoff performance can be seriously degraded due to hot, humid weather. If in doubt, look at your takeoff charts and carefully calculate your takeoff for the conditions of the day. Number two: Ground effect is more pronounced than most pilots realize, especially light aircraft in hot, humid conditions. Ground effect may help you or in my case this day may hurt you as your expectations exceed reality.

This story does have a happy ending; no one was hurt and the remainder of my summer float flying went uneventfully. I ended up joining the Canadian Air Force and to this day I still love what I do for a living, flying!

Bambi Bashing

IT WAS ANOTHER GORGEOUS SUMMER MORNING as I completed the walkaround on C-FDRV, the C-150 that I soloed in and my favorite of the fleet. I had spent the week completing and then going over my flight plan to make sure that this Saturday morning flight would be perfect. It would be my first real venture away from my home airport just north of Toronto and the first opportunity to use the skills I had learned over the previous eight months. After all, what good is an airplane if you can't go anywhere? I was 17 years old and worked part-time as a line attendant to help pay for my training.

Dave, my flight instructor, had gone over my calculations and map work and deemed them accurate enough to get us to Muskoka, Peterborough and home (Toronto-Buttonville Airport). The flight to Muskoka was uneventful and we cruised happily at 4,500 feet in smooth air as I kept track of our position and times. At Muskoka Dave had me practice a short-field landing even though the runway was paved and several thousand feet long, but as all good instructors do he took every opportunity to teach something new or have me practice a drill regardless of how proficiently or how poorly I had done in the past.

After a quick drink, a briefing that pointed out some of my errors, and a look at the current weather at the flight service station (and the requisite stamp in the logbook to prove I had actually been there, more important for my solo trip later on) we took off towards Peterborough. It was early afternoon now and the convective currents typical of summer afternoons in Ontario tossed us about at 3,500 feet for the hour and a bit that it took us to reach the uncontrolled runway. A soft-field landing (more practice) had us on the ground for a late lunch.

After another look at the weather and another stamp for the log, we taxied out along the grass next to the runway and waited for several aircraft to land. Dave told me that he would like to see a simulated soft-field takeoff, so as I taxied out onto the runway I held the control column fully aft, turned using rudder only, and applied full power. As the plane accelerated the nose of the little Cessna rose and I decreased elevator just enough to keep it at the correct nose-high attitude that I had been taught. At this attitude forward visibility was poor and as the aircraft lifted off the ground I began to lower the nose so I could accelerate in ground effect to climb speed. Just as I began to relax back pressure on the yoke, there was a loud crash and the airplane shook violently, struck the ground and bounced high above the runway. Only Dave's quick reaction saved us from plowing back into the runway as this startled and scared-stiff student pilot looked on, dumbfounded and unsure of what had happened.

At 500 feet with the airplane flying normally and me wondering how I could have hit the runway (my only rationale for what had happened), Dave, with a serious tone, asked me to look at the left main landing gear and see if it looked all right; it did. He then told me to lean over and look at the right gear, which I did after unbuckling my seat belt. My heart skipped at least two beats—the gear was gone, or rather it was bent right back and almost touched the fuselage.

Dave was silent, which had the effect of making me even more nervous. On top of that I still thought that somehow (exactly how, I had no idea) I had struck the runway as the plane mushed above it gaining speed. After turning downwind Dave motioned towards the runway. As I looked down I finally realized what had occurred: There on the runway was a dead deer. With the nose-high attitude of the 150 I did not see the deer dart across the runway, although Dave told me he had seen a brown blur. I remained silent, thanking God that it hadn't been an error on my part and at the same time asking Him to get me down in one piece.

Dave called clear of the circuit and spoke saying that we would fly back and land at our home airport, and then gave me control. In my long and distinguished flying career (all of 30 hours) I had never been scared, I mean really scared. Spins were nerve-wracking at first until I became comfortable with them, but this was, as they say, a whole new ball game. It was a short flight back to our base and the entire time Dave kept me navigating—I couldn't tell if he was nervous or not. The aircraft flew normally although some rudder was required to compensate for the drag on the right side. Ten miles out he radioed the tower and told them of the situation. They had us circle for about 15 minutes before directing us into the zone and onto the lefthand downwind for 15. As we approached the airport we noticed the flashing lights of the emergency vehicles. The airport fire truck as well as several local fire units, police cars and two ambulances had been called in. I was scared now!

Dave briefed me on the emergency procedures and how he was going to land. He made a single low pass so that ground observers could inspect the nose gear, which we could not see. We were told that it appeared undamaged. Dave turned final and set up the approach, the twinkling of the emergency vehicle lights all too obvious. I tightened my seat belt. As we crossed the threshold he flared normally but used left aileron to keep the right side off the ground as we decelerated. Slowly, as the speed bled off, DRV touched down and rolled out on the two good wheels until the fully deflected aileron lost its effectiveness and the right side settled onto the runway. The aircraft veered right and began to slide towards the side of the runway, the entire time feeling as if it was about to flip over. It came to a stop and we scrambled out—the step down on my side being much higher than normal. We were met by the fire crews and all of us stopped and stared at the Cessna. It looked just like a bird with a wounded wing. It was leaning to the right on the wingtip and the tail, with the nose angled up into the afternoon sky. I was happy to be on the ground.

Seven years later I am still flying (a commercial pilot now) and enjoying every hour. Looking back now I realize that the situation wasn't as dangerous as I had thought at the time, although I certainly would not want to repeat it. The deer, as I learned later on my solo trip to Peterborough, became dinner for several locals. The little Cessna, C-FDRV, was repaired and placed back on the line. To this day it is still known as the Deer Ramming Vehicle.

Breaking the String

THE ERCOUPE IS A THOROUGHLY ENJOYABLE AIRPLANE TO FLY. What a jewel Fred Weick created when he won the Guggenheim Safety Award in the 1930s. My aircraft was a 415C. It rolled out of the factory in Riverdale, Maryland, in the same year that I was born. Flying it was a déja vu experience, a trip back in time to "Walter Mitty" days that I had not had the privilege of experiencing. It was like being reincarnated in aluminum and fabric. The two of us were 50 years old and enjoying an aviation mid-life crisis.

I have owned three Coupes, and each one had its own personality. On a crisp fall Sunday morning, the sky was just beginning to lighten with the rising of the sun. The air was deathly still. One of my favorite pursuits was to trim the airplane for cruise at 1,000 feet with the side windows down. Then I could fly it through the still air by leaning forward in the shoulder harness to descend and leaning back against the seat back to climb. Turns were initiated by putting my hand into the slipstream on the right for a turn to starboard and out the left side for a turn to port. In this manner I was able to sail my Coupe through an invisible ocean of air with a number of swooping and diving maneuvers to my heart's content. My arms got so tired of this fun. The thought struck me that they were withstanding 1,465 pounds of airplane and pilot at 100 miles per hour. No wonder they were getting sore. This idea of being one with a machine led me to delusions of grandeur about my capabilities and the aircraft's willingness to perform on cue.

I was over the Oso Valley just north and east of Arlington. Below was the grass strip of an acquaintance situated on a sweeping bend in the Stillaguamish River. His invitation rang in my mind. "Why, sure I think it's long enough to land an Ercoupe on! I used to fly an old Cessna 150 out of there all the time. Just be at treetop level over the river bend and drop the flaps to full." I had a two-control Coupe, so there were no flaps. However, I felt that I was so adept at wagging the wings to spill off lift that I could work it out just the same as flaps.

I circled down over the strip and noted that the neatly mowed lawn glistened in the morning dew. At one end of the strip was the river bend and the tall fir trees. At the other end was a fence and a road with a meticulously maintained mobile home and shop to the left. There on the deck of the homestead were two boys and their dad. I'd even have an appreciative audience for my arrival.

As I let down further over the river, the trees loomed ominously, hiding the strip. I crossed their tops at 65 mph and settled in toward the runway wagging my wings to spill off lift. The wheels touched down at the half-way point, and one touch on the brakes turned the whole works into a slipping and sliding grass-born Sea-Doo that was rapidly heading toward the house. Another tap on the brakes and we careened in another direction. Two inputs were enough for me. I firewalled the throttle and held the nosewheel down as the barbed wire fence filled the windscreen. At the last possible moment I pulled the Coupe up in the air knowing I did not have enough airspeed to maintain flight but hoping for a miracle and to jump the fence. The nose rose, and I expected it to go end over end. I knew I hadn't come up high enough to clear the highest strand. But the airplane continued forward uninterrupted and settled into the adjacent grass field once...slowing with the contact...and then again with less resistance... before wallowing into the air like a wounded duck.

I couldn't believe I was in one piece; I got feeling a little weak. I established a climb out of the valley and back to my home base. Upon landing I taxied in and inspected the airplane. There was a hint of green on the propeller tips, and grass was stuffed into the main and nose gear but otherwise she appeared to be unscathed. I cleaned off the evidence, put away the airplane and drove my car out to Oso to the grass strip.

"I am so very sorry!" I said. "That was not like me to be so careless. If I damaged your fence or your neighbor's field I will pay for whatever the costs are." He smiled and said, "Well you gave us quite an exciting Sunday morning. My boys will remember that landing attempt for a long time. You didn't hurt the fence and the farmer next door is a friend. You can't even tell where you touched down in the grass. Didn't you know the grass would be wet?"

"I can't believe I didn't hit that top strand of barbed wire and buy the farm," I added. "Well there's a reason for that!" he explained. "I thought I'd give myself an extra measure of protection for flying out of here...so a while ago I replaced that top strand of barbed wire with a piece of string.

Looks like I'll have to replace the string." I drove back to Arlington realizing that I had been saved by a slender thread. Today a fellow pilot with some foresight saved my bacon. Tomorrow I will be more careful.

Adventure With a Hot Mag

THE JUMPERS WERE EAGER TO GO. It was late afternoon and we had to climb 10,000 feet into a simmering Idaho sky. New to the hustle and bustle of a busy skydiving operation, I jumped aboard, squeezed behind the yoke and dropped heavily into the seat, unaccustomed to the weight and bulk of my reserve parachute. As the last jumper slipped in beside me, I fumbled self-consciously with my headset, groped for a jack on the unfamiliar panel and buckled in. With no written checklist to go by, I jabbed the mixture, prop and carb heat, pulled the master and started the engine. Having checked the mags earlier, prior to the day's first load, I pulled down a notch of flaps, unscrewed the mixture an inch and firewalled the throttle.

Halfway down the runway, the Skylane still seemed reluctant to fly. Was it the density altitude? I eased the yoke back, trying to coax her off. Then I realized the engine was not its usual, boastful self.

"Stop!" cried the jump master. I pulled hard on the throttle and stood on the brakes, shuttering to a halt just as the concrete petered into ruts and weeds. Seated on the floor behind and to my right, the jump master had a clear view of the panel. "Your mags are off." I stared, confused, at the ignition key. How can the engine be running with the magnetos turned off? "We have a hot mag," he said.

In my haste to take off, I had forgotten to turn on the magnetos. But when I pressed the starter, an ungrounded magneto—the "hot" mag— fired the engine. Unaware we were operating on a single magneto, all seemed ready for takeoff. Although she was about to unstick when we aborted, I don't know whether we could have flown out of ground effect. Five souls, warm weather and incomplete combustion would have made for a lousy trip. That evening, I reconstructed the chain of events leading to the abortive takeoff. There were no excuses; I simply should have known better. After all, that Skylane had warned me—four times.

The first warning came during the mag check that morning. The RPM did not drop when the ignition was switched from "both" to "right." I sloughed it off, assuming the drop was subtle enough to be lost in my hasty switching. What I didn't recognize was the sign of an ungrounded magneto. When I selected "right," the left magneto should have dropped off line, registering the usual loss of power. But because the left magneto was not grounded—due, in all likelihood, to a broken lead—it remained on. What I mistook for a good right magneto was actually an ungrounded left magneto.

The second warning came from the magneto switch, which was in the "off" position, as I had left it when shutting down earlier in the day. In my haste—and without the guidance of a written checklist— I overlooked the switch when starting the engine, thereby setting myself up to launch on a single set of spark plugs.

The third warning came at engine start. Conscientiously maintained and carefully operated, the engine had a pleasing habit of starting instantly. This time it hesitated before catching—just for a moment, but long enough to notice. I chalked it up to the vagaries of carburetion.

The final warning came on takeoff, when the sound and feel of the aircraft were out of the ordinary. Had I glanced at the tach or manifold pressure gauge, I might have been alerted earlier; as it happened, the takeoff was not aborted until a passenger called out. Not the proudest moment of my flying career.

It had all the ingredients of an NTSB accident report: one part mechanical glitch, two parts pilot error. To the ungrounded magneto were added aviation's two greatest vices: haste and complacency. I've read plenty of accident reports over the years, ever amazed by the negligence pilots can demonstrate. Attempting takeoff with magnetos turned off? It's with a wry smile that I imagine other pilots' incredulity had I not been spared disaster that afternoon.

Today, I fly bigger and faster planes on much longer trips. But I haven't forgotten the lessons learned on that Idaho airstrip. I add fuel, perform a thorough walk-around, check avionics and charts and prepare my manifest well before departure. I do all I can to avoid haste and complacency and their inevitable, ignominious consequences.

SNOW AND
ICE AND
GLOOM OF
NIGHT

LIKE EVERY PILOT, when I read an installment of *I Learned About Flying From That* I put myself in the pilot's seat of that very airplane, an airplane that, in one way or another, is in trouble. Sometimes that cockpit is a scary place to be. Sometimes, it's downright terrifying.

As I read through 11 years of the column in editing this book, it became clear to me that winter weather is *not* a pilot's friend. Winter ratchets up the risk in several ways. Not only are the days short, but hazards of one kind or another seem to lurk in every corner. You've got the ever present peril of icing, which can literally pull an airplane out of the sky. Even the gently falling snow can be an aviation menace, cutting landing visibility to almost nothing. And even when you do succeed in getting the airplane on the ground, snow and ice on the runway can turn an otherwise well flown arrival into a high-speed bobsled ride of the worst kind.

Our readers have lived through some harrowing experiences with Old Man Winter and lived to tell the tale, from a couple who survived severe icing over the Appalachians in their Seneca, to the captain of a Metroliner whose airplane became an ice-encased lightning rod, to the otherwise cautious pilot of a Fokker commuter airliner who landed with a legal tailwind on an icy runway and barely escaped, along with his crew and passengers, becoming a terrible statistic.

Spring Snowstorm

IT WAS AN EARLY SPRING MORNING as I prepared to fly from the Spirit of St. Louis Airport (KSUS) to Destin/Ft. Walton Beach, Florida (KDTS) in my PA-24 Comanche 250. There was a low-pressure system in northern Alabama and Mississippi through which I would have to fly in order to get to my destination. The weather briefer reported that there would be isolated buildups of cumulus clouds but the weather would be reasonably good along the direction of flight because of a relative lack of moisture from the gulf. Even though it would be VFR en route, I always try to fly IFR to maintain my skills both in aircraft control and radio communications. This way, when I do fly in instrument meteorological conditions (IMC), those skills are more polished than they otherwise would be. After an uneventful preflight, I received the appropriate standard instrument departure (SID) instructions and launched into the air. It was not long before St. Louis Departure allowed me to fly direct. I climbed to 11,000 feet.

The flight was uneventful for about an hour until a seemingly innocuous comment from Memphis Center. He indicated that there was precipitation on his radar screen about 35 miles from my position and offered to let me deviate around it. The smoothness of my flight and lack of any real problems lulled me into a false sense of security. Looking at my StrikeFinder, I noticed that there was no indication of thunderstorms in the area. I could see the buildup ahead of me and it appeared to have tops of about 20,000 feet and perhaps 10-15 miles wide. I could see underneath the cumulus cloud and noted that there was no virga. It looked peaceful and quite beautiful. I responded by saying that I would go through the buildup. Memphis Center acknowledged.

Just prior to the cloud penetration, I turned on the pitot heat and the carburetor heat, as the temperature was at – 8° C. The first 10-20 seconds were uneventful. Then chaos ruled supreme. I was instantly engulfed in a blinding snow/sleet storm with seemingly every water molecule adhering to my subzero temperature airplane. It was like driving a car in a blinding snowstorm in northern Michigan in whiteout conditions, except I could not pull over to the side of the road under an overpass. Instantly my windshield iced over. Through the side windows I could see the green tip tanks become white with rime and mixed ice. Ice was clearly visible on the leading edge of the wing and it was increasing quickly.

The thermometer, with its four-inch probe sticking outside my side window, became completely engulfed in ice. Turbulence was severe, and despite my best efforts, I gained and lost hundreds of feet of altitude in surges of both up and down drafts. The folded maps on my knee flew throughout the cabin in their own free flight like malformed paper airplanes in their own futile efforts to find a safe haven.

Then, I could hear small ice pellets begin to hit the windshield and could see them go over the wings resembling "tracer fire" from antiaircraft bullets. They were perhaps a different color, but they could be just as lethal. Suddenly, I saw a lightning bolt out of my right field of vision, diffracted somewhat by the ice-covered windshield. I wondered whether I should turn off all the electronics. I decided against turning off the electrical system as my pitot heat would be lost and hence my airspeed indication would go to zero. This would make flight in IMC even more difficult. This was not the time to test my partial-panel skills.

I tried to slow the airplane down to maneuvering speed but was concerned about the ice buildup and the stall characteristics of the ice-laden airplane. I thought of turning the airplane around 180 degrees but believed that the best course of action would be to continue on a straight line as it would most likely shorten the duration of the IMC conditions. I wished I had never entered that "peaceful looking" cloud.

Then, just as suddenly as it began, the sleet/snow maelstrom ended and I was spit out of the cloud like a piece of flotsam. Completely covered in ice, the airplane looked like a distressed mongrel dog that had just come out of an icy river with icicles hanging from his bedraggled furry coat. Breathing a sigh of relief, I shut off the pitot heat. As I wiped the perspiration off of my brow, slowed my breathing and listened to the carotid artery pulsate in my neck and ears, I shut off the carburetor heat.

As I did this, the engine "stopped" and the airplane started to lose altitude. Instinctively, I added back the carburetor heat, as this was the last action I had done prior to the total engine failure. The engine came back to life again. I did not know what had happened, but I suspected that it had a lot to do with the ice covering my airplane.

I contacted Memphis Center and told them of my predicament and they immediately cleared me to 7,000 feet, which I estimated to be the freezing level. I kept the speed just below the yellow arc to minimize any structural damage due to turbulence but fast enough to avoid any unusual flight characteristics due to the ice on the airplane. As I approached the freezing level, the character of the ice adhering to the aircraft changed, becoming more "wet" and then melted off.

After an extra couple of minutes, while level at 7,000 feet and within sight of an airport, I took a deep breath, and removed the carburetor heat. The engine continued to run and reacted "normally." A review of the instruments revealed a set of normal operating engine parameters. I felt that my predicament was related to the ice buildup, although I did not know how. I continued on to my destination. Upon landing, I looked at my air intake filter in front of the airplane.

As it turns out, the air induction system and air filter of the Comanche are recessed somewhat from the air scoop. Taking measurements in the air scoop, it became painfully obvious that the amount of ice that I knew existed on the aircraft surface (e.g. thermometer stem) most likely filled up the air scoop. This essentially prevented adequate air from entering the engine, starving it of much-needed oxygen. By utilizing the carburetor heat, oxygen is obtained from the air traveling over the hot cylinders, heating it to a high enough temperature to melt any ice in the carburetor system. The mechanism for air entry in this system, however, is characterized by an opening that is much larger than the filtered air system, precluding its occlusion with ice. Hence, the mixture did not become excessively rich and the engine continued to run. I was lucky that the amount of oxygen getting into the carburetor from this aperture was adequate to allow combustion.

Although the lessons to be learned include the knowledge of how outside air feeds into the carburetor for combustion, a more important lesson to be learned is to stay out of a tall cumulus cloud that shows precipitation on radar at less than (or perhaps even greater than) the freezing level. This is especially true of a cloud that appears to be (potentially) developing into a cumulonimbus. The next time I drive a car in a blinding snowstorm in whiteout conditions I will be happy I am on the ground and not maneuvering an aircraft in turbulent IMC conditions two miles above the surface of the earth in a developing thunderstorm.

Icy Takeoff Spells Trouble for Touchdown

ILOVE TO FLY AFTER THE SEASON'S FIRST SNOW. That year it came on a Saturday. By Sunday afternoon it was sunny and a little warmer although still in the low 30s. Front Royal, my home field, had been nicely plowed and the snow that had been on the ramp had melted and evaporated. I pulled *Elizabeth*, my new Midget Mustang, out of the hangar and began my preflight. Everything was in order, although I noticed the tires looked slightly soft underneath their snug-fitting wheel pants. The cold affects the pressure to a small degree.

With the preflight behind me and the long nose in front of me, I sat on the ramp with the engine ticking over waiting to build a little oil temperature. The cockpit of the MM-1 is cramped, the instrument panel sits close. I think I'll probably need bifocals to read it someday. The racing canopy, when it's down, fits around my head like a helmet, my breath begins to fog the entire bubble. I raise the canopy a smidgen and the fog clears. No defrosters in a Midget Mustang, in fact no heat at all. On a really cold day the fog turns to a thin layer of ice.

With the cylinder head temps at 350° F and the oil over 100° I back-taxi 27. The Mustang is a piece of cake to taxi because of the locking Haigh tailwheel. I unlock the tailwheel and she spins on a dime. Looking down 27 I complete the run-up, check the radio, set the DG and apply full power.

There is virtually no tendency to veer with the cruise prop. Directional control in the MM-1 is done with the toes, repeat TOES, only. Just light pressure on the appropriate rudder pedal. On takeoff, the stick should float in your hand, ailerons neutral. No need to force the tail up; if you do, she'll want to bend to the left. The mains become unstuck around 80 mph and

I climb out in the 120-to-130-mph range in order to see over the nose and to put some miles behind me if I'm going cross-country. I've only got nine usable if I'm to maintain a 30-minute reserve.

I turn to the south and level at 2,500 msl. The Shenandoah River shimmers below, S-bending away to the horizon. The air is calm, crystal clear and cold; I can see 50 miles. Fresh snow blankets the farmlands beneath me.

Still level at 2,500 I let the engine accelerate to 2,700 as the IAS climbs to 170, reduce throttle to 2,500 and settle into a level cruise at 160 mph. Turning to the north I decide to head up to Winchester for a cuppa. The Shenandoah Valley is a feast for the eyes even on a bad day, but today is one of those perfect days that weekend aviators like myself live for.

"Winchester Unicom," I say in my best "Maverick" voice. "This is Mustang 15 Juliet, 10 south, 2, 500, landing Winchester. . . advisory please." I love to do that, everybody comes out to watch me land, I don't know why, I use my best West By-God Virginia drawl, a cross between Chuck Yeager and Hannibal Lechter's Clarice Starling.

"Thirty-Two is the active, sir, wind is calm, altimeter 30.03, no reported."

On downwind now, the airfield looks fine except for some snowy patches the plow has left on the taxiway. Easing the throttle off momentarily, the exhaust crackles and pops through the short exhaust stacks; I ease the nose up pulling the first notch of flaps at 140, the second at 120 and the third at 100. Coming back up to 1,500 rpm I begin my turn to base and then final, maintaining about 90, slowing to 85 over the numbers, leveling just an inch above the runway; the tires touch about 80. The landing is fine except I hit this enormous puddle of slushy water that really decelerates my little bird, almost causing a prop strike as this unintended deceleration causes the tail to pitch up.

With this unexpected little moment behind me I decide to forgo the coffee and head back to Front Royal. Taxiing slowly back through the scattered puddles of water I notice a small amount of slush has landed on the top surface of the right wing. "No problem," I think, "the wind will blow it off."

Taking the active I splash through some more slush and become uneventfully airborne, although probably somewhat farther down the runway. I turn to the south toward Front Royal and level at 2,000. Looking over at my right wing I see I still have the slush with me but now it is clearly frozen. "Fortunately, it's only about a cup." I think to myself." Eyeballing the northern tip of the Massanutten, I focus on my destination. I suddenly notice the artificial horizon and DG are flopping around. I don't understand what has caused the problem. Dimly the light goes on. The venturi is on the bottom.

"How much ice am I carrying?" I wonder, dreading the answer. I've got to find out how bad it is. I decide to try a little slow flight at altitude before entering the pattern. I find that as I slow through 110 with the second notch of flaps my little airplane wants to roll to the right onto its back, and the stick will only move a little to the left. Ice has loaded up the right wing, destroying the aerodynamics, jamming the aileron wells and putting too much weight out there.

At least I know what the plane will do at 110, so I have no choice but to fly it with power, at 110, down to the runway, then if it stalls it won't matter. This is precisely what I do, making one gentle continuous turn to final, concentrating on my airspeed and keeping the ball in the center. I am really sweating now. My breathing is tight and shallow.

Over the numbers, then down to one foot, one inch. . . "I've made it." I think. As the tires begin to touch I relax for the first time. Next thing I know I'm looking down the nose at the runway, both tires are screeching, locked solid and I'm veering toward the left edge of the runway at 90. I snatch the stick back into my gut. My first priority is to keep it from flipping over on to its back. The fact that I'm not on my back already is still unbelievable. Within three feet of the left edge of the runway, still going 70, the left wheel gets into an inch of remaining snow, and this instantaneous reduction in drag on the left wheel turns me back toward the runway center. Still keeping the stick firmly back, I head diagonally back across the runway. The tires finally begin to turn as I slow to taxi speed.

Back on the ramp, looking under the plane I find the entire bottom virtually covered in frozen slush one-half inch thick. The insides of the wheel pants are completely filled, solid.

When I got home my wife, Elizabeth, asked how my landings in her namesake Mustang were going. Alix, my cat, coughed on a hair ball, looked up from his perpetual nap and yawned. The neighbor's children were playing in the snow. . . I couldn't think of anything to say.

Experience Builder

IT'S LATE JANUARY. The weather at our Northeast destination is IFR—not extremely low IFR, but clearly weather no one should be flying in without the proper equipment and training. As the captain for a major airline, I am secure in the knowledge that the anti-icing systems aboard are more than adequate for the conditions. My first officer and I have just finished listening to the pilot of a light aircraft being worked into the airport ahead of us. By the sound of his voice he is quite shaken. His journey had ended with an ILS approach to Category I minimums while carrying a load of rime ice. My ex-Air Force first officer looks over at me and chuckles, "How do these general aviation types get themselves into such a mess?" Trying to look as fatherly as possible for my 37 years, I look at him and say, "It's called making a living," because I remember well a trip in similar circumstances I made a few years ago. As hard as I try, I will never forget.

Our company was a medium-sized flight school with a Part 135 charter department. All of the pilots did double duty either as flight instructors or charter pilots. Historically, businessmen would ask for a particular pilot to fly a charter trip. On one particularly dark and icy afternoon a good customer called to ask if I could fly him into the downtown airport in the nearby metropolitan city. The flight typically took about one hour, versus three hours on the interstate by car. After checking the weather I told him that the forecast didn't look good for an IFR flight in a twin-engine Piper Seminole. Icing was forecast from the ground all the way through 10,000 feet. He accepted my explanation and added that if things changed in the next couple of hours to call him back.

In the meantime, a couple of fellow charter pilots ask if I wanted to take advantage of the instrument conditions and practice local approaches. We all had Part 135 check rides scheduled the following week. Our plans were to go out for an approach and then if we encountered any ice we would high-tail it back to the airport and call it a day. After flying five or six approaches without encountering any ice, I called the company radio, who in turn relayed to my charter customer that I could indeed take him on the one-hour flight into Kansas City. After landing from our training session,

I quickly refueled the Seminole, checked the hourly sequence report, and filed a flight plan.

The flight progressed smoothly and at approximately 8,000 feet msl we broke out into clear, bright, sunny skies. The day was really shaping up. Not only had I impressed a good customer, but I was out there building IFR, multiengine time. Life didn't get any better for an airline pilot wannabe.

As we neared Kansas City, I noticed that I had to continue to request higher altitudes to remain on top. About 40 miles from the airport, ATC requested that we begin our descent and the next few moments will live with me forever. We were level at 10,000 feet msl, and while the clouds were for the most part flat on top, there was one little buildup that pushed up to what looked like only 11,000 feet. I flew through that little ridge and popped out the other side. While I was only in the clouds for a minute, the windshield was completely frosted over. Of course the wings, tail and everything else I could see had the same coating.

I told ATC the problem and that I would probably not be able to level off at very many intermediate altitudes, as we had already begun the descent. At that point we were only about 15 miles from the outer marker. It was now or never; the little Seminole continued to pick up ice at a very rapid rate. I ask for a vector directly over the marker, trying to get in as close as I could. The poor little Seminole wouldn't fly much longer. The controller informed me two miles was as close as he could go for the course reversal. I accepted his judgment and kept the airplane flying under full power with the gear and flaps up.

Over the marker I realized that there was no way I was ever going to be able to see the runway. I opened the little storm window on my side and asked my passenger to tell me when he could see runway on his side. Down we came with gear up and full power. The airplane mushed along like we were driving through a mud field. At the middle marker my passenger said he could make out the runway. I cycled the gear down and left the throttles at the stop. He shouted again that we were over the runway. I looked to my left and could see runway so I started the throttles back. The second I pulled the throttles out of the full-power setting the airplane stalled and hit the runway with a very firm thump. There was no way this ice-laden queen could bounce.

I taxied like the fighter pilots of World War II, weaving back and forth to stay on the taxiway. As I pulled up to the gas pumps I saw eight or 10 lineboys come spilling out and milling around my airplane. They were all laughing and pointing at the wings and tail. I shut down and my passenger and I climbed out of my faithful little Piper twin. What I saw absolutely amazed me. The airplane looked as though it had been dug up from some Arctic excavation. It was completely encased in ice. As I looked, my knees became weak, and I seriously thought that I would throw up. Undaunted, my friend and passenger looked over at me and said, "How soon do you want to go back?" Trying to look as professional as possible I looked at him and said, "How long will it take you to rent a car?" The Seminole sat in its ice cage for about a week before we could get it back home.

As I told the story to my first officer, I remembered how when I was young everything was possible. I was a good pilot and therefore invincible. My mistakes on that flight were many, but I feel the most grievous was never considering the option of simply turning around. My only thought was to get my passenger to his destination. This is a very dangerous concept for anyone, in any type of aircraft.

Killer Ice

WITH A FORCED CALM I DID NOT FEEL, I keyed the mike and announced, "Clarksburg Approach, I'm declaring an emergency." I had just flown into a wall of ice, and was in serious, life-threatening trouble. Suddenly, thoughts of dying and a deep terror were welling up as I struggled to control the plane.

On the ground only an hour earlier, all seemed so well. Hot Thanksgiving turkey beckoned as my wife and I carefully packed the twin Piper Seneca, struggling against the biting morning cold. We were making the annual trek to Memphis from Gaithersburg, Maryland to enjoy the holiday with my brother-in-law's family and his house full of five kids. Along for the ride were our 70-pound Golden Retriever and 176 pounds of luggage. Nobody can accuse us of traveling light. Each bag was weighed and tagged for either the front or rear luggage compartment, or the middle of back seats.

The Seneca has a great useful load, but has to be packed carefully to stay within the CG limits.

The weather reports from WX-BRIEF were consistent from the early morning to the time just before departure at 11:00: crummy winter flying. As usual, there were calls for icing in the clouds, with the day's special being light to moderate rime 6,000 to 12,000 feet. We were planning an early-morning departure, but I decided to delay to let a rainstorm pass through the area before lifting off. The route offered high clouds after breaking through a low deck, so I filed IFR at 6,000 feet to avoid any precipitation by cruising between the layers.

Departure offered that singular joy only achieved through IFR flight: lifting through the clouds in what seems to be silent slow motion to float serenely over the cotton below, basking warmly in the bright azure sky above. Somehow that sense of triumph over the clag below never ceases to diminish with time and experience. With the plane trimmed up for cruise at 6,000, we seemed set for an easy trip, and I settled in to experience the joy of commanding an aircraft. Ahead were what appeared to be some high clouds, but nothing to worry about.

As we approached the mountains of West Virginia, those high clouds were not seeming so high any more. As a precaution I put on the pitot heat and cranked the windshield defrost on high. And in fact before long we were smack in the middle of clouds. Telling myself I was only at 6,000 feet and therefore at the very lower end of expected icing, I decided to continue the journey. Beside, I convinced myself, I was in the clouds and not picking up any ice, so why not press on? I could always do a 180 if some frozen water started to accumulate, or go lower if necessary since I knew that 5,000 offered good terrain clearance. I foolishly ignored that tug in my gut telling me I was making a mistake—that uneasy feeling from experience that the picture is just not right, that makes you readjust your position in the seat just a little bit and raises your level of alertness ever so slight. No explicit threat of danger, but a sense of unease.

Sure enough, within five or 10 minutes of hitting the clouds, I started to pick up the very slightest traces of ice, which would stick and then melt. I mentioned to the controller that I may need to do a 180 since there were hints of a potential icing problem. He acknowledged, and requested that I coordinate with him prior to executing the turn. Just then, 10 miles to the north a Baron reported tops at 9,000 feet. Well, I thought, instead of turning tail, why not just climb on top and get out of the clag completely? After all, I was only picking up the slightest traces. I requested 10,000 feet and the controller quickly approved. That was probably the biggest mistake I have made in my life.

Somewhere between 7,000 and 8,000 feet, I ran into what can only be termed a frozen layer of sky. Within minutes, the plane was covered with two inches of ice and growing. At 8,000 feet the plane just could not squeeze out any more climb. With full power, the bird was not climbing, and there was nothing I could do to coax it—9,000 feet was never so close but so far away. I needed to keep the angle of attack low, both to ensure I stayed well above the stall speed, whatever experimental and unknown figure that was now, and to ensure that ice did not accumulate well behind the leading edge under the wing. Whatever delusions had led me to this point, all were gone now. I knew I was in serious trouble. I had a load of ice, I was over the mountains, I had no ideas what the bases were, and I still had at least 3,000 to 4,000 feet of clouds to descend through.

"I am going to go ahead and declare an emergency, and need to descend immediately." The controller acknowledged, and said that if at all possible I should stop the descent at 3,000 feet, but if necessary, I could go as low as 2,200 feet. My wife looked at me, understood we were in serious trouble, and had the wisdom of not asking any questions. She knew we were in trouble because she looked out the window and saw the ice—and I have always told her the one thing that will definitely kill you in a plane is ice. For my wife's silence and calm confidence (however misplaced), I will always be grateful because I had a full workload and could not handle additional distractions.

On the way down, the ice continued to accumulate, and I was getting difficult-to-control oscillations indicative of a tailplane stall on the descent. That careful packing job before liftoff was critical now because if the plane was even close to CG limits I would have lost it completely. The controls were getting mushy, and I was having difficulty controlling the airplane. The elevator had a weird response and was only partially effective. The controller then gave me the good news: "It is snowing at Elkins (to my southwest), with visibility 1/4 mile, bases at 2,000 feet." For the first time in my life, I thought I was going to die. Somehow, I was outwardly calm, and told myself to just keep flying the airplane as long as it will fly. Nothing else I could do. I told the controller I had "only minimal control of the airplane" and needed to land as soon as possible. I was still in the clouds at 3,000 feet, so continued to descend. Mercifully, I broke out at between 2,400 and 2,300 feet into about three miles visibility. I was no longer accumulating ice, but since the outside air temperature was at freezing, the load I had tenaciously stuck with me. I was able to level off just at 2,200 feet, but maintaining control of the plane was a constant struggle.

Still, once we were clear of the clouds, hope began to edge its way into my mind. The controller gave me a bearing to a small grass strip immediately to my left and told me that an asphalt strip was about five miles to my northwest. I elected to go to the hard surface, figuring that a landing on wet grass was probably as dangerous as trying to stay in the air to reach the asphalt. My hands were so full that I had to have the controller repeat three times the simple identifier for the field. He gently suggested that I need not worry about the airports identifier, but I told him I needed the information to punch into my handheld GPS. Perhaps I should have just hit the "nearest" key. In any case, I felt I needed all the help I could get in finding the field.

Between the controller and the GPS, I was able to find the field, which lies on top of a narrow ridge. But when I saw the airport, I was essentially on an angled short field (as if I had turned directly toward the runway from downwind instead of turning base), and therefore was not in a position to land. Now I had another problem. To avoid stalling, I could only make very shallow turns and therefore could not do a normal pattern to set up for landing. To position myself for final, I chose to do a wide 360 with about five degrees of bank (the plane was so close to stalling I feared any more would lead to a loss of control). The turn was so wide that I lost sight of the airport. During the turn I asked the controller if he was still with me and he reassured me that he was indeed with me and would do all he could to help.

During the wide turn to final, I had other problems to consider as well. I certainly could not lower the flaps on final because the aerodynamic effects on the new experimental airplane would be unknown. I could get actual or the equivalent of asymmetric deployment. I had to keep full power in, high airspeed and a low angle of attack to avoid a stall. Not exactly a good landing configuration for a short strip of unknown length. Finally, I feared if I lowered my landing gear, I would stall with the extra drag. I seriously considered an intentional gear-up landing, figuring I would rather land on the belly with control of the aircraft rather than stall short of the field.

As I completed the turn, I was fairly well positioned on final. I ultimately decided to lower the gear at a point near the numbers such that If I stalled, and tried to recover by lowering the nose, I had a chance of making it to the field. Turns out that lowering the gear had no ill effect. I came in low over the numbers at 120 KIAS with full power and no flaps. Having a choice of stalling, or possibly running off the end of the runway, I chose the latter. Only when the wheels were a few feet above the runway did I pull the throttle back. But somehow the landing was as smooth as if it were a calm summer day, and half the runway remained in front of the nose when I came to a full stop. From our ridgetopperch, I was able to contact the controller and inform him I was safely on the ground.

Stuck at Philippy/Barbour Airport, which is essentially just a strip of asphalt on top of a mountain, my wife and I were happy to be alive, but concerned about how to get somewhere, anywhere, to spend the night. After we'd spent about an hour discussing our options, a car pulled up at the end of the runway. Who should get out but the controller who helped me down! He realized we were stranded and gave us a ride into Clarksburg, where we spent a thankful and quiet evening. That controller's quiet professionalism during the emergency, and extraordinary act of kindness on the ground, should be noted by any pilot with a beef with ATC.

The lesson here is as obvious as it is painful. I got lulled by years of experience of winter flying in which nearly every day has a report of icing. I thought I had good "outs": turning around or going lower. Perhaps the biggest mistake was not executing that 180 at the very first traces of ice. Ice is an unforgiving killer, and if you ever forget it, the Grim Reaper is right behind to give you your last and permanent reminder. Personally, I will never fly IFR in the winter again without known icing equipment, and then only with extreme caution.

First Solo Flight

I **WAS FRESH FROM THE EXCITEMENT** of my first solo in the pattern. I had actually taken off, flown the pattern and landed an airplane all by myself. I had survived the event and the airplane was still flyable. I was now ready to make my first solo cross-country flight. I planned my flight from South Bend Regional Airport (SBN) down to Purdue University Airport (LAF) on the campus in Lafayette, Indiana, a distance of some 85 miles. It was a clear, sunny winter day on January 19, 1999. My instructor had reviewed my flight planning and had signed me off for the flight. I was ready for the next step in the incredible adventure of my flight training.

I filed my flight plan with Terre Haute Flight Service and headed for the T-hangars to preflight 94V, a 1975 vintage Cessna 172, one of three in our flying club fleet. Everything checked out, so I climbed aboard and I called South Bend Clearance for departure instructions. South Bend ground gave me taxi clearance to Runway 27R. After my run-up at the departure end of the runway, I called flight service to open my flight plan. I was cleared by the tower for takeoff and was on my way. The weather was absolutely beautiful with visibility from here to forever. The weather briefer had confirmed that I could expect no significant weather other than the possibility of some light snowshowers on my route.

As most pilots in the vicinity of the Great Lakes know, lake effect snow is always a possibility when the wind is blowing off the lake. SBN is only about 30 miles off the southeast corner of Lake Michigan, and the wind was from the northwest. However the wind was very light at about 10 knots at 3,000 feet and was not strong enough to drive any lake effect snow very far inland.

I had been in the air about 15 minutes when I saw a couple of dark spots ahead. They didn't look like clouds and they didn't look like rain. With my limited experience with airborne weather I did not realize that what I was looking at were several small, isolated snowshowers. As I got closer, the flakes started to fly around me. The snowshowers were very small and I thought I could see through to the other side. Forward visibility diminished rapidly, but I never lost sight of the ground. I could see straight down. Up ahead I saw another small snowshower and soon the experience was repeated. I really enjoyed the phenomenon.

Soon I was approaching LAF and was handed off to Lafayette Approach. I joined the flock of Purdue flight training students as I got closer to the airport. I was told to report the water tank. I asked ATC, "What water tank?" and was told the one with the great big "P" on it. After sighting and reporting the water tank I was cleared to land on Runway 23. After taxiing to the ramp, I sat in the cockpit for a few minutes to enjoy the satisfaction of completing my first flight from Point A to Point B without my flight instructor in the right seat. I went into the FBO and called Terre Haute Flight Service to close my flight plan and to file my return flight plan to SBN.

I talked to the weather briefer about my return flight and once again was assured that there was no significant weather between Lafayette and South Bend other than maybe some light snowshowers. I told the briefer about the small snowshowers on the way down to Lafayette and he assured me that there was nothing on the radar at the present time and nothing indicated any significant lake effect snow on the way back.

About 15 minutes after departure from LAF I contacted South Bend Approach for flight following. The visibility was still very good, but once again I saw some small snowshowers off in the distance. I figured I would see the same type of isolated patches of snow on the way back that I saw on the way down to Lafayette. Sure enough, again it started to snow around me but this time it lasted longer, and it took longer before I got through to the other side. I could still see the ground and did not feel at all disoriented. A few minutes later I flew into another snowshower much like the first, but this one lasted even longer. Realizing that the snow was obviously more widespread now than it was on the way down to LAF, I considered turning back. I knew from living in the area that lake effect snow usually comes off Lake Michigan in narrow fingers. I figured that I would be out of the snow more quickly by staying on my present heading than by turning around to fly back through the stuff behind me.

I called South Bend and told them that I was a student pilot on my first solo cross-country and that I was in a snowshower with zero lateral visibility. Just as I contacted them I flew out of the snowshower. South

Bend told me that there were several more fingers of snow coming off the lake. They vectored me to the east to fly around the snow, but soon I was back into another snowstorm and this time it was really thick. I could still see a small circle of ground below me but had absolutely no forward visibility. I still was not disoriented or panicky. I felt that I could keep the wings level and would be able to fly out of the snow. Fortunately I had refueled at LAF and had about four hours of fuel for what would normally be a 50 minute flight. ATC seemed to be a lot more concerned than I was. I guess I just didn't know enough to be scared.

ATC now advised me that they would vector me to the Plymouth, Indiana (C65) airport that was clear of snow. Although I was able to keep the airplane under control, I didn't have a good idea where I was. The vectors took me right over the Plymouth Airport but the snow had followed me. However, I could see the airport in my ground circle. The winds indicated a landing to the west on Runway 28. I was flying on a heading of about 80 degrees as I overflew the airport. As I maneuvered to line up for a final approach I lost sight of the airport as it moved out of my ground circle. ATC vectored me back until I could see the airport again underneath me. I maneuvered again to line up on final and again I lost sight of the airport.

Now I was starting to worry. I had to get this airplane and myself on the ground—in one piece. Fortunately, Runway 28 runs parallel to and just north of Interstate 30. As ATC vectored me back to the airport, I saw not only the runway but also I-30. I figured if I flew east above I-30, I could then fly a 270-degree turn to the north and re-intersect I-30 and then follow it west back to the airport. As I completed the turn, I saw I-30 and turned west. I just hoped I would be able to see the airport to my right and north of the highway. This was giving a whole new meaning to IFR—I follow roads. I had to get down below pattern altitude because I knew that I would be almost abeam the threshold when and if I saw the runway. I would not have time to lose the altitude after I saw the runway. Please let there be no obstacles down there!!

A moment later I saw the runway off to my right. I slid over to line up and realized that the runway was now covered with snow. The only reason I was able to see it at all was due to the edge lights protruding through the snow. I thought to myself, "This landing has to be smooth and slow." Thanks to my instructor for all that soft-field landing practice. Hold it off, hold it off. Stall horn. Touchdown. Okay, no brakes—just let it roll out straight and slow. As I slowed, I realized that there was about four inches of snow on the runway. I did not stop but kept rolling to the far end of the runway and the ramp. As I turned off the runway onto the ramp, I saw a twin with its left wing pointing skyward. I learned later that the poor guy had lost it and slid into a snow bank along the edge of the runway just the day before.

Again, I sat on the ramp for a few moments, savoring the fact that I still had an equal number of successful takeoffs and landings. Actually, I think I was probably shaking too hard to get the door open! I walked into the office and before I could say hello, the airport manager said that the tower at SBN wanted me to call them right away. He handed me the phone number. I called the tower and thanked them profusely for their help before they had a chance to chew me out. It was obvious that their only concern was that I was safely on the ground. My instructor was in the tower and had followed my adventure from there. He was almost—but not quite—as relieved as I was that I was safely back on the ground. Later, we had a lengthy discussion about snow.

Snow can be light and nothing or it can get heavy and blinding very quickly. It is no place for a student pilot and can be lethal to an experienced VFR pilot. Without the help from Interstate 30, I would have had to find some VMC somewhere to land (maybe back where I came from). The sure out was to make a 180 degree turn back to where I knew there was VMC. I got lured into heavy snow thinking that it was just some more light snow-showers like I encountered on the way down. I decided for sure that very day to get my instrument rating, which I just completed. This flight would have been a non-event for an instrument rated/instrument proficient pilot.

The Nick of Time

IT HAS BEEN SAID that an accident is often the result of an unbro-ken chain of events. If something breaks the link, disaster is averted. Rarely do pilots get to stand at the edge of the abyss, peer over and step back, the chain broken at the last possible moment. It can be a powerful learning experience.

As a fairly new captain at my airline, I was scheduled to take the twin-jet Fokker F28 to one of our smallest stations—Worcester, Massachusetts. Not blessed with overly long runways or impressive facilities, Worcester Regional Airport also had the worst weather in the region, especially in winter.

It was the middle of January as I talked to the flight dispatcher about conditions at our destination. He assured me that while it had been snowing heavily, the runway was being kept clear by the plows. The previous company flight, another F28, had reported braking action fair, well within our operating limitations. The wind was from the west at 15 knots, which ruled out the ILS 11 approach, the obvious choice. But he helpfully added that the NDB Runway 29 was available, with the weather just above minimums.

I wasn't too enthusiastic about that idea. Domestic airline jet crews rarely have to fly an ADF approach in the real world; and the two or three a year practiced in the simulator never feel like enough. The dispatcher's parting advice—"It wouldn't hurt to go take a look"—was amusing, because at some critical point "taking a look" becomes either a landing or a diversion, and guess whose decision that would be? Thanking him, I hung up and returned to the airplane.

I found Dave, the first officer, relaxing in the passenger cabin and briefed him on the situation. Then, like any captain using his best CRM training, I asked his opinion. Dave was a conservative and thoughtful airman. He felt that while conditions were less than ideal, he couldn't think of any reason why we shouldn't launch.

I agreed, but recalled the main source of my concerns: the Dutch-built F28 was the only jet transport this side of the old Iron Curtain that was not equipped with thrust reversers. Short of throwing out an anchor, the only way to stop the aircraft was with its wheel brakes.

The flight to Worcester was uneventful, with the usual light to moderate chop present in a northeast low-pressure system. Listening to the ATIS during the descent, Dave relayed the first piece of interesting news—the NDB Runway 29 was out of service. On questioning the approach controller, we learned that it had been OTS for three weeks—a fact somehow unknown to our dispatcher. The other big news was that the wind was now 290 degrees at 10 knots, exactly at limits for landing on ILS Runway 11.

Mulling over this turn of events, I asked for the latest braking action report. The man in the dark room said that an ATR commuter reported fair to good, and the runway had been plowed within the hour. The small-town nature of our destination became apparent when he casually added that an airport authority pickup had just finished a mad dash down the runway, weighing in with a report of "good friction." The weather was holding at a 500-foot ceiling, with four miles visibility in light snow.

Airline pilots are paid for days like this. If every less than ideal situation was turned down by the captain, schedules would become a joke. I had yet to hear the words "poor" or "nil" regarding braking action, so I made the decision to shoot the ILS 11. During my briefing for the approach, I told Dave—assuming good visibility on breaking out—I would drop one dot low on the glideslope to ensure touchdown well before the 1,000-foot mark. There was no sense wasting runway on a day like this. On touchdown and auto-spoiler extension I would use maximum braking, and if it didn't feel right, I would pour on the coal and perform the maneuver known as getting the hell out of there. The Rolls-Royce Spey could spool up from idle to takeoff thrust much more quickly than most jet engines, and this was the procedure in our Flight Manual for landing on snow and ice-covered runways.

As we slid down the ILS everything was routine, except for less power than usual to hold the glideslope because of the tailwind. Breaking out at 500 feet agl, the runway appeared dead ahead, and I announced that I was going one dot low. Dave got a final wind-check from the tower, 290 at nine; one knot to spare. Crossing the threshold right on speed, I made a low flare, landing about 500 feet from the end of the 7,000-foot runway. The spoilers immediately deployed and when the nose wheel touched down I applied maximum braking.

We slowed very nicely at first, now committed to a full stop. And then the games began.

Suddenly we were no longer decelerating. The change was so abrupt it felt like taking off. Too late for a go-around, we had run into an ice-covered part of the runway that had all the friction of a skating rink. At 90 knots, the Fokker began to slide sideways, and I fought to regain control by releasing the brakes and holding full right rudder. After a few moments, which seemed much longer, we straightened up and I applied brakes again, desperately hoping the anti-skid system would kick in.

I've heard from pilots who have been involved in crashes that everything moves like a slow motion dream. They're right. I found time to reflect about the lack of reverse thrust, and what a stupid place that was to save a few bucks. I also remembered the steep drop off and rugged terrain waiting past the end of the runway. A broken airplane and serious injuries (or worse) would not exactly be a career-enhancing event. All these thoughts drifted through my mind as I heard myself tell Dave to shut down the left engine—at this point we hardly needed its 400 pounds of idle thrust.

The end of the runway was coming up fast and we were barely slowing. Passing the intersection of Runway 33, I was on the verge of shutting down the right engine as well when suddenly we were past the ice. The anti-skid took hold, cycling the brakes as we quickly slowed in the last 1,000 feet. Snow was falling again as I very slowly taxied to the gate, the tarmac so slick the nose wheel slid in the turns.

In a droll manner that made me envious, Dave reported to the tower that the runway "reports" left a lot to be desired, with braking action nil on at least half its length. We sat in stony silence as the jetway pulled up and the 70 passengers deplaned without a single comment. Even the flight attendants apparently didn't realize how close we had come to making headlines. I turned to Dave and said I was going to inform the dispatcher we were not taking off until spring.

During the post mortem, I discovered a few interesting sins of omission (and one of commission) committed by me. If we had known the ADF approach was OTS, we couldn't have departed in the first place, since the tailwind made the ILS illegal. The company had the information about Runway 29, some electronic gremlin kept us from getting it on our paperwork. Once in the Worcester area, the wind subsided, luring us into a tailwind landing on an ice-covered runway.

Another critical piece of information we didn't get was that the ATR braking action report was nearly three hours old. Besides, I should have disregarded a braking action report from a truck, there being a considerable difference in stopping a 70,000-pound jet and a pickup.

The fact remained, however, that it was my decision to land with a barely legal tailwind. I'm sure the Feds would have jumped immediately on that, and on the fact that runway conditions were drastically worse than advertised would have made a nice footnote in the accident report. The accident chain was broken by a quirk of nature that allowed less ice to form on the last portion of the runway. If it weren't for that, I would probably be in another line of work.

When listing pilot error, the NTSB often manages to miss the process that went into making a mistake, as if judgment and decision making exist in a vacuum. In a tradition dating to sailing ships, we are held accountable for our decisions. Any other way would erode the power we have as pilots to make judgments based on the best available information. In an imperfect world, that information can sometimes be very wrong.

WHEN ALL
GETS QUIET

IT'S NOT A COMFORTING THOUGHT, but it's important to remind ourselves regularly that the only thing keeping our powered airplanes from become really bad gliders is the powerplant. And when you think about how complicated an engine is, how much stress its individual parts are under and how little we know about its day-to-day health status, it's even less comforting. Pilots of twins get a break, because if one mill stops turning they've got another one to fall back on. But the literature is full of stories of that exact scenario working out badly, much worse in many cases than if there'd been no second engine at all.

If many of the stories in this book fall under the category of foreseeable problem or even fool mistake, the ones in this chapter don't. In almost every case, the pilot was a victim of circumstances beyond his control, like the pilot who experienced a total engine failure on climbout at 500 feet agl, or the one whose instructor decided to simulate an in-flight engine failure on a perfectly good engine that was lacking only a perfectly good starter. And there's a story (one of the most remarkable in this entire collection) from a pilot who lost the engine and his DG in his Turbo 182RG at 21,000 feet and who, with the help of an air traffic controller, was able to deadstick the iced-up bird in for a safe landing to an airport that was 80 miles distant when trouble began.

These are real adventure tales. While we hope we never have to come up with the kind of quick thinking and grace under pressure demonstrated here, the fact of the matter is that someday we might have to. And while simulated failures are the best we can do in our recurrent training to approximate the experience of unplanned glider flying, there are certainly things to be learned from pilots who have gone through such a harrowing event and come out safe and sound—save the engine repair bills—on the other side.

Who Needs a Starter?

I T WAS FRIDAY, OCTOBER 30, 1998 at about 11:20 EST. The weather was cloudy and the winds were 090 at five and the ceiling was at 2,500. I just finished up my preflight on a Cessna 172 for a routine training flight. Due to a low ceiling, my CFI decided that we would stay in the pattern and practice takeoffs and landings. He thought I was ready to solo and he said we would practice together before cutting me loose to make my first solo for the last 20 minutes of the day's lesson.

I went through the prestart check list and announced "clear" just before turning the key. This is the part I enjoy, just like a NASCAR driver hearing the words "Gentleman, start your engines." I turned the key only to hear the starter motor whining with no propeller turning. I looked at my CFI and told him it sounded like the bendix was bad on the starter motor. When the motor quit spinning, I tried it again. After a couple of tries, the bendix finally kicked into the flywheel and the engine started. I didn't have a problem with the bad starter motor because we were only going to be in the pattern, and that didn't have anything to do with the airplane's flying ability. I did mention to my CFI that I hoped we did not need an inflight restart.

After starting, I did the usual routine of a radio check and airport advisories. I taxied to the end of the taxiway where I pulled out the pre-takeoff check list and did the engine run-up. Everything appeared and sounded normal so I made the call to announce that I was taking off and remaining in the pattern. I rolled out onto Runway 9 and did a normal takeoff. I had already done two normal takeoffs and landings, and on my third downwind leg, my CFI told me to do a go-around a few feet from touching down. I did the go-around exactly the way he taught me and then entered my downwind leg. I got abeam of the runway and all of a sudden, I lost all power with my hand still on the throttle. The pucker factor started at a three on a scale of one to 10. My CFI asked me "What are you going to do now?" I immediately set up my glide speed and skipped the best place to land and went to the cockpit check. I had the runway to the left of me and I already knew I was going to land there. I immediately found that my CFI had pulled the fuel mixture out all the way to idle cutoff.

At an 80 mph glide the propeller was windmilling. I entered my base leg and got the aircraft a little slow. With that, the propeller quite turning, I said "Oooooops" and my CFI said "Uh oh" at the same time. The pucker factor just escalated to an eight. My CFI pushed in the fuel mixture and leaned over on my lap, reached up under my yoke and tried to restart the engine. Guess what? Same problem that was on the ground when I first tried to start the plane. The bendix wouldn't kick into the flywheel. My CFI told me that he would try to keep restarting the engine and for me to keep the airplane flying like he taught me.

By that time, I had turned for my final approach. After making my turn on the final approach, the pucker factor reduced to almost a zero because I knew I had the runway made. I leaned over and put in full flaps to slow me down and just make a normal landing. My CFI asked me what the hell I was doing. I told him I needed flaps: He said "You better have that runway made." He then jumped up and saw that I was about 100 feet above the runway and just making a normal landing. He told me not to touch the brakes and to let the plane coast off the runway. I did that, and we tried to restart the engine a few more times. It finally started and that ended my lesson for the day.

That following Friday, we flew out to the practice area, did some stalls, returned to the airport and did more takeoffs and landings. After the second landing, my CFI told me to pull up to the FBO. He jumped out and told me to give him three takeoffs and landings. I did it with no difficulties. After I landed and parked the Cessna, it was the traditional cutting of the shirt tail and another advancement in aviation for me.

Pop Quiz

YOU TAKE A LOT OF EXAMS before you get to be a professor, like I am. So, my private pilot checkride was just another exam. The theoretical engine out procedure was easy. Set up the glide, switch fuel tanks, mixture rich, carburetor heat on, electric fuel pump on, check magnetos, find a suitable landing place, and, when you have the field made, extend flaps. A snap, theoretically.

Then I bought a quarter interest in a Cherokee 140 based at Corpus Christi International. The partnership worked out fine. My partners flew for recreation on weekends. I flew to Laredo during the week to teach.

A year after the purchase, I took a real engine out exam. The Cherokee needed fuel. Why not buy it at Rockport? RKP was just an enjoyable 15-minute flight over the bays, islands and farms of South Texas. And they had a good price on 100LL. It was a superb day for VFR flying. The temperature was in the upper 70s, CAVU and light wind from 140 degrees. The preflight revealed nothing. The Lycoming started as the first blade passed over the cowl. Navy trainers frequently practice landing at RKP, so I requested VFR traffic advisories from CRP Approach. I landed RKP with a slight bounce on zero nine, refueled to the tabs, and gulped a soft drink.

A quick preflight and I departed, spent a minute or two viewing the mansions and yachts on Key Allegro Island during the climb out, got CRP ATIS and contacted approach. Five minutes into the return flight I was on radar at 1,500 feet, a few miles north of Portland assigned a straight in approach for runway one three at CRP. The Lycoming was running smoothly with the power set at normal cruise of 2400 rpm.

Then, immediately after "radar contact" notification, the airplane began to shake like a sports car on a washboard road. It sounded like the internal engine components had initiated total war against each other. No abstract theory involved here. This was one final exam the professor had better pass. I self-administered the following six-part test in under three minutes. The grading I've done myself in hindsight.

1. What should I tell ATC? And should I switch to emergency frequency 121.5?

I decided to stay with approach, advise them I had a rough engine, and request vectors to the nearest airport.

Grade: C. Staying with approach and requesting the nearest airport were fine. But the term "rough engine" did not specify the situation. I should have said that total engine failure was probable and I was losing altitude.

2. Should I make a precautionary landing or try for Hunt's Airport five miles away?

I decided to try for Hunt's. After all, I could cover the distance in less than three minutes.

Grade: D. There were suitable emergency landing sites below me and the probability of the engine running much longer was low. By waiting until I had no power I would lose options.

3. To declare or not to declare an emergency? If so, how and when?

Two miles from Hunt's at 700 feet the engine quit. I called: "Mayday, Mayday 1803T."

Grade: D. A better call would have been "Mayday, Mayday, Mayday, Cherokee 1803T. No engine power. Two miles northwest Hunt's Portland. Pilot alone. Full fuel."

4. Should I try to stretch the glide to the airport?

NO!

Grade: A+. The end of a stretched glide is a smoking hole. Inside is a shattered airplane and pilot drenched in 36 gallons of blazing avgas. Sure, the airport is a seductive mistress, but hardly worth dying for.

5. Where to land? Within easy gliding distance were two roads and three fields. One road had power lines on both sides, the other deep ditches. The three fields looked better.

I chose the one that had shallow furrows matching the wind direction and no obstructions.

Grade: B. Good choice, but dumb luck to have a good field below when I had no option but to land in less than 90 seconds.

Suspecting a soft field, I used back elevator pressure after touchdown to prevent a nose over. A Bonanza pilot relayed CRP Approach my message that I had landed with no damage in a cotton field one mile northwest of Hunt's. Approach then vectored a nearby helicopter to me. It gave me a lift to Hunt's Airport. I telephoned the CRP Tracon and answered their questions.

Then I returned to the Cherokee. I was met by two crews of television reporters.

6. Should I talk to the media? If I did not, they might fabricate a "Daredevil Pilot Defies Death" headline.

I gave an interview. I explained that pilots are trained—and light airplanes are designed—to land safely off airport when necessary. I also said that ATC had responded very professionally. As a result, the television reports generated no hysteria.

Grade: A

Final grade: Pass (no flying colors). Although I'm hard on myself, I did a few things right. Despite the broken crankshaft, no one was hurt and no damage was done in landing. I believe that I passed the exam. I hope I never take the test again, but if I do, I'm a little better prepared than I was before.

Basics to the Rescue

FOR MY AIRPLANE CO-OWNER, Steve Carter, and me, expanding the boundaries of IFR flying and developing weather skills has long kept the "newness" in flying. Sophistication has crept in with the affordability of GPS receivers. Our Piper Arrow IV is home-based at Palomar Airport in southern California and satellite navigation through nearby complex airspace is a real benefit.

December 22, 1996, found our home airport with scattered, fast-moving clouds at 800 and 2,500 feet, and cold gusting winds out of the southwest at 14 knots. Some rainshowers were in the region. The new portable GPS receiver had arrived during the week, and a "trial by flight" was in order, even if it meant a bumpy ride. In view of the blustery conditions, the GPS unit was mounted to the copilot's yoke. I would "fly" the new GPS from the copilot's side, and Steve would be free to fly the airplane.

Engine run-up showed everything well within normal limits. Just 200 hours were on the overhauled engine, and it was proving to be a strong and satisfying performer. A short local-area trip plan was loaded into the GPS unit. Ready to go! Moving map navigation coming up!

The westward takeoff on Palomar's single runway was as normal as one can be with a 14-knot crosswind, and the liftoff was crisp. The gear was up and the Arrow bounced and yawed through gusts as it climbed toward the turn to crosswind. Steve commented on the wind-whipped whitecaps on the nearby Pacific Ocean, then scanned the engine gauges again. "The oil pressure is really dropping," he remarked, with a tell-tale edge of concern in his voice.

Both of us stared at the oil pressure gauge for an instant in disbelief. The engine sounded good and the climb out was strong—was that gauge wrong? Please let it be wrong... but now it was showing zero! During the early left turn to crosswind at 800 feet I was on the radio: "Palomar Tower, 70 Kilo is showing zero oil pressure. We need an immediate return for landing." Still in my mind was the image of the Cessna 414 and the Archer that had been beside us in the run-up area. Was one of them on the runway already? The controller's response was welcome and without hesitation, "70 Kilo, understand, cleared to land on, Runway 24, left traffic."

Steve immediately reduced power and started to bank towards the downwind leg, to get a low, tight pattern going. If that oil pressure was really zero, any more flight time was borrowed flight time, and it was running out fast. Part-way into the turn, a sharp jolt from under the cowl was followed by heart stopping heavy engine shaking and frightful, cockpit-filling mechanical clatter. Things were not going well up in the engine department! More throttle pullback, push the nose over and keep the turn going right back toward the center of the field. "70 Kilo has a full engine failure now! Emergency... landing down-wind!" I wondered if the tower could hear me over the cockpit din. "Roger, 70 Kilo, cleared to land, any direction" came the anxious reply.

Stop the engine, kill the vibration, still the din? No, not yet... no smoke, no fire. Let the prop keep turning. Maybe, just maybe, there was one burst of power still left in that engine. Maybe, just maybe, it would help us later.

The Arrow had continued turning and was now approaching the departure end of Runway 24 at almost a right angle, but still too high to simply turn and land. Now what? Steve's words captured my next thought: "Too low to circle down!" Some high-voltage power lines to the west of the field seemed to take on momentary life—they glared up at us, bared their teeth at us, dared us to come down to their level. Forget circling. A moment's discussion found us agreeing to cross the runway end and "S" turn back to the center of the field, losing excess altitude along the way. Getting the landing gear down brought more drag into play, and our "short final" was a curving one to the middle of Runway 06. The Arrow was somewhat low but still had plenty of flying speed. That 14-knot crosswind was now a quartering headwind, but it helped push Steve through a very low left turn to the runway centerline that had me wondering if we would scrape a wingtip. The left wheel touched first followed by the other two, quite smooth in spite of the late turn and the wind. Touchdown and roll-out were met by "That was a great job!" from the tower, and how sweet those words did sound!

Braking to a stop at the runway takeoff end, the temptation was to immediately shut down our poor hammering, barely-running engine. However, not wanting to force an airport closure, we hobbled off into the run-up area, clattering, shaking and dripping our way past the startled pilots in the still-waiting Cessna 414 and Archer. The engine could barely produce taxi power, and the propeller stopped with a wicked suddenness the instant the mixture was moved into cutoff. We sat for a few seconds in our new-found silence, then both said together, "It's great to be down." And then, looking at the forgotten GPS unit, "We didn't make much use of that moving map."

A look at the outside of the airplane showed an oil-streaked cowling but no other damage. A pool of engine oil formed on the ground behind the nosewheel. A small bevy of well-wishers who had seen our airshow-style return arrived to shake our hands. Later, back at the shop, removing the cowling revealed a three-by-tour-inch hole in the engine case near the base of the right rear cylinder, apparently knocked out by a separated and flailing connecting rod.

Nothing that really mattered on our short flight that day involved satellite navigation, complex procedures or anything else very sophisticated. Everything important involved gut-level flying, presence of mind and doing the things rehearsed in VFR airwork. How fortunate and timely were our recent on-the-numbers landings over the hills to the short desert strip at Agua Caliente, and the crosswind work at gusty Chiriaco Summit near the Salton Sea. Yet how humble these sessions had seemed next to instrument approaches in the Los Angeles area, and how basic compared with satellite navigation. The "new and sophisticated" may keep us interested in aviation, but the "old and basic" still flies us home.

Mayday at 500 Feet

IT WAS MAY 13TH (BUT NOT FRIDAY), and for the first time in days the wind had finally died down. I decided to take the day off and put some time on my Mooney, which had just come out of annual.

I couldn't find anyone to go with me, so I took off on a solo mission to Gainesville, Florida. It was hot but dry, with almost no wind. The short trip over was uneventful and after getting a soft drink, I fired up for the return trip. I was cleared to taxi to Runway 06, the shorter of Gainesville's two runways at 4,150 feet. With little traffic and no wind, I had expected to be instructed to Runway 24, with its departure end right next to the FBOs. I guessed that construction on a nearby taxiway had prompted the change.

During the pre-takeoff checks, the engine seemed to idle a little rough. However, it smoothed out during the run-up, and everything checked out. I decided that if all the gauges weren't in the green on the takeoff roll, I would abort and go look.

I called the tower "ready" on 06 but was cleared for takeoff on Runway 10. At 7,500 feet, Runway 10 is Gainesville's airline runway. It joins Runway 06 at the departure end to form a short-sided "V." The takeoff roll was normal, and as I cleaned the airplane up, I was pleased to note the 800 to 1,000 feet per minute rate of climb. Not bad for 180 horses on a hot day, even if I was fairly light. At 500 feet, just as I was thinking ahead to an afternoon on the golf course, the engine quit dead. My first thought was that I was too low to return to the runway I had just departed. I called "Mayday!" and started a gentle turn to the left while going through the emergency procedures. It was my intention to enter a left base for a landing on Runway 24, and so I informed the controller.

I was over trees and swamp, so the airport environment looked like the best place to be when I ran out of altitude. The tower controller cleared the area of other traffic and asked if I could make Runway 28. A quick look to the left gave me hope that I could, as it was becoming clear that I was not going to make it anywhere near Runway 24.

Continuing the turn, I aimed for the corner of Runway 28. When I had it made, I lowered the gear, kicked the nose to the right and touched down in one of my smoothest landings in some time.

Less than a minute after the engine quit, I rolled to a stop and shut the airplane down. It had all happened so quickly that the emergency equipment was still rolling as I exited the airplane.

I half expected that I had somehow caused the engine failure and that I would taxi in with my tail between my legs, contemplating a call to the tower. Those thoughts changed when I saw raw fuel gushing out of the cowling. Something in the carburetor (probably a sunken float) had failed, flooding the engine.

I had been lucky; being cleared for takeoff on Runway 10 instead of 06, having a tower to clear the area and suggest a return to Runway 28 and not catching fire. But what did I learn that day? At the slightest sign of a problem, stay on the ground. If it turns out to be a problem, it's a lot easier to deal with on the ground than at 500 feet, and the only thing you lose is a little time.

The other valuable lesson learned is that every situation must be evaluated as it occurs. This must be done by reference to the common wisdom of flying but without rigid adherence to that common wisdom. Faced with a similar situation in the future, turning back might not be an option. But given the circumstances that day, doing so saved my airplane and quite possibly, me.

The Right Stuff—In The Wrong Order

HIS WIDOW CALLED WITH THE SAD NEWS. Walter had been a good friend and a fine pilot, with almost 40 years of impressive flying experience; over 20,000 hours of accident-free flight time. The heart attack was completely unexpected and had claimed him quickly. She asked if I would be a pallbearer. Of course I would.

The funeral would be in Superior, the northern Wisconsin city on the western tip of Lake Superior. I was living in Madison, in the southern part of the state, and flying a Beech 18 for a living. After contemplating the six-hour drive on winter roads I planned to set out on the day before the funeral.

Avery was a mechanic in our shop, and the owner of a Beechcraft Musketeer. "Hey, Jim, why don't you take my airplane instead of driving?" He reasoned that the flight was less than two hours and I wouldn't have to leave until the morning of the funeral. This alternative would require less rescheduling of my flights in the Twin Beech and should make for a more relaxed trip altogether. It was a generous offer, which I quickly accepted. I'd never flown a Musketeer, and so we made plans for an early morning check flight before I would depart.

I arrived at the airport at six a.m., a few minutes before Avery. The place was socked in, sky obscured and the runway visual range was 1,600 feet. A delayed Northwest flight was parked at the gate waiting for things to burn off. I untied the Musketeer and shoveled the snow from around it while I waited for the owner to arrive. When I drained the sumps the fuel streamed out clear, a good indication when the temperature is around zero. Any water in the tanks would have settled in the sumps and frozen solid.

Avery arrived and suggested we push his airplane into our warm shop for awhile, as it probably wouldn't start without preheating. After doing this I called flight service about the weather. The tops were around 3,000 feet, clear above, and the northern two-thirds of the state, including my destination, was CAVU. The weather bureau wasn't expecting our visibility to improve much for several hours.

A check flight was out of the question, and so prospects for completing the trip in time for the funeral seemed doubtful. Walter's family and mine were very close, and he had been a mentor years before when I was finishing my instrument training. Failing to attend his funeral was not something I wanted to consider. "Heck, you really don't need a check ride," Avery said. He assured me that the Musketeer flew very much like most light airplanes—no bad habits, no gear to retract, no prop control to fiddle with. The instruments and radios were up to date, and I wasn't hard to convince.

We sat in the cockpit and went over the simple panel, locations of the few switches and knobs and talked about trim settings. I read the flight manual. With an ATP ticket in my wallet and a lot of recent wet instrument time in my logbook, a climb on the gauges through 3,000 feet of cloud was about the easiest instrument flight I could ask for. I filed a flight plan and called for a fuel truck to top off the half-full tanks.

The preflight and run-up were comforting. The vacuum-driven gyro instrument spun up and stabilized quickly, a fast VOR receiver check was on the money, and the current altimeter setting parked the needles right on field elevation. When the ground controller read my clearance the radio sounded crisp and clear.

The tower cleared me for takeoff, adding that the RVR was now 1,400 feet. Out the windshield it looked like a lot less than that as I shoved the throttle ahead. When the centerline of Runway 31 was slipping nicely under the nose of the Musketeer, I took another fast peek at the instruments and saw everything was in order. With the nosewheel off the runway, the little Beechcraft soon went airborne and I went on the gauges. The airplane handled as Avery said, docile yet responsive, stable in the calm morning air. My departure clearance read straight out, and in a few minutes I was on top, cleared to 6,000 feet.

With the sun shining in the cockpit and the cabin heater beginning to warm things up, I sat back for an easy trip to Superior. Going through 3,500 feet the unthinkable happened. The engine stopped. There had been no indications on the engine instruments, no warning noises, just two or three sputters and then nothing. And nothing I did in the next few seconds—carb heat, boost pump, fuel tank selector check—improved the condition.

The fact that there were no options to consider, no decisions to make, probably made the task easier but no less emotionally stimulating. The airplane was heading for the ground, and, with the visibility little better than zero, there wasn't much I could do about selecting the spot. I trimmed for a 60-knot glide and listened to the gyros slowly spooling down. They were still working but were doomed, of course.

I'd always suspected that flight instructors were overly optimistic when they talked about maneuvering IFR with only needle, ball and airspeed. Tentatively I practiced the primitive exercise for a few seconds while the directional gyro and horizon were still functioning. Just before settling into the cloud layer I told the controller I'd lost power and was coming down. I don't remember his exact words but they were along the lines of, "Give us a call later and let us know how it turns out."

I'd decided that I could handle a straight ahead descent without gyros. When the "off" flags appeared on those instruments I concentrated on holding the turn needle upright, ball in the center, maintaining 60 knots of airspeed. At least I didn't have to be concerned about my heading because I had no idea where to point the Musketeer anyway. I'll admit now that there was a little porpoising and wobbling going on, but I think I averaged roughly level descent and 60 knots.

I was familiar with the countryside as I was over a few miles northwest of Madison. It was gently rolling, snow-covered land, a farming area with many harvested fields. On the negative side, there were lots of tree lines, barns, silos and fences. I prayed that with some luck I might emerge from the obscured sky at a place where I could put the crippled airplane down without killing myself. Nosing over in the deep snow was a probability, and I thought of how hard it was going to be to tell Avery he should not have trusted me with his airplane.

Descending through about 200 feet, I began sneaking quick peeks down ahead of the wing. The first earthly thing I spotted through the mist was the most marvelous sight I'd ever beheld in 20 years of flying—the orange wind sock at the Waunakee landing strip. It was about six miles from the Madison airport, five miles from my home, and I'd never landed there.

The runway hadn't been plowed since the last snow and was hidden somewhere under a foot of the white expanse, but I recalled that it ran about east and west. A row of T-hangars appeared dimly through the haze, and a short strip of plowed blacktop road whisked beneath the wing. I took a guess, which required only a quick turn about 60 degrees left to line up with what I hoped may be the runway.

It wasn't pretty. I'd let the airspeed build a little in the turn, and a lot of airport went sliding past after I jerked the flaps down. Then I missed the flare by a few feet, but came to a stop undamaged about 50 yards short of a barbed wire fence at the airport perimeter. To this day, the only landing I've ever made in a Beechcraft Musketeer was a little long, featured a bounce and was done dead-stick.

I tramped through the snow on shaking legs and roused the occupant of the nearest house. He was the manager of the little airport, and when I told him I'd just landed he looked out the window at the fog-shrouded airplane and asked, "How did you manage that?" "Fate," I shrugged.

I used his phone to make a couple of calls and Avery arrived within the hour. The first thing he did was attempt to drain the fuel sumps. They were frozen. We went over the sequence of procedures that morning and solved the mystery. The airplane had sat out in the cold for several days with half-full tanks. With the temperature below freezing most of that week, water vapor in the air had condensed and formed frost in the tanks above the fuel level. When I drained the sumps shortly after six that morning, clean fuel streamed out. Then we put the airplane in the warm hangar and the frost became water and ran down into the fuel. Some time after that is when I should have drained the sumps.

The rest is pretty obvious. Up in the bitter cold air above Madison's winter, the water migrated to some strategic location and froze again.

I take no credit for the miraculously happy ending to this event. The blame was all mine. I thought I'd done all the right things: Read the manual, done a thorough preflight inspection, drained the fuel sumps, been briefed by the airplane owner and the weather bureau. All the right stuff—but done in the wrong order.

The Luckiest Day of My Life

I FLY A 1983 PIPER TURBO SARATOGA SP that I bought two years ago with a few partners, and I have done quite a bit of traveling in it with friends and family. I hold a private/instrument certificate with about three years and 400 hours under my belt. The aircraft was well maintained by a major shop. The engine had 1,400 hours on it, and a top overhaul was just completed about six months and 60 hours before the incident I am about to describe occurred.

This was the first flight in N4292K since an annual inspection and oil change had been completed the day before. Sound familiar? On October 21, 2000 I departed my home base of Wilkes-Barre/Scranton, Pennsylvania (AVP) with my fiancée, Madelyn, and her brother Mark as passengers for a day together at Foxwood Indian Casino and Bingo near Groton/New London, Connecticut. The trip out was completely normal, and the early morning autumn mists and scattered foggy patches clung beautifully to the bright orange and red foliage of the Catskill Mountains. It was that perfect kind of day that gives us a reason to fly. We had a great time at Foxwoods, and Madelyn even won $1,500 in a bingo game.

We got a late start home and would be flying directly into the setting afternoon sun for the first half of the trip home; the remaining 45 minutes would be completed in the dark. Despite being behind schedule, I conducted an unhurried preflight, added a quart of oil and found nothing abnormal whatsoever during the subsequent engine start and run-up. I asked Groton ground for VFR flight following and a briefing on noise abatement procedures, was cleared for takeoff and departed Runway 23 turning left out over Long Island Sound to avoid overflying the houses.

As we leveled off about 15 minutes into the flight and I finished leaning and fine-tuning cruise power, almost immediately, I saw the engine oil temperature start to climb toward redline. Checking further, the oil pressure was in the green range, and the graphic engine monitor was indicating EGT and CHT evenly and in the acceptable ranges. I simultaneously dialed up the nearest airport list on the Garmin GNS 430 installed a few months before and called New York Approach, saying "4292K would like to divert to the nearest field." He gave me a few options, none of which I heard. I pulled the power back to 15 inches of manifold in an attempt to reduce the oil temp, but it just kept on climbing.

There is a suspension of the thinking processes that happens in these few seconds that I can only describe as a "locked up" phenomena. It's as if your brain refuses to accept the reality of what is happening to it and it literally stops processing information. I was seeing the list of nearest airports on the GPS but not comprehending what I was looking at. I somehow transmitted, "We request priority handling," but my finger never released the mic button on the yoke. After about 10 seconds or so of this brain fibrillation, I finally let go and New York Approach said "92K, I think you had a stuck mic and can you tell me what the problem is?" I replied, "We have a high oil temperature indication," and asked him to tell me the closest airport again.

My brain finally clicked into gear and I scanned the list of airports. There were two behind me, but with short runways. The one that caught my eye had a 5,600-foot runway and was 12 miles distant more or less on my present heading. After a quick estimate of the available glide but without thinking about it too much I said, "I'll take New Haven" as I punched in direct HVN on the GPS and turned left to the indicated bearing. Just then the engine started "missing." There was no loud noise or pop, just a rough intermittent interruption of power. My plan at this point was to limp into New Haven under reduced power, but the engine had other ideas.

I remembered those articles I had read about people waiting too long to declare, and the rough running engine obviously told me I had more than an oil temperature gauge problem. In my most authoritative tone I said, "New York Approach, 4292K is declaring an emergency." He answered with "Say souls on board," to which I resignedly replied "Three." As if the engine heard me, within seconds thick white smoke poured into the cabin and oil and smoke started streaming out of the cowling. I opened the pilot's storm window to vent the smoke, and Madelyn let out a feeble, "Oh my God" from the back seat. In my only opportunity to say anything to my passengers, I said, "Relax, we're going to be fine," although I said it more for myself and probably didn't sound too convincing.

As the oil blew out of the engine onto the windows, my visibility was becoming increasingly impaired, and I felt the panic and helplessness welling up inside me. Although it was very difficult at first, I forced myself to remain calm and fly the airplane. I was concerned about fire and the engine seizing, which sometimes makes the engine shake loose from its mount and throws the airplane out of balance. Not wanting this to happen, I proceeded to shut things down. I told New York that we had smoke in the cabin and oil on the windshield and said, "We could really use some help here," as if there were anything he could do. He replied "Airport 12 o'clock and eight miles, just remain on your present heading, we have emergency equipment responding." I told him I was shutting the engine down and pulled the mixture and prop back simultaneously, then reached down to engage the gear override to prevent the landing gear from automatically extending.

At this point the front and side windows were completely coated with golden oil, and I had zero outside visibility. I trimmed for best glide at 80 knots and started a circular scan of the GPS, turn coordinator, airspeed indicator and pilot's storm window. Wanting to conserve battery for the GPS and gear extension, I shut down the transponder and strobes, but with all my attention devoted to keeping control of the airplane, failed to turn off the fuel valve or move the magnetos to the "off" position.

With the gear warning horn blaring and the prop windmilling, we continued gliding toward the airport with the stall warning horn intermittently chiming in. At four miles out, I changed to the tower frequency obtained from the Garmin without informing New York Approach. I called up and said that I didn't have the field in sight yet, and the tower operator said that he's looking for me as well, had turned up all field lights to maximum and turned on the beacon. I continued inbound, passing through 3,000 feet, turned 20 degrees to the right to try to find the field out of the three-inch window. "4292K, you are cleared to land on Runway 20 or any runway. All traffic remain clear of New Haven airspace, emergency in progress."

At two miles out and 2,500 feet, I saw the beautiful runway and the emergency vehicles flashing lights nearby. I dropped the gear, dropped full flaps, and entered a massive forward left slip while diving for the runway. The slip was the only way I could track the runway by crouching down and looking through the spit window as the windows were still all completely covered with thick oil. Beyond the runway were houses and the open ocean, and I was in serious danger of overshooting the field. I engaged full right rudder and left aileron and dropped 2,000 feet in about 30 seconds with my airspeed at the top of the white arc. I killed the master switch and was still flying literally sideways approaching the numbers at 500 feet. I saw the centerline come up and held it in the window off the left side of the airplane so I could track the runway.

Somehow, about halfway down the runway, I simultaneously kicked out of the crab and flared before digging a hole in the ground and held the airplane a few feet from the surface to bleed off airspeed while holding that centerline in that little window. The mains touched down very firmly and I began a gentle bounce. I kept the wings level and pushed forward ever so slightly to plant the wheels softly on the ground. I immediately raised the flaps and began full braking, slowing enough to take an instinctive left turn off the runway onto Taxiway Bravo just as the prop windmilled to a halt. The aircraft came to a stop just clear of the hold short line as the fire engines and ambulances raced toward us. We sat in stunned shock and silence for a moment, surprised to be alive, and then I said, "Get out of the airplane now." There were no physical injuries, and the airplane appeared undamaged other than the oil dropping off of all visible surfaces.

The aftermath of the incident left us shaken and full of questions. Foremost in my mind was a need to have an answer to what went wrong. Was it a mechanic who did something wrong during the annual and oil change the day before? Was it just chance catastrophic engine failure? The FAA investigator said that the visible engine damage, which consisted of two holes through the top of the case near the camshaft and a sloppy exhaust valve, was very unusual and neither he nor the head mechanic at New Haven had ever seen anything like it. Since I shut the engine down almost immediately, it was still intact and it may be possible to determine exactly what happened. The engine was crated and shipped for teardown and analysis. The engine analysis revealed that the catastrophic failure was the result of a setscrew coming loose and getting caught up in the engine. The NTSB documented this as having been the result of the mechanic who performed the last engine overhaul using unapproved parts and procedures prior to our purchasing the aircraft.

It took me two weeks to summon up the courage to get into an airplane again, with my friend Mike Rencavage, a CFI-I, there to lend moral and emotional support for that short flight. I was acutely aware of every firing of every cylinder the whole way. But I did it.

I highly recommend a disciplined program of recurrent training in engine-out procedures. Mike trained me for such an event, and I supplemented that training with a great deal of study. The one thing you can never fully prepare for, even in a million-dollar simulator, is the shock, surprise, fear and uncertainty that accompany the situation. Always fly with the assumption that you will have an engine failure at some point, and be prepared to handle it. Are you ready today? Complacency can kill. Also, if you're not already instrument rated, become so. Sometimes zero visibility has nothing to do with the weather. With proper preparation, and if you don't panic, a positive outcome is nearly always possible, and you should never give up.

In the wake of these events, beyond the mechanical investigation, is the reconciliation of circumstances in my mind and the recognition of exactly how close we had really come to having our existence ended. "If" was the key word: If it happened on takeoff over the water, or not within gliding distance of an airport (without forward or side visibility, surviving an off-airport landing was unlikely, at best). Or what if it was 30 minutes later, at night? Or in IMC? There was certainly a great deal of good fortune on our side, but as Mike said to me, pilots make their own luck. I didn't panic. I flew the airplane correctly, managed the emergency properly, and extended the glide almost to its limits. I definitely made good use of my instrument rating all the way to the ground. I used every piece of knowledge and skill I ever learned to get us on the ground safely. However you slice it, this certainly was the luckiest day of my life, so far. I hope I don't need to have one luckier.

A Big Debt to an Air Traffic Controller

MY FRIEND AND I FLEW TO LAS VEGAS from Salt Lake City in October to see a few races. The weather was lousy for several days, and I knew that it would beat me back to Salt Lake City.

The weather cleared that morning before our flight, but I knew I would run into it. I called for a briefing. To my surprise it was 6,500 broken... 8,500 broken and 10. "I can do that," I thought. For 21 years in the air I have maintained my policy of not flying passengers into doubtful circumstances. My gut was churning and didn't rest until I told my passenger to fly home commercially, a decision for which he was later very grateful.

I climbed my Turbo 182RG up to 13,500 for VFR on top. Then to 15,500, then to 17,500 VFR on top. I was nearly home but could see no breaks in the clouds to drop through. My IFR rating had long lapsed. This was decision time, and I missed or ignored the moment—for which I would nearly pay with my life. I got on the radio to find where there was VFR flying. While trying to do so, the cloud tops came up into my belly. I pulled on the yoke and noted that I was climbing through 18,000. I jumped on the radio and asked for clearance into controlled airspace. The controller was furious. Pop-ups had become a thing of the past.

As I was involved with this irate controller, I noticed that my HSI had failed. Was I now going, for the sake of this controller, to attempt a 180-degree turn in IMC with no HSI? Not for him or anybody else would I do that except if someone else were in danger by my flight. I told him of my "no DG" conditions. He was still mad. I was cleared to 21,000 and popped out VFR. Just then my engine rpm dropped from 2200 to below 500 and the manifold pressure nearly fell to zero. I lied to the controller that I'd had "partial engine failure" and dropped right into IMC... rain, snow and icing with no HSI! I could not get the engine back and would later discover a fractured turbo shaft. Both my imminent death and John F. Kennedy, Jr.'s death hit me in the gut, and I was scared more than ever before in my life. "Well this is it" echoed in my head.

By now the controller was asking me to take down phone numbers. I ignored him and responded "negative" to his inquiry as to whether I had taken down the number. By now other fliers were silent, except one who, when sent to another frequency, asked to "stay on this frequency to hear this." "He wants to know what happens to this village idiot," I thought. It occurred to me that if I ever got down, I would find this controller and box his ears. No DG, no engine, IMC and he is writing me up.

Just then heaven intervened in the form of a controller who saved my life—new voice, new guy. I knew I had to listen and also maintain 70 knots, the best glide ratio. I knew I had to be glued to the turn and bank and attitude indicator or I'm augered in. When the controller confirmed my DG and engine loss he came back calm and reassuring. "Turn left and I'll stop you at a heading of 270 degrees—going to Wendover." I couldn't resist a quick peek at the compass 12 inches above me. When I came back to the panel the attitude indicator was 25 degrees left and I was climbing toward stall! "How could that happen in 10 seconds?" I thought. As I pulled the airplane back, I could feel the pull in the seat of my pants. Why did I not feel it go? I wanted to disbelieve the attitude indicator for that reason, but I knew better.

Holding 70 knots, I could see rime and then more on the leading edge of the wing. I increased to 80 knots. At some point I turned on the pitot heat but don't remember doing it. It was deathly quiet and I was scared to death. The windscreen was frosted over. Just me, three instruments, a quiet airplane, ice and a controller who to me was God. At 17,000 feet I was holding and alive. Then the warrior in me stepped up. "I can do this. I'm going to make it." At 14,000 feet I asked the controller who had been there all along, "How am I doing?" His response brought me to tears. "You're doing just fine, you're going to make it fella." If he suspected I was a long shot, he never let on—thank God.

I remembered the Cedar Mountains, 40 miles east of Wendover at 9,500 feet. Not the place to end my flight. The controller called on my frequency and asked for anyone with a pirep on ceilings at Wendover. Someone said 10,500. The controller called me with "You are going to break out in two minutes," and I did. Windscreen fully frosted over. I could see the ground out the side window but nothing forward. Then, as mentioned in the preflight briefing, I hit the freezing level and the ice came off in chunks. There was Wendover, still a long way to go. I could hear the elation in the controller's voice when he knew I was VFR. Could I make Wendover?

Then I could see I might make it. The controller asked me if I wanted to declare an emergency. I should have said "Yes," but, self sufficient to the end, I said, "No." He then asked me to call him "when I got down." Sounded good to me. I had one shot at a runway with a quartering tailwind. I put the wheels down. No time to blow that one, and I made a very iffy landing. As I pulled up the airplane was engulfed in smoke. Smoke that had followed me from 21,000 feet. I got out, leaned against this great airplane and simply cried like a kid... great emotional sobs. I was on a military airfield and the flashing truck came out. The officer got out and started to chew me out but quickly saved the day and I had a new friend.

In the aftermath I called that controller and had an emotional talk. I got his wife on the phone and told her what I still believe now, that without him, I'd be dead. I never talked to Mr. Furious controller.

The FAA didn't believe that I came 80 miles with a blown engine from 21,000 feet, no DG. Nor did I. Do the math, not possible. They came out to see the airplane. Yup! Then they didn't know what to do with me. Nor did I. In the end the FAA sat me down for a long chat; no need to see if I could fly the airplane, they said. Fair enough. I should have turned back at 17,500 feet. Of that there is no doubt. However, my engine and DG failed at altitude. I had the best controller on the planet and I made a runway. Most days I flew without controllers. That has changed. I still owe one controller very big time.

LEARNING DIFFERENT THINGS FROM FLYING

I LEARNED ABOUT FLYING FROM THAT is most often a story of a close call with an accident. But occasionally we get a contribution that tells the story of a different kind of lesson learned. And sometimes, if the subject is just different enough, we decide to put it in the magazine.

Sometimes the contributor's impulse is to educate *Flying* readers, as with the piece written by a flying spouse about the pinch hitter's course she attended, or by a wizened buyer about how much harder it can be to purchase an airplane than to fly one, or another, by an accident investigator, who shared lessons learned from a particularly difficult crash scene. In each case, we get interesting and unusual insights into of flying from very different perspectives.

Sometimes these lessons are reflections on some deeper theme, insights about ourselves, or about others, that we've learned from flying, such as the story written by a pilot who gave a terminally ill man his last flight, or another tale, in part a tutorial, by a pilot who successfully scattered the ashes of a good friend over the waters of the Atlantic Ocean.

So while the name of the piece is always *I Learned About Flying From That*, it is sometimes from others' experiences that the lessons are learned. More often than not, those lessons go straight to the heart.

CHAPTER EIGHT

The Wrong Impression

A FEW YEARS AGO I was talking about flying to a patient I was treating who was also a co-worker in the local Scout program. It was a one-sided conversation as I am a dentist and he had his mouth full of fingers, cotton and a dental drill. I could tell that he wanted to ask me a question; a dentist learns to recognize the expression on the face of a frustrated patient who, due to the crowded mouth, can only speak in monosyllables. I stopped long enough for him to catch his breath and ask his question. "Doc, how about giving some of my Cub Scouts a ride in your airplane?" After explaining that my Alon Aircoupe would only take two people and that I could just take one passenger at the time, he still seemed interested. After more discussion and more work on his teeth we set up a date for the outing.

I had not owned the Alon for long and while I was not a new pilot, giving rides was something I had only done for family and a few hangar buddies. I was pleased at the opportunity to get some young seven-year-old interested in aviation and the thrill of flying in a small airplane.

The appointed time proved to be a lovely Saturday morning with unlimited visibility and calm winds—an ideal day to introduce to the young troop the beauty and excitement of flying your own plane.

The youngsters gathered around the plane, their faces glowing with interest and excitement. I gave a brief lecture on aerodynamics, mentioned the rules of operating around an uncontrolled field ("Where is the tower?" was the first question) and we all did a careful preflight. This was going to be a day they remembered, the day when they learned all about flying. There was some reluctance when I ask who wanted to ride first. The cub leader had assured me that he had signed permission for all to go.

A timid hand went up and I summoned its owner into the cockpit. I buckled him in on a cushion that I had brought for the occasion, proving that I had thought of everything to introduce a youngster to aviation.

The takeoff was as smooth as I could make it from the dirt runway, and we climbed out over his home town. A few steep turns over his home and school got his attention. A circle over the main intersection on the interstate allowed him to see our superiority over travel by car. I then insisted that he put his hands on the control column and pull the aircraft up into a climb and then push it down to see how easily it followed the controls. I keep thinking what a great experience we were having and how he could tell his buddies how he "flew" the Alon. I then feigned a little confusion and ask him if he could find his way back to the airport, which was just below us. He shook his head to let me know he had no idea where it was and I dropped a wing so he could see where we were. I then quickly descended into the pattern and landed as smoothly as I could so that I could give the others their big chance to become aviators.

After taxiing to a stop and helping him out of the cockpit I noticed that he was a little unsteady on his feet and that his color was somewhat more pale green that I had previously noticed. I stood next to him and his buddies expecting to hear the compliments on the exciting flight before the others crowded in. He looked at me with an expression that I will never forget and said with the sincerity that only the young can project, "Mister, I'm sick and you scared the hell out of me."

I was stunned, as was my friend, his Cubmaster. The other boys backed off. After a brief discussion with the pack and the leader they decided it was time to leave. The Cubmaster shook my hand weakly and said in a voice that carried some sarcasm he guessed that it was just a little too much for the youngsters.

Too late I saw the flight from the eyes of the insecure child. My haste to find his home had not given him time to orient himself to the additional dimension of flying. The abrupt turns had made him uncomfortable. The noise had distracted him from any comments I had made, and my suggestion that I did not know where we were frightened him. The aircraft controls and instruments confused him, and worst of all, I never appreciated his distress. I was so taken up with my concept of the morning flight that I ignored his concerns. Not surprising that he was anxious to get back to his buddies safely on the ground.

I was appalled as I realized that I had done just the opposite of what was intended. Instead of instilling confidence I had generated fear. My enthusiasm was built on many hours in the air but this was their first experience. My whole approach to the first ride of the young, or the old for that matter, should have been to build confidence and to make the passenger comfortable. No steep turns, no abrupt changes of attitude and a confidence by the passenger that you are in full control. I had broken almost every rule for the first flight of an apprehensive passenger. Worst of all I missed that most unique of opportunities: Make a good first impression.

Final Flight

WHEN A FRIEND OF MINE RECENTLY PASSED AWAY after a long illness, I learned that he had requested in his will that I scatter his cremated remains from an airplane over the Atlantic Ocean coastline at Rehoboth Beach, Delaware. This had been the scene of some pleasant sightseeing flights in a Cessna 182RG for the two of us before his illness. Implementing this last request turned out to require a bit of planning, and I thought my experience might be useful for other pilots faced with a similar mission.

I was advised by a flight instructor not to use a single-engine Cessna for this "funeral flight" because the large side windows create a swirling turbulence when opened that cannot easily be sealed off. Such attempts have led to the unpleasant experience of having portions of the remains blown back into the aircraft, coating the interior and occupants alike.

The best aircraft is a low-wing airplane with a small pilot's storm window, such as a Mooney or Bonanza. I selected a Piper Arrow from my flying club and took the following equipment. I purchased a large oil change funnel from an auto parts store and cut off the bottom six inches to eliminate the narrowest constriction. I also bought a large car-washing sponge that was slightly larger than the storm window, masking tape, resealable plastic bags, paper towels and a camera. Rounding out my supply list was a friend to serve as copilot on the flight.

We took off from Leesburg, Virginia, and flew east past Baltimore across the Chesapeake Bay. On reaching the Atlantic coastline, we flew along the beach about a half mile offshore at 1,500 feet msl to stay above the occasional coastal traffic at 1,000 feet. It was a beautiful morning, with sunshine and scattered cumulus clouds above and surf below.

Once over the drop zone, I slowed to 80 knots, with gear down and one notch of flaps to make the aircraft as stable as possible. I engaged the single-axis autopilot in "heading select" mode and trimmed for level flight. After reminding my copilot of her responsibility to assist with maintaining see-and-avoid vigilance for other traffic, I set up the equipment for the drop.

First, I turned off all cabin air, heat and vents to minimize the outflow through the storm window. (You don't want to lose the sponge at the outset) I opened the storm window and placed the sponge over the opening. The strong suction held the sponge securely in place.

Next, I pushed the funnel spout out through the lower right corner of the storm window and used masking tape to hold the wide end of the funnel upright against the window pillar. We then slowly opened the front cabin air floor vents all the way, directed down towards the floor. With the rest of the window blocked by the sponge, this created a strong airflow from the cabin flowing down the funnel.

The funeral home had delivered the cremated remains in a cardboard box with an inner plastic bag suitable for scattering them; the whole package was about the size of a small toaster. After a moment's quiet reflection and a silent farewell to my friend, I slowly poured the contents into the funnel, watching as they were whisked off into the slipstream. The cabin airflow created a strong suction, which made it seem as if the funnel were connected to a vacuum cleaner.

It took about 10 minutes to complete the drop. The ashes dissipated instantly from the end of the funnel, looking like the spray from a perfume atomizer. Not a trace of the remains was left on the aircraft's wings or fuselage. The process was so neat and efficient that we did not have to use the paper towels and bags that we brought along in case of problems with the drop.

With the window secured and the aircraft back in cruise configuration, we took a final pass down the beach to photograph the scene and preserve our memories. As the disposition of a good friend's physical remains, the occasion was solemn. Yet at the same time, the process was curiously exhilarating. The last memory of my friend will forever be of that final flight over the ocean, mixing his ashes with millions of molecules of air and sea. I felt he was there with us watching it.

Pinch Hitter

IT'S EVERY GIRL'S DREAM: four days in a flight simulator with your husband, his friend, and a total stranger. And one of those days was Valentine's Day.

So how did I get there? Simple. We turned 40. I wanted a new kitchen; my husband, Bob, wanted to fly again, after an eight-year layoff. (Kids will do that to you.) Well, I got my kitchen, and in an 18-month period my husband got his instrument and multiengine ratings. The remodeling never bothered him. He was at the airport!

At one point, his buddy and partner, Tom, who was coming back to flying after a 10-year layoff, said, "I really need to fly and so does Bob." I remember basic biology: there's a need for food, water and oxygen. But flying?

There's got to be something about turning 40. Some guys need fast cars or boats or even a new wife. And then there are the guys who "need to fly." My husband tells me it's cheaper than a mistress. I'd love to see the numbers on that!

So you know what's coming next: They needed their own plane. As near as I can tell, this process entails talking to people from all over the world, spreading out airplane pictures all over the kitchen table, and spending countless hours on the Internet. Of course this didn't include the hours of conversation discussing the merits of each particular plane. I became fluent in the discussion of VGs, hot props, boots, HSIs, Stormscopes and the like. Finally they found the plane of their dreams: a Cessna 310Q. They told me it was sexy. I said I thought it was cute. They were horrified.

Once they bought the plane, Bob and I loaded up the kids and went on vacation. My parents were apoplectic—I was putting their grandchildren's lives in danger, if anything happened to Bob. I began to see a pinch-hitter course in my future.

Tom and Bob had decided that the best way to get to know their new plane and become safer pilots was to go to simulator school at SimCom in Scottsdale. When I asked Bob if I could tag along and learn to land the plane, it was like asking a kid if it's okay to go with him to Disney World. Truth be told, this wasn't on my "List of Things To Do" this week, month or year. But hey, I went to the School of Good Sports. And besides, no one is going to die in a simulator, except of natural causes.

And I'll confess, it was fun. In fact, at times it was kind of a rush. . . especially on takeoff. The simulator is a large room with video screens surrounding a plane fuselage. Inside are all the controls you need to fly the plane. At the back of the plane is the control booth, where our instructor, Bob Kuplin, sat like the Marquis de Sade, programming in disasters to plague the pilots. We trained on a Cessna 421, which was programmed to fly like our 310.

Each day, we had a couple of hours of classroom work, which, at first, meant a lot more to the guys than it did to me. Then I observed while each one did their two hours of simulator. Sitting behind them, I started to understand the fundamentals. By the time I was sitting in the right seat and was pilot in command, I discovered it wasn't so hard to hold it straight and level.

If I only have to worry about holding an altitude, attitude and heading in VFR conditions, it will be a piece of cake. At first, my eyes never left those instruments. Eventually I began to learn to scan the instruments and watch the horizon. The first day, the instructor talked me in on an emergency landing and I nailed it.

On the second day, I was taking off, flying the plane around the pattern and landing it. One of the greatest features of the simulator is being able to say, "Hey, I don't like that landing. Back me up and let me try it again." You can't do that at home.

By far, the hardest thing for a nonpilot to master was the concept of taxiing. You drive a car with your hands, you don't steer with your feet. And the toe brakes! Time after time, I'd get it on the ground, stomp on what I thought was the brakes and start careening around the airport at 120 mph. (Fortunately, when you drive through a hangar in the simulator, it just pops out of your way.) I finally got to the point where I'd only put out a few landing lights. However, I did walk away on every landing.

Power is tough, too. I have a hard time knowing just when to decelerate on landing. They had me land without flaps, because they thought that would be easier. I can handle leveling off and flaring the nose for touchdown but it was difficult to ease back the throttle at just the right time.

Remember, I've never flown before and I'm starting out on the right side of the airplane. And to top it off, this is not your father's Oldsmobile. It's a Cessna 421/310 going about four times the average speed of my mini-van. But the more I flew and observed, the more I figured things out when I was pilot in command. For example, when I ascended with full power on takeoff, it was easier to level off if I started easing the power back 200 to 300 feet from my goal. This was a revelation to me. The guys were nice enough not to say, "Well, duh!"

Whenever I was flying, one of the guys was the designated dead man. Occasionally, it became too much fun for whoever was playing dead and they'd shout out instructions. I'd have to remind them that they were dead. What power! That's not to say that my companions made it easy. One day I was flying along at 2,000 feet, straight and level. All of a sudden, I see a body hanging on to the pilot's window. It seems Tom was reenacting his favorite *Twilight Zone* episode, the one where the gremlin appears outside the plane's window. They also thought it would be great for me to fly into a flock of birds. Sure, and I thought it was funny when both their engines failed.

From the right seat, it is very difficult to make sure you are "above redline" or "going for blueline," because you can't see them. We remedied this with post-it notes with extended red and blue lines. At home, we're going to get out the red and blue nail polish and extend the lines onto the panel. The guys will love it.

Was the experience worth it? You bet. I already feel safer flying with them. As Tom told our instructor, "You guys really save a lot of lives." Can I land the 310 in an emergency? After six hours of simulator time, probably. Will I panic if I'm ever pilot in command due to an inflight emergency? No. . . and I hope the opportunity never arises. Would I do it again? Sure. Will I get my private pilot's license? Maybe.

Buyer Beware

ISTARTED LEARNING TO FLY IN MAY 1990. In July of that same year I purchased a 1971 Piper Arrow that had a good paint job and a nice interior. Unfortunately, learning to fly and learning to buy an airplane are two entirely different things.

The Arrow had been owned by a pilot who'd had a heart attack while flying. His nonpilot wife had taken over and landed, with assistance from ATC and an instructor in an accompanying airplane, but she couldn't keep the Arrow on the taxiway; the prop hit an embankment, and the engine needed rebuilding as a consequence—but not a major overhaul, at least not officially. However it did—and still does—run well. I go on about this just to draw a picture; it's not a bad airplane under the skin. (In fact, we've just gotten back to Vermont from a three-week vacation in Florida using our '71 Arrow.)

I'd had the plane inspected; it was a "nice" airplane and sound mechanically, so even though I had some uneasy feelings about the broker, we made the deal, for $29,000.

The next month our local newspaper had an article about a local airplane broker who'd had an accident while ferrying an airplane—the same broker we'd bought the Arrow from. The plane caught fire after landing on a road and colliding with a car, and he had to wait for the seatbelts to melt before he could free himself from the wreckage as the releases were jammed. Needless to say, he was a hurting individual and spent months in the hospital. Since he was a one-man operation, there was no one to "take care of business."

Two months later, I received a phone call from a company in Massachusetts, asking about the N number of my Arrow. When we confirmed we were both talking about the same airplane, he informed me that there was a $29,000 lien on the Arrow by a bank and he'd been instructed to repossess it. Apparently the broker from whom we bought the Arrow had not had the opportunity to repay the loan before events had overtaken him, and after the bank got as much from him as it could, there was still a balance of $16,000, which we had to pay in order to avoid repossession.

In the meantime the broker declared bankruptcy, and although our claim against him was still valid, it was like trying to get blood out of a stone.

Six years later, the broker finally made a mistake. He bought an Aztec and registered it in his own name. We attached it, and it went up for Sheriff's sale last year. We recovered approximately $16,000 from the sale, and later the broker cleared up the balance he owed us, but after considering the fees needed to recover these monies, we certainly didn't come out ahead.

The moral of this story is a simple one that could have saved us a lot of grief: Get a title search by a reputable firm. No one had told me about the FAA records office in Oklahoma City when I was wet behind the ears, and I believed that the piece of paper the broker showed me a title, like a car title, and that if the title wasn't clear the broker wouldn't have had it in his possession. I know better now. The FAA records bills of sale and liens on airplanes, and issues registration certificates, but there is no automotive type of title for an airplane. The only way to be certain that the person you are buying an airplane from owns it free and clear is to have one of many qualified companies in Oklahoma City perform a "title" search.

Don't Blame the Engine

IS THIS A SINGLE-ENGINE AIRCRAFT?"** the reporter asked. I cringed at the thought Torrow's headline in our state-wide newspaper, *The Burlington Free Press*, "Single-Engine Airplane Crashes Onto Lake Champlain."

The date is February 19, 1993, and I have been called to the site of an airplane crash on the ice in West Addison, Vermont. As county State's Attorney, I am responsible for investigating untimely deaths in Addison County. I am also an instrument-rated pilot and the proud owner of a Beech Debonair.

Upon arrival at the shore of Lake Champlain, I am met by law enforcement officers who take me to the crash site by snowmobile, about three-quarters of a mile out onto the ice. At first glance, the ball of aluminum is unrecognizable as any particular aircraft. After a few minutes I realize that this heap of scrap is a relatively new Grumman Tiger. Three hundred feet north of the twisted fuselage is the start of a trail of airplane parts which begins with the nosewheel of the airplane. A short distance south is an aileron, followed by the wings, pieces of the windshield, seat cushions, personal effects of the pilot, one of the main wheels, a multitude of small pieces of aluminum, plastic and Plexiglas, all of which lead to the main fuselage of the plane.

The fuselage has the appearance of a wrung-out towel. The engine is open to view and twisted around so that it now points toward the tail of the aircraft. The instrument panel is also twisted around 180 degrees. The fuselage, aft of the firewall, is upside down, exposing the belly of the airplane to the sky. The horizontal stabilizer is still attached, but just barely. The vertical stabilizer is 75 feet away, somewhat upright in the snow, displaying an American flag decal. The remains of the pilot lie south of the fuselage in the snow.

Preliminary indications are that the pilot had crashed the afternoon before at about 3:30 p.m. Unfortunately, due perhaps to the way the fuselage blocked the signal, the ELT transmission was not picked up until 0230 the following morning. I made a mental note not to rely too much on my ELT for rescue should I ever experience a crash.

Media people began to arrive, a testament to the fact that airplane crashes are so rare that they are still considered big news, particularly in a small state like Vermont. I had formed a theory about the cause of the crash in the hour I had been at the scene before the media arrived.

By chance, I had been at the Middlebury State Airport, about 15 miles east of the crash site, at the time of the crash. A local pilot had just landed and reported snowshowers over the lake. Snowshowers had been forecast for the area and we watched them advance on the airport from the west. An ice fisherman reported hearing a plane over the lake near the time of the crash. The fisherman reported that the plane seemed to be traveling back and forth over the lake as if it were looking at something. In hindsight, the fisherman thought that maybe the pilot was looking for a place to land. He did not hear the crash.

The pilot logbook, located at the scene, indicated that the pilot received his private pilot's license on September 24, 1992. His total hours were reported to be 118.

The aircraft appeared to be relatively new and was loaded with avionics—dual KX 155 radios, an HSI, an S-Tec autopilot, a KLN 88 loran, intercom, headsets, the whole shootin' match: the kind of panel that most of us can only dream about.

The two obvious questions I was asking myself were: Why did this pilot crash? and why did it take so long to discover the crash? The answer to the second question may help to answer the first.

The clock on the panel, which apparently stopped on impact, indicated a time of 3:30. This time corresponded with the report of the fisherman. At 10:30 a.m. the following day, two snowmobilers traveling across the ice decided to investigate what looked to them from a distance to be an overturned fishing shanty. Upon closer inspection, they discovered the remains of the airplane and the pilot. At about the same time, reportedly, the ELT signal was traced to the crash site by the Civil Air Patrol. Nineteen hours had elapsed from the time of the crash to the discovery of the crash site.

The pilot had reportedly left the Morrisville Airport, near Stowe, Vermont, on the afternoon of February 18th. He was en route to Glens Falls, New York, a distance of approximately 95 nautical miles. Apparently he had not filed a flight plan, as no rescue operations were launched when he failed to return.

Not only were snowshowers forecast for the area that afternoon, but snowshowers were reported by the pilot I'd spoken to at Middlebury State Airport. The pilot had experienced the snow and had described the complete whiteout that he had flown into. Undoubtedly, the accident pilot had flown into the same snow conditions.

Had he become disoriented and lost control of the aircraft? It appeared from the crash site that the plane had hit the ice at a significant speed in a nose-down attitude. The fact that the engine was rotated 180 degrees indicated to me the nose of the airplane had experienced the brunt of the force.

Why hadn't the pilot used the autopilot to hold his attitude and keep his wings level? An autopilot coupled to the KLN 88 loran could have flown him to Glens Falls while he was asleep in the back seat! Did he panic? Why hadn't he communicated his trouble to anyone before the crash?

Like many crashes, we will never know exactly what happened to cause this crash, but one theory seems very likely. This low-time VFR pilot took off on a hundred-mile trip into an area that, if he checked, was forecast to contain snowshowers. He did not file a flight plan and was not totally familiar with the operation of the avionics in his plane. Having flown into a snowstorm, he either lacked the skills to get out of the trouble or his panic overloaded his thought processes to the point that he was unable to execute the skills he possessed. He did not communicate his trouble to anyone (perhaps out of fear of the trouble that declaring an emergency might bring him with the FAA) or did not realize the seriousness of his situation until just before impact.

I don't know if he checked the weather before he took off. If he did, and still decided to make the trip, he made an error in judgment. His failure to file a flight plan was another error in judgment. Failing to understand and be able to use the sophisticated avionics in his plane was another mistake. Failure to communicate his emergency to Burlington Approach Control as soon as he realized he was in trouble was yet another error in judgment. As I expected, the FAA concluded that this VFR pilot flew into IFR weather conditions and crashed.

"Is this a 'single-engine' aircraft?" the reporter asked. "Yes," I said, "but you can take that tone out of your voice when you say that. I fly a single-engine aircraft and that is not why this crash occurred," I explained. We didn't need this reporter telling the world that this plane crashed because it only had one engine. I couldn't let him go with a simple yes. I had to give him some background on VFR versus IFR flying and what might have caused this crash. He listened intently as I described how flying into a snowstorm removed all points of reference for a VFR pilot and that additional training was necessary to fly in clouds or snowstorms. He thanked me politely and went on his way.

The next morning the plane crash was reported on the front page of *The Burlington Free Press*. Nowhere in the article was the fact that the Grumman Tiger is a single-engine airplane mentioned. The reporter talked about the fact that the pilot was relatively inexperienced and that snowshowers had been reported in the area at the time of the crash. Hopefully the readers of the article would understand that the reason for the crash was the weather and lack of training on the part of the pilot. Hopefully no one would think that single-engine aircraft are accidents waiting to happen.

Fred's Gift

FRED'S MOVEMENTS WERE STIFF that Labor Day morning. His speed had slowed from the days he flew Corsairs off the carriers in Korea. Impeded by a heart attack, Parkinson's disease and the stress of weekly dialysis, he could barely be helped into the pilot seat of my Cessna 182. At that time I did not know this was a last wish.

Fredrick Hilton Mershon, Jr. had a distinguished career flying in the Navy. However, in August of 1952 he was struck by ground fire over Korea and lost one eye. He landed safely back home on the *Princeton*, but in the wake of that mighty carrier he left his Navy Wings.

He returned to the States as a private pilot and continued to fly through the years. He loved his airplane, a Cherokee 235, and his 35-foot Cal sailboat. He later enjoyed developing a marina on Chesapeake Bay.

His health declined and since his heart attack 20 years had passed since he had held a yoke in his hand. More health problems chipped away at his abilities, but the pilot in him still lived on. I had come to know his daughter, Michele, and knew that meeting Fred was something I wanted to do before he died. As she told me of his illness, I knew he did not have much time left. Something in my heart told me to offer the chance for his one last flight.

As an instructor, I knew the risks. Some might say I was a fool. I was placing a man that I did not know on the pilot side of my airplane with the trust that he would not do anything to cause loss of control during the flight. Over the previous three days I had observed him. He was a proud, powerful man trapped inside a body that could barely respond. He obviously comprehended his surroundings but was unable to communicate except in occasional brief words.

That Monday while I was preparing to return home to Arkansas, Fred had been up early waiting for me to take him flying. I flew from Freeway Airport outside Washington and met him and his family at his base at the Lee airport in Edgewater, Maryland. As I turned final at Lee, I barely cleared the trees on Runway 30 as I saw him and his family standing by the FBO. I taxied around to where they stood and we loaded up. Michele put the headset on him and buckled him in. Few words were said. Fewer were needed.

We taxied out and flew over Annapolis and the Academy. Since we were fairly low, I kept the controls, but then I climbed up to 2,500 feet and gave him the yoke. At first he tested the controls, but before long he had the trim adjusted and flew us around the bay. He turned us back to Lee and placed us in a position to enter the downwind. I asked him if he wanted us to land and he nodded yes. I took the controls back and we landed on the numbers. As I taxied back to the hangar, a chill swept over me as I knew these were his last moments in an airplane. He smiled at me as we shut the engine down. He muttered something about how flying a high-wing airplane was different. We went into the FBO to wait for his wife and daughter to return. There I could see him reliving past days, no words exchanged, only understanding.

As I left Lee and headed home I realized that though I gave him his last flight, he instead gave me a deeper appreciation for the privilege of flying. The smile in his eyes followed me as I boarded the airplane and headed home. Climbing higher into the haze of Washington, I said a prayer that someday some young pilot would give me that chance.

They told me weeks later that he asked for me on the day that he died. My guess is that he wanted to feel the joy that only pilots know, just one more time.

PATIENT AT THE CONTROLS

UNDER CERTAIN CIRCUMSTANCES, which are voluminously illustrated in these pages, flying an airplane can be a difficult thing to do safely, even when the pilot is in prime condition to fly.

But when the pilot is incapacitated in some way, even keeping the airplane straight and level can be a nearly impossible task. And unlike the driver of a car, a sick pilot doesn't have the option of pulling over to the side of the road and calling for help. In fact, for a pilot who's flying solo, or for one who's flying only with non-pilot-rated passengers, incapacitation to any significant degree presents a life and death challenge.

Even minor health issues can become life threatening events. This happened to a pilot with a garden-variety head cold, which due to changes in altitude, caused a debilitating onset of sinus block while he was flying an instrument approach with his young, non-rated son in the right seat.

Sometimes the incapacitation is life threatening by itself. One story here is told by a rusty pilot flying with his grandfather. When the grandfather suffers a stroke in flight, the grandson has to take the controls and get his grandfather to medical care as soon as possible. Another story here is by the captain of a Boeing 737-200, whose first-officer (who was the pilot flying at the time) passed out while on short final, which went unnoticed by the captain until it was almost too late to save the flight.

The stories in this chapter might motivate some readers take a look at their personal health and maybe make some changes. And it might prompt others, especially older pilots, to fly with a safety pilot, as some of my older pilot friends already do. But these stories should make us all realize that no matter how wonderfully designed and constructed our airplanes might be, they're only safe when the pilot flying is healthy enough to keep them under control.

Saved by a Copilot

MY PERSONAL "MINIMUM EQUIPMENT LIST" for our A36 Bonanza did not include a functioning autopilot, since nearly all my flying was done with my instrument-rated wife as a backup. At the time these events occurred, our autopilot had been removed and sent out for servicing at the factory. Although we have backup redundancy for air-driven instruments and radios, I had never really given much thought to such redundancy for the pilot.

I had recently joined an organization that provides free, non-emergency transportation to needy medical patients. After a thorough checkout by the organization's CFI, I received a call and agreed to fly my first mission. The flight was to be demanding in several respects. First, besides a copilot supplied by the organization, there were three patients to be retrieved from the Palo Alto airport, just south of San Francisco. The airplane would be at max gross weight even without full fuel, not a common situation for our A36. In addition, the Palo Alto airport has a rather short runway, a fact that was noted by the Malibu pilot who was to deliver the patients several days before my flight: He had elected to land at San Jose instead. Because the airport has no instrument approach, IFR conditions during the early-morning hours before the flight would mean a harried attempt to contact my passengers for alternate arrangements.

The weekdays before the Sunday flight were busy with flight preparations and arrangements. Because this was my first mission, I had requested that the sponsoring organization find me a copilot who had experience with the paperwork and procedures. I also asked that my right-seat companion be current and checked out in a high-performance aircraft. I had an ulterior motive: This would be a chance to do some instrument flying under the hood.

By Friday, things seemed to be falling into place. Arrangements had been made with the patient/passengers and the copilot. Time to have a little fun. Some longtime friends were having a surprise anniversary dinner at the local country club. Saturday found me doing a final weight-and-balance calculation and a DUAT check of the weather. Unlike the past few days, the forecast suggested clear weather for my nine a.m. arrival at Palo Alto.

Sunday morning brought an unpleasant surprise. My wife became very ill with vomiting and fever. I considered how this might affect me. Because I felt fine, I assumed that she had been exposed to someone at work and that I had at least a few days' grace before being infected.

Another DUAT call confirmed that the CAVU weather would not be a factor in the day's flights. The drive to Whiteman Airport in the San Fernando Valley, the preflight and the departure went smoothly. After waking up Burbank Approach, and switching to L.A. Center, things relaxed to the point where I had a chance to talk to my copilot. As luck would have it, he was in the process of getting checked out in a Bonanza. The northward trip was spent comparing notes.

The arrival at Palo Alto was expedited by Bay Approach. The landing and patient pickup went smoothly. I carefully monitored the limited refueling, and with the paperwork completed, we taxied for departure. My careful calculations paid off as the wheels left the ground just about where the POH suggested they would. As we turned south, I marveled at how smoothly things seemed to be going.

About halfway into the return flight, I said to the copilot that it felt warm in the cockpit. As we continued, I began to feel lightheaded. My stomach felt slightly cramped. Suddenly I noticed perspiration pouring from my face as I struggled to control my unfocused thoughts. Could this be hypoxia? The CO detector sat silently, showing only green. (Because we have had occasional exhaust leaks in our A36 Bonanza, I had purchased an electronic carbon monoxide detector and found that it did its job remarkably well.)

The other occupants chatted comfortably. As the outside world seemed to recede from my vision, I realized that I was losing my fight to remain conscious. What if I didn't have a copilot? A feeling of helplessness washed over me as I imagined trying to locate the nearest airport for an emergency landing. I knew that I was unable to find, let alone read, the proper chart. I imagined telling Oakland Center that I was becoming disabled. What could they do? I could barely speak. I turned to the copilot and asked whether he would like to fly for a while since I wasn't feeling well. He agreed, and I unlatched and rotated the throw-over yoke.

My eyes closed and I began to relax. This seemed to help me retain consciousness. My symptoms began to disappear almost as quickly as they had come. After a few minutes I was able to think more clearly. I realized that the whole episode had lasted only about 15 minutes and that there had been no communication from ATC. Our passengers had continued with their conversations. Only my right-seat partner had the slightest idea what had transpired. As he continued the flight, I continued to improve so that an hour later, I felt comfortable making an uneventful landing at home base.

On the ground, my only symptom was a very slightly feverish feeling, although by the time I got home I felt exhausted. By the next day, I had recovered enough to go to work. We later learned that several people who had attended the Friday night festivities had fallen ill.

There is no doubt in my mind that I would not have been able to maintain level flight by myself. Fifteen minutes is not a long time, but it is long enough to lose control of an airplane. The latest entry on my minimum equipment list says that the autopilot must be in working order if the right seat is not occupied by a pilot.

Second in Command Savior

IHAVE LOVED FLYING WITH MY GRANDFATHER, Pop-Pop, since I was very young, and one Christmas Eve I was grateful that I learned to fly with him and did so as often as possible.

On a mid-semester break, I came home from college especially anxious for some flying time with him. He reserved the Piper Cherokee Six for December 24th, his 78th birthday. After preflighting the airplane and warming up the engine, we were all set to head up to Groton, Connecticut, for a bit of lunch. With Pop-Pop flying and me as copilot we were cleared for takeoff on Westchester County's Runway 34.

As the airplane began its takeoff roll and speed gathered beneath the wings, we gently rose from the ground and began what would become one of the most horrifying experiences of either of our lives. As we approached Bridgeport, Connecticut, and an altitude of 4,000 feet, Pop-Pop leaned over and said, "You have the plane." He would often hand over the controls for a short time during a flight just to give me a feel for the airplane. I took over a bit reluctantly this time, since I had trouble reading all of the instruments from the right seat.

I soon discovered that Pop-Pop was handing me the controls for no reason that I could possibly have imagined. Just after I took over, he said, "I don't know what's wrong. . . but I can't move my right arm." He said that he felt fine, so I assumed that he had a pinched nerve or a muscle spasm in his shoulder. Still, I figured we would be smart to check it out, so I asked him if we should land instead at Bridgeport Airport, just to make sure that everything was okay. He assured me that he was absolutely fine, but I thought that we should head to Bridgeport to land. He said that maybe we should just head back to Westchester; he was sure that his arm would be fine by the time we got there. We agreed that this was a good course of action, so I trimmed the airplane for a descent.

I began a 180-degree turn to the left. While in the turn, I called New York Approach and told them that I was about 50 miles away and intended to land at Westchester Airport. I did not mention any particular reason for our change in plans. I completed my turn and continued to descend. I looked to my left, and Pop-Pop's appearance was drastically altered. His face was flushed and his eyes looked tired and lacked the presence that they normally held.

Something was terribly wrong. Fighting an impulse to panic, I asked him again if he was okay. He seemed startled by the sound of my voice. He said that he was all right, but he spoke slowly and looked exhausted and confused. His speech was drawn out and slurred. He certainly was not okay. I had no idea what was wrong or how to help him, and I decided that the only thing I could do was to get the airplane on the ground as quickly as possible. We were already headed for Westchester, so I unhooked my shoulder harness and leaned across my grandfather to see the altimeter. We were at 1,100 feet above sea level. I had become so focused on trying to figure out what was wrong with Pop-Pop that I had lost command of the aircraft. We had dropped almost 3,000 feet and I had not even noticed. I had to snap back to myself as a pilot, stop panicking and fly the airplane.

The cockpit seemed lonely and unfamiliar. I could not see the airspeed indicator or the altimeter from my seat, the airplane was far larger and more powerful than the Cessna 172 I usually fly, and I was all by myself watching my grandfather seemingly dying before my eyes. Summoning all the focus I could muster, I quickly pushed the throttle to full and began to climb back to a safe altitude. I continued toward Westchester, which was about 40 miles away.

New York Approach radioed to tell me that I should contact Westchester Tower. "Westchester Tower, Saratoga 8694N is with you," I radioed. Westchester Tower responded, "Saratoga 8694N, you are off course for your instructed pattern for landing." I had been so completely caught up in my racing thoughts, my grandfather and regaining control of the airplane that I had not even heard my instructions. I responded that I now had the instructions but that I was off course because I had a serious problem on board. "The pilot is no longer able to fly. I'm not sure what is wrong with him, but he needs an ambulance immediately upon arrival." I explained that I was also a pilot and felt that I could land the aircraft, but that I was second in command. I was cleared on Runway 34. I turned left in order to enter an extended downwind and continued on toward the midfield point of the airport.

I began to feel that I had no control of the airplane. I did not know how fast or at what altitude I was flying, and I had not landed an airplane in over four months. I looked around the cockpit for a way to help myself, and I noticed the GPS located in the middle of the instrument panel, easily within my field of vision. It was still set on a moving map display of the course to Groton, Connecticut, and I punched in the identifier for Westchester Airport and changed the display to the navigational page. I had groundspeed and altitude instantly in front of me. I decided to trust that I would be flying into a headwind on final and therefore that I should maintain a safe speed during my approach.

As I passed the midpoint of the runway, I went to put on a notch of flaps, only then realizing that my grandfather had no control of his right leg. I pushed his leg aside as best I could and put on a notch of flaps.

I called the tower and said, "Saratoga 8694N is midpoint right downwind for Runway 34 cleared to land and, again, I need an ambulance on arrival." The tower responded that I was cleared to land and asked what was wrong with the pilot. I responded that I had no idea, repeated that I needed an ambulance and told them that I would taxi directly to Westair. Knowing that I was bit out of practice and in an unfamiliar airplane, I decided to give myself a little more space for final, so I extended my downwind slightly, figuring that the extra time I spent making sure I was going to land safely was far more important than the few seconds that I would save by making a short approach.

As I banked rather hard to the right and onto my crosswind leg of the approach, Pop-Pop, who at some point had unhooked his shoulder harness, slid over onto me. I eased him back from me once or twice, but, afraid that he would interfere with the controls if he fell forward, I decided to leave him where he was. I tried to reach the flaps, but with my grandfather's weight up against my shoulder and his right leg leaning up against the flap lever, I decided that with the long runway, I could land with just the one notch of flaps.

I turned onto final, made one last check and ensured that the prop and mixture were set full forward. I played with the throttle setting until I found one that put me a little bit faster than normal landing speed, figuring that too fast was better than too slow. I continued on the pattern, and once I got within about a wing's length from the runway in height, I cut the power and flared the airplane. The landing was smooth, and once the wheels hit the ground, I realized that I had no brakes on my side of the airplane. I pushed Pop-Pop as hard as I could and lunged across his leg to grab for the parking brake. After some pulls on the parking brake, we slowed down enough to turn off the runway.

The tower told me to taxi directly to Westair, whatever way possible. I pumped the throttle a bit and taxied as fast as I safely could to the Westair office, weaving down different taxiways. Once I arrived, I parked the airplane and waited for help.

Pop-Pop had suffered a cerebral hemorrhage, a stroke. He is recovering, and he says that he has changed his mind about flying alone in his advanced years. He urges older pilots to consider flying only with a trained copilot.

Sinus Scare

IT WAS A BRIGHT SUNNY SPRING MORNING as I prepared to fly to Dexter, Missouri (KDXE) to get my recently purchased Piper Comanche 250 painted a new color scheme, which would be its final renovation for the year. My 10-year-old son, Aaron, accompanied me on this trip, since he had been taking a major interest in the plane. He was equally excited to fly down with me to pick out the paint scheme and to spend some valuable father-son time.

As we departed Spirit of St. Louis (KSUS) to Dexter on an instrument flight plan, we were vectored direct to our destination. Climbing to our final altitude of 7,000 feet, I looked at my son as we broke through the clouds at 3,500 feet. I could sense his amazement and excitement, as parts of the plane ducked in and out of the clouds as we climbed.

Finally we broke free and reached cruising altitude. That's when I noticed that my ears did not clear as rapidly nor as easily as they usually did when I climbed to altitude. I attributed this to the cold and hay fever that I had. I'd taken some Benadryl (an antihistamine) earlier and I could tell it was beginning to go to work. While Benadryl is not banned by the FAA, it is known to cause drowsiness. Since it had never caused me any problems in the past, I felt it would not interfere with the flight.

The flight was uneventful. Fifteen miles from KDXE, I realized this would most likely be a full instrument approach, as we were above the cloud deck. The nearby Cape Giradeau, Missouri ATIS (KCGI) did indicate that the clouds were about 1,500 feet, so it really would not be that much of a challenge to fly the VOR approach.

I began the descent at 1,000 feet per minute, I had my approach plates in front of me. As we descended into the clouds, I suddenly had a sharp stabbing pain over my left eyebrow. It was so painful, that I instinctively closed my left eye, holding my head with my left hand, trying to fly the plane in IMC with my right eye. I howled in pain.

My son, who has had some VFR flying experience, volunteered to fly the plane: "I can fly it dad!" "Over my dead body," I thought to myself, which I realized could very well happen. The pain was so sudden and intense that I had no idea what was going on. At first I thought of a cerebral hemorrhage. As a physician, I have treated many patients with this type of sudden excruciating pain. But I did not have a stiff neck. A quick neurological evaluation revealed I could move all the parts of my body and there really was no other deficit except for the excruciating sharp pain localized over my left eye.

A more likely diagnosis, I realized, was sinus barotrauma from unequal sinus pressures. A few minutes earlier, I had been at 7,000 feet; now I was at 2,500, and, as Murphy's Law dictated, this was the busiest and most demanding part of the flight. I had only two options: immediately climb back up to 6,000 feet and come back down more slowly. This would mean having to notify Memphis Center what the problem was. I was loathe to do this. I might have to answer a lot of questions and perhaps be forced to get another medical examination. Besides, climbing back to altitude would take three to four minutes during which time I would still have to put up with a lot of pain.

Option two was a more immediate solution: I tried to clear my nasal passages, since it was the unequal pressure between the now more denser atmosphere in my nasal passages versus the less dense air in my sinuses that was causing the excruciating pain. I forced air into my nose while pinching my nostrils closed. This would force air into the sinuses. I only hoped that it was only my left frontal/ethmoid sinus cavity that was unequalized, so I would not have to contend with a double-barreled dose of borotrauma.

Suddenly, I heard a slight groan from my facial bones and sinuses. Air was beginning to move into the cavity. With the pressure between the sinus cavity and nasal passage equalized, the pain immediately dissipated. And the landing, which a moment before seemed almost impossible, was uneventful, even anticlimactic.

As an emergency physician, I know all too well the anatomy and physiology of barotrauma and what can happen to the sinuses when unequal pressures are at play. I have treated many patients with scuba diving injuries, but interestingly no pilot has ever graced my emergency department. I should have realized the potential for a problem when I needed to take an antihistamine prior to the flight.

I should have also realized that the Benadryl would have worn off by the time I would be preparing to land, setting myself up for an unpleasant re-equilibration problem. Now whenever I fly, I first decide if I am physically fit enough, with special attention to my sinuses and the risk of sinus occlusion severe enough to prevent sinus equalization of pressures upon ascent or descent. If there is any doubt, I either do not fly, or I fly at a lower (4,000-foot) altitude. In addition, I carry some neosynephrine nose spray inside the aircraft at all times. Thus the potential "antidote" is right at hand.

Reprieve From a Silent Killer

THE MORNING AIR IS SOMEWHERE IN THE MID-40S, the sky is a brownish overcast, and Flight Service is predicting very acceptable VFR for the duration of our Boulder–Cheyenne–Boulder journey.

Picking up the keys to our 172, I ask the man at the FBO for a current chart, since the one I have has expired and Cheyenne is 69 nautical miles away. The keys he happily gives me, but he's all out of charts, so I hope it's okay with everyone to modify our original plan.

Just as I'm finishing the preflight, Linda and Steve pedal up on their mountain bikes. Linda climbs into the right seat, all smiles, and Steve takes up the rear. After an explanation of how we're not chart-legal for Cheyenne, we all agree to an hour or so of local cruising. Our itinerary settled, we strap on the plane and launch. Our easterly takeoff and climbout are uneventful, and the air is severely smooth.

After climbing straight out for about five minutes, I begin a slow right turn to head us back west; Linda doesn't much care where we go, but I at least want to see the mountains. We level off at about 8,000. I'm too warm now even with my vent open, so Linda holds the wings level while I take off my jacket and drop it in the back. After a few minutes I'm too cold, of course, and close my air vent and pull on the cabin heat. Linda just leaves her coat on and her vent open.

Around five minutes of general sightseeing later, Linda says, "I smell exhaust in here." I hadn't noticed until then, being preoccupied with the view and piloting, but she is definitely right; that tailpipe odor is really pretty strong. I push the heater back closed, and the odor goes away.

I ask Linda if she'd like to drive now, and she accepts in an instant. She turns us gently back north, paralleling the foothills, and she even holds her altitude. In the middle of watching the plane and watching the mountains, I hear something funny from the back seat. Looking back, I see Steve unfastening his seat belt and lying down as much as possible, his eyes closed. I tell Linda what he's done, and she says he's just really tired. I shrug it off and get back to serious mountain-and-copilot watching. Looking back at Steve again, I'm quite certain that he's asleep.

Now, that is really weird, I think. Why would anyone agree to split the cost of a sightseeing trip and then go to sleep without seeing any sights? Having no answer, I turn my attention back to Linda, who is still doing a decent job of flying. And a small inner voice starts telling me that I should land this plane right now. But the instruments are showing nothing to cause alarm, and a 15-minute flight is nowhere near what I promised.

So on we fly, a little north of Boulder now. Looking down, I see what seems to be an airstrip running north and south, about three miles directly in front of us. Funny, I think, I don't remember any airports down there, and I've been this way a dozen times. But the closer we get, the more it looks like a runway—a dark path surrounded by brownish fields. And again something tells me, "Land. Land this thing right now!" Then I remember an article about teaching passengers to land an airplane, and begin wondering if Linda could set us down there if something happened to me.

After a few more seconds of staring, my "airport" transforms itself back into a simple field. I blink at the ground a few times and wonder how I ever could have thought there was a runway down there. Still staring at my "airport" I tell Linda to turn us east. And even though the instruments are still telling me that everything is fine, I keep hearing the voice that's telling me to land.

Linda takes us eastward and into the practice area of another airport. As she does a pretty good 360 and a few random maneuvers, I begin to wonder if she could land the plane at Jeffco, a larger airport to the south of Boulder. I'm feeling my body start to tighten against a fear I can't identify. But the tanks are almost full, all the gauges are in the green, and the weather is fine. We could even glide into the nearest airport. Everything I'm seeing says we're more than okay, so I do my best to relax.

Linda does a few more turns as the Hobbs closes in on an hour. It's finally time to head for home, so I tell my friend to steer us west. I call for the advisory, and, as usual, it's left traffic for Runway 8.

I make a power reduction for our altitude loss, still letting Linda hold us on course. We eventually level off at 6,100 (pattern altitude for Boulder) and I reach back and shake Steve's arm. He jolts awake and I tell him to put on his seat belt. He sits up slowly and looks strangely groggy, and his hands move uncertainly as he straps himself back in.

Linda sets us up to enter our downwind, and it's time for me to be the pilot. I lean over and tell her, in my best flight instructor imitation, "I'll take it now." She lets go of her yoke as I take mine. When abeam the number "8," I pull the carb heat and throttle out, watch the nose fall, and reach for the trim knob. Instead of the fine adjustments I've practiced hundreds of times, I give it two mighty spins, turning it hard and fast each time. Not quite understanding why, I watch the nose balloon up in front of us. Wondering what in the world ever made it do that, I push the yoke forward to level us out. A bizarre sensation has come over me. Whatever it is that relates my senses to each other no longer functions the way it should, and I can barely control this airplane.

In a lot more confusion than fear, I begin the left turn back toward the runway, and then remember reading a few weeks before about how many people spin in the traffic pattern. Not wanting to get overanxious on the turn, I start holding a little right rudder against the left aileron. Something about this just doesn't feel right, but I can't figure out what it is. I do not budge from my controls, and add some power to keep us in the air. We're just barely managing to turn at all. This looks really abnormal but I don't know how to change it. I can't seem to think anymore, and I'm locked into my left aileron/right rudder inputs.

We're about two miles out when we finally get turned upwind. I pull the power out some and line us up on the longest final I've ever seen, wondering what in the world we are doing way out here. Roads that shouldn't be there begin to pass beneath us, and after a minute we're down to 400 agl, over a block of townhouses. I watch the buildings for about five seconds before I realize that I'm staring at the ground. Then the threat detector in my mind finally succeeds in going off, and I know that something is terribly wrong.

A second later I'm unconscious.

Something manages to open my eyes just 200 yards from the threshold. We're still more or less on runway heading, but south of where we need to be. I hurl us back to the left, then overcorrect to the right, losing altitude all the time. We cross the number, still zigzagging. I wonder why this thing just won't line up, see that we are only three feet from touchdown, and pass out for the second time.

A muffled "BOOM!" and the loudest screech of tires I've ever heard shocks me back to consciousness. I open my eyes to see us on the runway, but we're 10 degrees off heading and the grass is coming up fast. My feet somehow keep us on the pavement; we swerve as much now as we did in the air, but make it to the ramp intact.

Wondering how I ever could have made such a horrible landing, I shut down the engine and we all climb out. None of us can walk straight; it's all we can do to stand up. After a few seconds of collective staggering, one of my companions says, "Carbon monoxide. That heater. It was carbon monoxide." My numbed brain can only agree. We make it into the FBO and I collapse on one of their couches. Linda and Steve are in about the same shape, a tangled pile on the other couch. Twenty minutes go by before we try standing, and even then we are wobbly. I finally remember to say something about the malfunction, and tell the woman at the desk about the heater leak. She says she is glad I told her; she had a student taking that plane on a cross-country in about half an hour.

Looking back, it is easy to recognize the warnings I'd been given—exhaust in the cabin, Steve's going to sleep and fumbling with his seat belt, seeing an airport where I knew there wasn't one, "hearing the voice" that kept telling me to land, and even wondering if Linda could get us down. It's very obvious (now!) that something was amiss. But in my oxygen-deprived condition I ignored everything except my promise of an hour-long flight, and the instruments that told me everything was normal.

All in all, we were incredibly fortunate. No one was injured, nothing was damaged, and my "horrible landing" started to look like divine intervention: Something had made me wake up coming down final, I was too incapacitated to think of the go-around that surely would have killed us, and that radical overtrim had held the nose up when I'd lost consciousness over the runway. The noise from our impact had even shaken me awake, and (most miraculous of all) that impact was more or less in a landing attitude.

A few days after our flight, I spoke with the owner of the FBO about what had happened. His first words were, "If you ever smell exhaust in an airplane, you should open every window you have." To this I would add, "Land as soon as possible. You have a major problem." A molecule of carbon monoxide will bind to your blood's hemoglobin 284 times more readily than will a molecule of oxygen. In other words, inhaling even a small amount of carbon monoxide will diminish the amount of oxygen which will be taken into your bloodstream, and symptoms of oxygen starvation can begin to manifest. But the onset and progression of those symptoms can be so subtle that you never know anything bad is happening.

The other thing I learned from this flight is to trust your instincts, and never make your instruments responsible for your safety. All those dials make wonderful servants, but always remember who is in command. In the same way that you scan your panel, look at your feelings from time to time. They can tell you things no instrument ever can. If something really seems wrong to you, it probably warrants checking out. Land when you can, take a break, get a ground-based point of view. Everything may be perfectly fine, but if you ever err, err on the side of caution, and make sure your mistakes cost nothing more than time.

A Hypoxia Scare

IWAS EXERCISING AT THE LOCAL GYM with a banker friend of mine when I was surprised to hear myself being paged. A fellow pilot, John, whom I knew casually, was to ferry a Baron from Galveston (where we were) to Houston Hobby, where he was to leave it with the Beechcraft dealer. From there, he and his passenger needed a ride home to Brazoria County Airport, a short trip from Hobby. He said that the local FBO owner had suggested that he call me to transport him and his friend in a Beech Debonair based at the FBO. I readily agreed and asked my buddy Larry (an aspiring pilot) if he'd like to go along. He was excited about the prospect, so we ended our workout and headed over to the FBO.

The trip to Hobby was pleasant as we picked up John and his friend and took them to Brazoria County. We dropped them off, leaving the engine running, and proceeded to take off. When climbing, I noticed an odor, sort of like fresh paint "burning-in" on an engine. I asked Larry if he noticed it and he did. I recalled that there had recently been some major work on the engine and attributed the odor to that and the fact that perhaps the cylinders were a bit hot from the long ground operation.

As we headed back toward Galveston, the odor became stronger, and I thought I detected the smell of exhaust. The view outside was total darkness, with no moon or stars to light the terrain, which consisted of swamps, bayous and Galveston's West Bay. That, along with the increasing exhaust smell, led me to decide we would return to Brazoria County. After turning, the odor got much worse. I pulled the red knob provided in all Bonanzas to cut off any firewall openings in case of fire. That had little or no effect, and I found myself feeling the physical effects of hypoxia. My lips began to tingle, and I rather strangely found myself feeling relaxed.

I remembered the vent window on my side. It is placarded not to be opened at over 145 mph, so I slowed the airplane and opened it. The air rushed in, but, unfortunately, it smelled heavily of exhaust and only made matters worse. I closed it. By then, I felt I had the runway made and decided that, if the engine was not running, it could not produce exhaust. I pulled the mixture and began the long glide to the runway. I opened the window again, this time finding fresh air, and instructed Larry to open the door immediately upon touchdown. I proceeded to execute my first dead-stick landing in a Bonanza.

When the wheels touched, I reminded Larry to open the door; he did not respond. I glanced over and noticed he was unconscious! I opened the door on roll-out, and he immediately woke up. As we rolled onto the taxiway I looked at my fingernails and they were a rich hue of blue. Even after such a traumatic experience, I still felt that inexplicable relaxed state. After getting out of the airplane, I began coming back to reality. That euphoric state quickly disappeared and I realized I had just come very close to death. I proceeded to open the cowling and discovered that there was a large crack in the exhaust port of the number two cylinder (the one closest to the pilot) and much of the exhaust had been escaping from there.

That experience taught me always to err on the side of caution. The trip to Galveston would have only taken another 20 minutes, and it was a temptation to make it home. There is no doubt in my mind that, had I made the decision to continue home, I would not be sharing this account today.

One-Two Punch

"**F**ALCON FLIGHT, THIS IS LAREDO GROUND CONTROL.** You're cleared to taxi runway one-three. Wind is one-five-zero at eight, barometer three-zero-zero-four."

It was a typical South Texas afternoon in early June of 1960. The temperature was in the mid-90s as our two-ship formation of T-33 jet trainers taxied out for takeoff at Laredo Air Force Base. "Hot and dusty" was how the locals described this weather; my own description contained some saltier language.

I was in the front cockpit of the lead aircraft with my instructor, Dan, in the rear. Another student and lieutenant—I'll call him Charlie—was solo in the second aircraft. Charlie was not one of Dan's regular students but he was flying with us today because his instructor was on leave. Charlie and I were due to graduate from pilot training in two weeks and, to fulfill curriculum requirements, we both had to log some day navigation time. Since Charlie also needed some solo formation time this was to be a combination navigation/formation mission.

Our formation takeoff was normal and we headed north toward Carrizo Springs, the first checkpoint on the round-robin navigation portion of our flight. After completing this phase back in the Laredo area we planned to practice rejoins and other formation maneuvers before landing.

The planned altitude for the navigation portion was 25,000 feet. Everything seemed to be going smoothly. Since Dan was on board it was his responsibility to monitor Charlie.

"Falcon Leader to Falcon Two. You're flying loose and out of position, Charlie. Move it in," Dan barked over the radio. We were climbing through 21,000 feet at the time.

Apparently Charlie did not make the necessary correction because Dan repeated what he had just said, but this time he added some volume as well as a few expletives. Shortly after this I took a quick look at the other aircraft and saw that even after Dan's second radio call Charlie was still out of position.

Things were getting hairy! It didn't make sense that someone with Charlie's experience and proficiency in formation flying would have trouble with something as basic as holding normal wing position, absent any adverse conditions. Dan and I had the identical thought at the same time but he blurted it out first.

"Falcon Leader to Falcon Two. Charlie, I think you might be hypoxic. How do you feel?" Charlie responded saying he felt a little lightheaded, a common symptom of hypoxia. It appeared that our diagnosis was correct. My level of concern escalated rapidly as I knew that Charlie must recover soon, before becoming too incapacitated to either control his aircraft or successfully eject from it.

"John, I have it," said Dan, and I acknowledged. Regulations required that the instructor take control of the aircraft during an emergency. Dan informed both of us that he would throttle back to 60 percent rpm and descend at close to the maximum allowable airspeed to facilitate a rapid descent. Charlie had to get more oxygen as quickly as possible. Charlie hung right in during our steep descent and Dan and I were both relieved when, as we passed through 5,000 feet, he announced that he was feeling better. Dan said we would level off at 2,000 feet.

After we accomplished this and flew straight and level for a minute or so, Dan asked Charlie how he felt. Charlie said he was back to normal and would have no problem with the landing. We entered the traffic pattern at Laredo, executed our standard 360-overhead fighter-type approach and landed without incident.

Charlie was given a complete flight physical, standard procedure in cases like this, and was pronounced completely fit. Not so his oxygen mask; a small hole was found on the right side of his mask, a hole which should have been detected during a routine preflight inspection. Charlie admitted that he had not inspected his mask. While the hole was not large it nonetheless was cited as the cause of Charlie's hypoxia. Case closed.

After Charlie's close call I became even more diligent in terms of inspecting my oxygen mask and other gear. The motivation certainly was there. After all, hadn't Dan and I nearly witnessed a disaster due to Charlie's negligence?

Our class graduated on schedule and I never had the opportunity to discuss the incident with Charlie. Since we had chosen different assignments we went our separate ways. After some advanced training I moved on to Dover Air Force Base in Delaware as a C-124 copilot. In June of 1962 I upgraded to Aircraft Commander.

Conditions had begun to change in Southeast Asia and the United States increased its military presence in that area. In October of 1963 I flew from Da Nang to Clark Air Base in the Philippines and after a quick shower headed for the Officer's Club to zero in on one of the T-bone steaks it was noted for. As I entered the club, who did I see but Charlie. We decided to have dinner together and after ordering, Charlie said there was something he wanted to share with me.

Just before our unusual flight, he said, he had experienced some bothersome nasal congestion and had taken a decongestant. Air Force regulations were quite specific; except for aspirin and certain nasal sprays, self-medication was prohibited. Anything else had to be authorized by the Flight Surgeon. While Charlie knew he was wrong, he didn't think one pill would hurt. He found out he was mistaken. It was impossible to determine how much of Charlie's problem had been caused by the hole in the mask and how much by the unauthorized pill but the combination provided a potent one-two punch that was nearly lethal.

Nightmare on Final

IT WAS ONE OF THOSE MOMENTS OF ANXIETY which on rare occasions punctuate the hour upon hour of fortunate boredom.

From our vantage point six miles east of the airport and 1,500 feet above the ground, the visible dust in the vicinity of the airport was blowing in opposite directions. Consequently we viewed the report of "light and variable" wind with skepticism.

Another wind check confirmed the reported wind and the controller added, "You're cleared to land, Runway 26." Due to the obviously capricious wind and its potential for mischief, we added 10 knots to our calculated no-wind approach speed.

The first officer was at the controls, the Boeing 737-200 was in landing configuration, and our indicated airspeed included the additional 10 knots as we approached the outer marker. Though the skies were clear of clouds and visibility was unlimited, we tuned in the ILS as a backup for the visual approach. As we crossed the outer marker, all was well. We were aligned with the centerline of the runway, our rate of descent normal; there was nothing to indicate what was about to happen.

At 1,000 feet I began the procedural calls of altitude, airspeed and sink rate. As we left 800 feet, I noted and called attention to an increase in the indicated airspeed. From the planned plus-10 it quickly became a plus-15, then 20, and stabilized at plus-25 as we approached 500 feet. The rate of descent had increased accordingly and we were less than 30 seconds from touchdown.

At this point I was concerned but not yet alarmed; this appeared to be a classic, though a bit extreme, wind shear, from which we could expect to emerge with the excess airspeed dropping off as rapidly as it had built up.

When the excess airspeed did not drop off, I expected the first officer to react by reducing power; he did nothing, and I shouted, "We're too fast!" Incredibly, the aircraft was still on the glide path and aligned with the runway. The thought that he was no longer flying the aircraft did not enter my mind.

When he did not respond to my emphatic warning, I reached for the power levers, intending to initiate a missed approach, and as I gripped them I glanced to my right, wondering why he had done nothing to correct a now-critical situation. Just as I touched the power levers, the aircraft suddenly "slewed" to the left in a wild, still descending, uncoordinated turn. As I pushed the power levers to their forward stops and applied back pressure on the elevator, the 737 began a circling climb from what had become a dangerously low altitude. Later, one of the flight attendants who was seated in the rear of the airplane where the aircraft's motion was most violent, knowing only that something was drastically wrong, described her thoughts as, "This is it, we've had it and we're going to crash."

My questioning glance at the first officer was frightening—he was obviously unconscious; that he was no longer alive appeared to be a very real possibility.

We had flown together, he as first officer and I as captain, hundred of hours and thousands upon thousands of miles. During the course of a 15-year period we frequently flew the same monthly schedules. We knew each other's likes and dislikes, moods, idiosyncrasies and jokes. We trusted each other's skill and judgment. Together we had experienced the usual mechanical problems ranging from minor to major, in short, the "normal" events an airline flight crew would experience over a period of time—up to now. However, those years of routine and relatively uneventful flying resulted in a dangerous and nearly fatal complacency on my part.

Now motionless, my first officer and good friend was held in his seat by belt and shoulder harness in a nearly out-of-control airplane. While I stared at his contorted body, one simple question burned through my mind: "My God, what happened?"

For some unknown reason I was unable to "roll" out of the left turn; the turn could, however, be coordinated by use of the ailerons. A 45 degree angle-of-bank turn was a simulator training maneuver, not something to be done in a "real" airplane 200 feet off the ground—unless one had to.

With maximum power now set, I repositioned the flaps to a "go-around" setting and retracted the landing gear. That extra airspeed which moments before had been a liability suddenly became an asset of immeasurable value by enabling us to begin this wild and unplanned maneuver with our airspeed well above stalling speed.

Though we were continuing the steep turn, we were gaining altitude, and I had a moment to think about the plight of the first officer. I signaled for a flight attendant to come to the cockpit and the attendant seated in the forward part of the cabin responded immediately, asking, "What's wrong?" Nodding toward the first officer, I said, "Get the oxygen mask on him."

In the process of following that brief instruction, the flight attendant, who was a licensed pilot, discovered the cause of the still-uncontrollable turn when he realized—and told me—that the first officer's stiffened left leg was holding full left rudder. I didn't need to tell him to forget the oxygen and take care of the "control" problem. Supercharged as he was, he flexed the first officer's leg at the knee, thus freeing the rudder. This allowed us to recover from the turn that by now had progressed through some 270 degrees. We were level at 1,500 feet and the aircraft was once again under control.

A second flight attendant was called and she assumed the duty of making certain the first officer continued to breathe an uninterrupted flow of 100 percent oxygen. In a matter of moments, the first officer appeared to be regaining consciousness to the extent that we needed the third flight attendant to assist by keeping the FO's hands clear of switches and controls. (Incidentally, and incredibly, five people *can* get in the cockpit of a Boeing 737—all at one time.)

Until we could fly straight and level we had not advised the tower of our predicament, and no one in the tower had asked questions. Tower personnel observing our unusual missed approach were probably as perplexed, but not as alarmed, as our 72 passengers must have been. Fortunately, no other aircraft were in the pattern.

With the aircraft and my voice once again under control, I advised the tower of the onboard medical problem and requested that emergency medical assistance stand by to await our arrival. I also requested and received landing clearance. Our passengers were then advised that the copilot had suddenly become ill, thus the missed approach. They were assured (if such was possible) that he was now much improved and that we would soon be landing.

As we turned final for the second time, two of the flight attendants returned to stations in the cabin. The remaining attendant belted himself into the center jump seat. From this position he was able to assist by reading the checklists (particularly important, I believe, when operating under such unusual circumstances) and by monitoring the now-recovering first officer; we landed without further complications.

As we parked at the terminal, waiting paramedics boarded the aircraft to assist the first officer, who was soon able to walk to the waiting ambulance. In the hospital it was determined that his seizure had been triggered by a chemical imbalance. With proper treatment he regained full health.

We eventually completed our delayed trip with the help of a reserve first officer. Arriving at our layover stop for a much-needed rest I found that sleep did not come easily. During the time that I was awake that night and on many subsequent nights I reviewed the known factors which contributed to the safe outcome of a situation that was, for a brief moment in time and space, touch and go.

Without the flight attendants' skilled and calm assistance in the crowded cockpit the outcome would have been unpredictable at best. Until they could lend support, the aircraft was literally out of control.

Another factor was our skepticism about the reported wind that was in such contrast with our observations of the actual wind in the vicinity of the airport. As a consequence of this doubt, we planned a higher airspeed on the approach and allowed the airspeed to increase even further due to what was probably a "phantom" wind shear. I will always believe that because of the additional airspeed we were able to keep the aircraft from stalling, rolling over and plunging that short distance to earth when the sudden and unexpected full application of the left rudder took effect.

Following this incident, someone unknown to me sent an article entitled "Pilot Incapacitation in Flight" published in *The Cockpit* (United Airlines, May 1980). A summary of facts gleaned from that article quoting various sources follows:

During a seven-year period prior to 1980, there were 17 instances of pilot deaths in the cockpit. Five of these deaths led to accidents that resulted in 148 fatalities. Of those five, four deaths occurred during the approach phase of flight. Two-thirds of the 17 pilots who died were under the age of 50. (The first officer in this story was 40.)

When total incapacitation, ranging from unconsciousness to death, occurs, the pilot simply ceases to function. A second and more dangerous form of incapacitation is subtle or partial incapacitation, in which the pilot flying remains conscious but with reduced analytical capacity. The subtle type is more dangerous because it happens more frequently and is more difficult to detect.

Between March 30, 1983, and January 8, 1993, National Transportation Safety Board records reveal 36 instances of crew incapacitations on Part 135 and Part 121 air carrier operations.

Pilots should realize that a crew member's incapacitation is always a possibility, and as with any aircraft emergency it must be dealt with in three phases: 1) recognizing the problem, 2) maintaining or regaining control of the aircraft, and 3) solving the problem.

In the personal experience described in this article, earlier recognition would have lessened the impact of the illness by allowing me to take control of the aircraft at a higher altitude and before the seizure resulted in full application of the rudder. Several days after the incident, my first officer stated that he remembered nothing of my calls about the high airspeed; he probably suffered a partial incapacitation before the total incapacitation occurred.

And last but not least—always expect the unexpected.

Barry Ross

WEIRD, WACKY AND WONDERFUL

W

WHILE WE LOVE JUST ABOUT EVERY *I Learned About Flying From That* we publish, every now and then we come across a submission that really catches our attention. This chapter contains some of those. Some are downright strange, like the story of an Air Force cadet who was encouraged to go for a wingwalk on a real flying T-28 trainer, or the tale of a C-130 military transport that had an in-flight run in with a boat! Others still, like one pilot's tale of being rescued from potential disaster by, well, Santa Claus, are downright bizarre.

The one thing that all of these contributions have in common is that our readers loved them and let us know it. Whether it's the story of the pilot who tried his best to spread his beloved aunt's ashes over the Wasatch Front, or those by two different pilots who had run-ins with UFOs of very different descriptions, each of these stories was memorable in its own special way.

I saved a couple of my favorites for last. One is a hilarious tale of a near ditching in the Pacific Ocean, with the student pilot being the one who was able to exhibit remarkable cool under pressure.

The other is the simple story of a woman's first solo cross country flight into what would normally have been a perfectly appropriate airport for the purpose but which that day was anything but a good place for a student pilot. It did, however, make for one of the most unusual student solo cross countries ever. And, as is the surely the case for every pilot/author in this book, it made for one of the most unforgettable flights of a lifetime.

Crosswind Turkey

AS I REACHED MY 40S and my career became far less rewarding and far more lucrative (funny how that works), I started yearning for something new. Flying! It took one introductory flight for me to know that I was hooked. Five months and a few well-deserved gray hairs on my instructor's head later, I had my ticket. The very next week I marched into my flight school and booked a Cessna 172RG (Cutlass), and my instructor of course. A complex endorsement seemed to be the next step. I really wanted out of 152s. With that signature I was finally ready to carry passengers in style. So there I was that beautifully clear November morning, clutching the keys to the Cutlass. I was planning a pleasure flight the upcoming weekend, but before subjecting passengers to the terror of a new pilot's landings in an unfamiliar airplane, I thought some solo touch-and-goes were in order.

Napa Tower ATIS advised that the winds favored Runway 18 (left or right). Landings were my objective, so I opted for the mile-long right. Taxiing out I noticed that a very indecisive but full windsock had varying opinions as to where the wind was coming from. The temperature was increasing rapidly and there was that extreme dryness that we Californians associate with the Santa Ana winds, which are strong winds from the east. But if this was indeed a Santa Ana, shouldn't I be using Runway 6?

After runup, while I was holding short, the tower mentioned the wind had shifted and was blowing from the north. The Piper just ahead of me, who asked to remain in closed traffic, did not seem to experience any problems doing a tailwind takeoff, so I took the runway despite the wind direction. With all that concrete ahead of me, it was a long but uneventful takeoff.

As I turned downwind, another pilot entered the pattern behind me. The new arrival asked for a wind check. The wind had shifted again to 090 at 14; it was indeed a Santa Ana. The pilot behind me (with certainly more hours than I) chuckled to the tower that a 90-degree crosswind at that velocity was more than he cared for, and asked for Runway 6. The tower granted the request. Meanwhile I was number two for touch-and-go behind the Piper.

On final everything seemed in order. I had run my checklist and was correctly set up for a stiff crosswind landing. Suddenly a turkey buzzard appeared from below and flew directly into my flight path. This happens occasionally at Napa, which has a large bird population. As I had seen before, he glided down and out of the way. After all, who was the bigger bird here anyway? With the runway made I added the final notch of flaps. It was then that my feathered fellow aviator returned, only this time he was totally out of control. Tumbling up the left side of the engine cowling he spread his enormous wings out just as he hit the windshield.

A blast of Plexiglas, bird body fluids, feathers and hot air hit my face. It is funny how slow this all seemed to happen, unrealistic, not like real life at all. I was having trouble believing that the windshield had actually given way, but there was some pretty good evidence to support this fact. During all my study and training, I couldn't remember a single reference to bird strike procedures. The checklist (which at this point had blown back into the baggage compartment with almost everything else) had no emergency section on flying without a windshield. I was getting real suspicious that I might be on my own on this one. Little did I know at the moment that things could get worse. . . a lot worse.

I soon woke up and started flying again. Assessing the situation, I was still on short final and somehow still at an appropriate orientation to the runway, what little I could see of it. There was an 18-inch jagged hole in the windshield directly in front of me. My feathered hitchhiker had lodged himself there rather securely, blocking my view. One of the poor creature's large three-foot wings had flopped down over the instrumentation, blocking the basic six instruments and the radio. I decided not to try to dislodge the bird. The potential of being hit and knocked out by a Thanksgiving-sized bird did not appeal to me.

As the shock wore off I became vaguely aware of the radio chatter. For some reason the touch-and-go in front of me had decided to become a stop-and-go—probably that pesky crosswind. I apparently was barreling down on an occupied runway. The tower, unaware of my situation, issued a go-around to me. At moments like these you want to sound like John

Wayne; unfortunately what came out was closer to Roseanne Barr. In a shrill voice I announced that I had to land because I just hit a bird. Later while talking to the tower over the phone, I learned that my lack of detail as to how critical my situation was led to a slack reaction from the tower. Hitting a bird is one thing, not having a windshield is another.

Somehow the airplane in front cleared in time and I did a rather good crosswind landing. But either shock or inexperience caught up with me and I failed to follow through on the ground roll. The 172RG started to weathervane and I knew I was going to lose it. No matter how good the earth felt at that moment, I decided I had to go around after all. Applying full throttle and jamming carb heat in, I announced my intentions to the tower. Even after removing two notches of flaps that Cutlass didn't want to gain velocity or altitude.

For those of you who have not had the pleasure of flying a single-engine aircraft without a windshield, there are two things that stand out about the experience. The first is that the noise and wind generated by the prop are astounding (my headset blew back off my ears from the force). The second is that the craft no longer seems to be interested in flying. Passing the end of the runway, I was maybe 50 feet above some very hard fields.

Birdie remained lodged in the gaping hole despite some violent fluttering. I was rather fearful that he might work loose, hit me and expedite the landing process. Adding to the chaos, the tower was attempting to switch runways. I informed the controller that I no longer could hear the radio (I did not want to take my hands off the controls to reposition my headset) and that I was having difficulty gaining altitude. I learned later that there were airplanes everywhere in the runway shuffle; and there I was, floundering around without communication in the middle of it.

I continued in a slow upwind climb till I felt that I had sufficient altitude to maneuver. Announcing my intentions into the headset microphone resting on my chest, I started a slow right turn toward Runway 06. On final I could see out the left window that big pink sock pointing right at me; nothing could have felt better. I brought the airplane in with almost full power. Under the circumstances I think I made a rather nice landing. Taxiing off the runway I pulled to a stop, and found I was physically shaking. I could hear a squeaky voice coming from the headset around my neck. It was the tower calmly instructing me to contact ground, followed by the clearance for another aircraft to land.

After taxiing to the maintenance hangar, I found "the boys" on a coffee break in the back room. I told them I hit a bird and they indicated I should write it up. "No, I think you should come take a look," I told them. Within minutes I was surrounded by landing pilots who had heard the drama over the radio. Many had words of congratulations and praise for handling the situation so well. But I knew different.

If I had better judged my abilities, it never would have been as critical at all. The bird strike was unavoidable, but the go-around was due to lack of experience with crosswind landings. Maybe without the bird I would have been able to make the landing; but why land in unfavorable conditions when there are other options? I accepted the prescribed runway without question, but now I know to ask for the runway that best suits my abilities. The other mistake was not informing the tower as to exactly how critical my situation was. Without that knowledge they didn't know to clear the area. Thankfully this did not complicate the situation, but just think of what could have happened.

Of course I felt like I would never fly again, but after sitting around the airport for a couple of hours, I calmed down. Still in a shirt covered in bird juice, I checked out a trainer and flew the pattern a few times. It seemed I would never escape the 152. After landing, and feeling much better, I contacted the FBO for fuel. The lineman asked if I was "Buzzard Bob," a nickname that I hoped would not stick.

Midnight Sun

I AM A PSYCHIATRIST, and I have always been interested in aviation. In the 70s I owned a Part 135 operation based in Houston. Texas which flew freight all over Texas and parts of Louisiana. While I had multi-engine and instrument ratings and over 1,000 hours, I had never bothered to get a commercial license. So, I never flow any of our revenue producing trips. However, I did like to go out to the airport at 5:00 or 5:30 a.m. and help load the freight and see the planes take off. Also, I was often the one who had to fly here or there to pick up parts or do the other countless myriad of tasks necessary in that kind of business.

On the day in question. I was going to fly to Wichita, Kansas to look at a used Navajo Chiefrain we were thinking of adding to the fleet. My plan was to work at my psychiatric practice a whole day (or at least most of it), take off in the afternoon, inspect the Navajo and return that night.

On this day one of the patients was a twenty-something man with a variety of neurotic problems. I had known him for a while and he was doing much better. However, on this day he was complaining of fear of flying. He had to make a business trip that involved flying in a week and he was terrified. I thought about it while I listened and let my enthusiasm for flying overcome good medical judgment.

I told him that I prescribed "behavioral therapy" for his fear of flying and that he could go with me that afternoon in my plane to Wichita. He turned pale and started to protest, but I told him to meet me at the airport at 3:00 p.m. and we would put an end to this fear of flying for good.

My personal aircraft at the time was a Seneca I, which I had turbocharged. The weather was perfect CAVU all the way from Houston to Wichita and predicted to be the same for the return. A fall cold front had just blown through and except for some moderate north winds at low altitudes the high pressure meant pleasant flying.

My reluctant passenger arrived on time, but was full of excuses why he couldn't go and dripping with perspiration from terror. I showed him the Seneca and that scared him even worse. He was thinking more of a ride in a 727 where he wouldn't have to look out the window. I told him that was silly. Half the fun was looking out the window.

I told him I could hypnotize him, calm him down and give him the post hypnotic suggestion that "flying is fun." He was skeptical but agreed to the plan. After the hypnotic session, I put him in the right seat beside me. Our chief mechanic had performed the preflight and pronounced it A-OK. I had filed IFR direct from Houston Hobby to Wichita. We taxied out to Runway 35 and the tower cleared us for takeoff. The clearance I got was Hobby One Departure, Leona, direct Scurry, around the east side of the Dallas TCA to Ardmore then direct Wichita. This was the long way around but reasonable, considering the 8,000-foot altitude I had filed.

The afternoon sun was bright, and it was one of those rare afternoons in Houston when you can see 50 miles. The weather front had blown the pollution away—at least for a few hours. After takeoff I set the climb power, turned on the autopilot, and gave my attention to my passenger.

The gusty winds after the cold front created some mild to moderate turbulence. With each bump my passenger yelled: "Oh my God! Oh my God!" But passing through 5,000 feet the ride smoothed out and he started to relax a bit. I tried to distract him by pointing out the landmarks as we went by: downtown Houston. Intercontinental Airport, Lake Conroe. By the time we got to Dallas, he was feeling much better and started picking out landmarks on his own.

The flight from there to Wichita could not have been nicer. I made a good landing and my passenger commented that maybe flying wasn't so bad after all.

The business in Wichita went well, but took longer than I'd expected. The salesman insisted on taking us to dinner. When we got back to the airport it was late and dark. I decided to fly back VFR direct at 15,500 feet and go directly over the Dallas TCA, which you could do back then.

We took off and headed southeast. There was no moon and it was dark, but there were a zillion stars. It was a beautiful night. The Seneca did not have Loran or GPS in those days, but my navigation plan was simple. Fly a VOR course out of Wichita for Dallas, find the lights of the city, correct course for Houston, find the lights and let them guide me to Hobby. I backed up the plan with the VORs. But on this night it was hardly necessary.

It seemed like as soon as we leveled off at 15,500 feet we could see the Dallas lights a hundred miles away or more. On climbing through 8,000 feet, my passenger and I put on oxygen masks. He complained about feeling claustrophobic, but soon settled down. He was really enjoying looking at the stars and the lights of the cities as we passed by.

It was about midnight when we were passing right over DFW airport. Everything was going fine. All of a sudden the cockpit lit up like it was daylight. I could not figure out what was going on. I thought maybe we were in the headlights of a big jet going into DFW. I told my passenger to look for planes. The tone of my voice really scared him and he was frantically looking around. I started to make a clearing turn to the left, but I could see nothing. The daylight seemed to go on for minutes, although it must have been only seconds.

Then all at once I saw it: a big glowing ball of fire coming right at us at 12:00. I instinctively pushed in on the control wheel as the object kept coming at terrific speed. As it got closer I could see that it was solid rock about 10-15 feet in diameter. The flames extended out another 10-15 feet. It soared about 2,000 feet over us and then we were plunged back into darkness.

All the while my passenger had been screaming at the top of his lungs. His oxygen mask was off and he was hyper-ventilating. I was monitoring center frequency and I punched the button and asked "What the hell was that?"

A calm voice came back that there had been reports of meteors. My passenger panicked to the point of uncontrollability. I, who am normally the picture of calmness in an emergency, was anxiety ridden. My heart was pounding and sweat was pouring. It was all I could do to keep myself under control.

My passenger stopped screaming and started to cry. "What else is out there?" he asked, sobbing.

"Ducks," I said.

He cried harder and pressed his face to the window frantically looking for ducks.

By then I had regained my composure and said calmly, "Don't bother, you can't see them. They don't have lights."

My passenger started begging me to land so he could get out. I didn't. I continued on to Hobby airport.

Later we learned it was a fairly large meteor that crossed over Dallas and hit the ground in Arkansas. My instinctive descent probably had no role in the meteor missing us. It had all happened so fast. It was, however, probably a good thing that I hadn't selected 17,500 feet for the flight.

What are the odds of an airplane being hit by a meteor? Most of the time, infinitesimal. In October, however, there are two annual meteor showers, which come when the earth passes through the remains of old comets. We ran into one of these showers.

I didn't see my patient until about a month later. He told me that, yes, he had gone on his business trip and no, he'd had no problems flying. He was cured!

"How can that be?" I asked.

He said that when he got home that night he started thinking that the light had been a religious experience—maybe even the presence of God. He said that if the meteor were meant to hit us, it would have. This fact relieved him of his anxiety and he overcame his fear of flying.

Lesson One: In flying, no matter how much experience you have, expect the unexpected.

Lesson Two: In medicine, sometimes patients get better in spite of their doctor's help.

Planes, Trains and Power Lines

THE NIGHTMARES STILL PERSIST, not as often as before. They are generally the same with little variation. I find myself in the cockpit of some unknown aircraft, 10 feet off the ground, no sound, moving slowly through a chick, molasses atmosphere. As I look ahead I see a vast array of trees and power lines reaching into a bleak, featureless sky. All too aware that I am on the losing side of the altitude/airspeed equation, I use all the strength I can command to urge the airplane above and around the web of obstacles. When all is lost, and an instant before I meet my demise, I awake with a start, heart pounding. I spend the next several minutes trying to convince myself it was just a dream. But there was a time when it wasn't a dream—and that is what this story is about.

My Aeronca Champ climbed on takeoff from the Newton, Kansas airport, and I was intent on doing some late afternoon exploring across the central plains. It was Labor Day, and the fall air was cool and clear, perfect for skimming the treeless Flint Hills that stretch across eastern Kansas. Due to the shallow rock formations that give the land its name, these rolling, grass-covered hills have been better suited to cattle grazing than farming. The annual spring burns have done an effective job of keeping the trees and larger "woody" plants from taking root, thus leaving the area much as it was when the Indians, buffalo, and limitless wildlife ruled its graceful swales of bluestem grass and sparkling streams.

As the plane turned to the northwest, I was greeted by a picture-perfect view of a lone cloud dumping a sheet of dark rain down to the thirsty prairie below. It was getting late, so I decided to turn back toward my home base in El Dorado, Kansas.

As I flew the 30-some miles home, I spotted a long Santa Fe train with its three engines and some 40 cars snaking through the distant hills. This was too much for the Walter Mitty in me to resist. As I gently pushed the nose over I rolled to the left for a 45 degree intercept of the train's tail. If all went as planned, I would meet the train on the other side of the highway viaduct 10 miles away. A mile from the bridge I noticed a car parked on the overpass and two people watching the long train passing beneath them. I decided that it would be best if I gave the train watchers some clearance, so I made a graceful arch up and over the bridge. On the down side I lined up with the train which was now less than a quarter-mile away. The airspeed indicator showed 90 mph giving me an estimated closure rate of 40 mph. I continued descending so I would be about 30 feet above the train as I ran up the train's back-side. Concentrating on alignment with the train, which had just begun to pass beneath my nose, I noticed something on the horizon—power lines!

Adding power, I sharply pulled the nose skyward. For a split second I thought I had missed them. Then I began to slow. Gently at first, almost as if due to the steep climb angle. Then I began to be pushed into my lap belt as if on a roller coaster at the end of its run. I knew it was over. The nose of the Champ was pointing toward the sky.

The power line, stretching pole to pole across the tracks, created a giant guitar string twanging an ever-higher pitch as the plane stretched it to its limits. As the plane pulled the line taut, the poles pitched inward until they could hold no more. Thrust, lift, gravity, and drag were no longer significant forces in this flight; the new forces were power line tension and momentum.

BANG! With a shotgun-like blast, the poles gave up and the plane rotated about the fulcrum of the lines. As I hung from my lap belt, I looked straight down at the white dusting of track ballast, which, most likely would be my last view of this earth—so much for dying in my sleep at age 95.

In a matter of seconds, these thoughts streamed through my mind:

Gosh, I think I've just killed myself.

Boy, THAT was pretty stupid!

How sad that my two children, Lynn (10) and Jack (5), won't have a father.

Boy, those tracks are getting big.

Ouch!

All said and done, I ended up with a compound fracture of my left elbow, fracture of my right pelvis, broken right toe, "many" stitches in the forehead, face and scalp and a newly acquired weather prediction accuracy of 85 percent. After three days in the hospital and two weeks at home, I returned to work to face all of the train jokes which still persist.

I expected the worst from the FAA and figured I deserved everything I got. Ninety days after filling out the accident forms I received a certified letter from the FAA stating all of the things I did (which I knew), and all of the rules I had violated (which I didn't know). They gave me the choice of protesting the action, filing a NASA witness form or returning my certificate for a 60-day suspension. No problem, I hot-footed it to the post office and returned my certificate.

I'm back flying now and am the proud owner of a 1947 Stinson 108-2 Voyager—the family insisted on a four-place airplane so we could all fly together. (Surely it wasn't that they just wanted to keep an eye on me.) I'm cured of train-chasing and enjoy the Flint Hills from a more elevated "plane" as well as the cross-country advantage a Stinson has over the shorter-legged Champ.

Model Midair

IGOT HOOKED ON FLYING when I was a child, when the pilots of a jet in which I was a passenger gave me the million-dollar tour of the cockpit. The dream stayed with me for more than 30 years, with one difference: What I really wanted was to fly a helicopter. Finally I stopped procrastinating, called a helicopter school at MacArthur Airport on Long Island, bought all the books and flew three times a week—all this while working full-time and supporting my family.

With my license in my wallet, as my confidence grew the thrill never left me, but after many solo hours I felt I now could share the awesome feeling with my family and friends. The Statue of Liberty, the Connecticut shore, all over Long Island and Manhattan—I've flown my wife, my mother-in-law, my dad (on Father's Day), my girls on their birthdays, and many friends to many places.

I felt very strongly about sharing this awesome hobby with everyone interested, and on this particular day I had set some time aside to fly my old buddy Mike in a Robinson R22 over his home and other areas of interest to take some pictures. One of the areas he wanted to see was the Queens side of the Throgs Neck bridge, just outside of La Guardia Class B airspace. We were squawked in, and identified just for good measure.

Suddenly, just as I was switching frequency I felt a solid jolt and heard a very loud noise. It felt like I had hit something sticking up from below with the tail, and I looked behind me to see what it could have been and what I might have done wrong. What, I thought, could be sticking up 600 feet from the ground?

Mike asked what had happened, and I told him I didn't know. He asked if the helicopter was still flyable; I said, "So far." He nodded, and went on taking pictures.

Meanwhile the main rotor rpms were dropping, to 95. The horn didn't come on, but I decided I'd be better opting for autorotation now while I had some control rather than later, when maybe I'd lose the tail rotor. I dropped the collective and started autorotation. After I checked engine and rotor rpm—all were in the green—I went back on LGA frequency and stated that we had been hit by something, and they responded, "Are you declaring an emergency?"

I checked the pedals, left and right, and milked the power; the helicopter was still responding. My ego said, "No, we are in control and will fly for Farmingdale airport and report the strike." I took the helicopter out of autorotation and headed for home.

Some minutes later, sanity set in and I realized that I was pushing my luck and should put down immediately, so I located a heliport nearby and headed for it, all the while realizing I could lose the tail rotor and really have my hands full. The area of the heliport, Sands Point, was an industrial park, surrounded by wires, fuel tanks, buildings, houses, you name it, so I opted for the beach. If I lost the tail and headed straight down, I didn't want to do any damage to other people.

The landing was uneventful. But when we got out to examine the damage, to my surprise there was a sizeable dent in the tail cone, and some kind of box with wires and cables connected to it was wrapped around the tail stabilizer. From the control box and balsa wood shrapnel I identified the UFO as a radio-controlled model airplane. We had just survived a billion-to-one chance encounter with an RC model at 600 feet agl in Class B airspace.

Well, so much for those guys who knock the R22; I'm sold on its resilient structure, and its nimble responsiveness. The model airplane had taken out the position light, and there were some scrapes of the model's coating on the R22's tail surfaces, but the helicopter seemed mechanically sound. I saw nothing defective or damaged, nothing that looked as if the aircraft was structurally inhibited. I spun up the rotor, checked for vibration, put some loads on it, and it behaved normally. I deemed it airworthy and flew it home; later, after I contacted the FAA, they counseled me that, since I am not the FAA or an A&P mechanic, I should have left the aircraft there until an authorized mechanic could check it out (and, luckily, the FAA left it at that). Live and learn—thanks to God, my instructor, and autorotation.

The "pilot" of the RC never did come forward.

The Milk Run

THERE MUST BE SOME COSMIC LAW that the worst emergencies—the real nail-biters, the ones where your consuming thought is, "Get me out of this and I'll never do it again"—always have to happen when you've got your mental trousers at half-mast.

Back in the late 1970s I was flying C-130 Hercules transports for the Military Airlift Command out of Elmendorf Air Force Base, Alaska. We were basically the trash haulers for all of Alaska, and prided ourselves on delivering the goods to thousands of GIs at godforsaken outposts where the Cold War lived up to its name in a very literal sense, in a kaleidoscope of weather, terrain, and airports that other people only saw in their worst nightmares.

We routinely shoehorned our four-engined bush planes into one-way runways with 13 percent slopes and mountainsides in the overruns, and eased into wind-blasted strips on the back doorstep of the late, lamented Evil Empire. We felt our way into North Slope whiteouts along the old DEW Line and fought the fog and winds at remote islands in the Aleutians that might as well have been on another planet. We weren't supermen, though. Our real secret was nothing more than caution, experience and teamwork, something we older heads spent months pounding into new pilots who took the "unique, harsh, Arctic environment" a little too lightly.

But knowingly going in harm's way with all your senses at full alert is one thing, and getting blindsided on a milk run is quite another. These come-as-you-are situations are the ones we always remember and never boast about, because they're the worst. They always have an element of total surprise and undiluted terror, and result in more than enough spur-of-the-moment gropings to diminish any enthusiasm for hangar flying afterwards.

One winter night we were returning from Shemya, at the very tip of the Aleutians, after dropping off a VIP who actually wanted to spend a few days there on an inspection tour. (As island inmates say, Shemya isn't the end of the world, but you can see it from there.) In keeping with our VIP policy, my crew was top-notch: I was one of our senior instructors and so was my copilot, and he was the safety officer to boot. Our navigator outranked all of us, and had had the dubious distinction of bailing out of an AC-130 Spectre gunship over Cambodia and living to talk about it. Our flight engineer and loadmaster were likewise among our most experienced.

We were empty, with only a few pallets of backhaul odds and ends, cruising comfortably at 25,000 feet and 280 knots in our aging but reliable E-model Herc. The five-hour run from Shemya to Elmendorf was pretty much on airways, but we were in the weather. Below us, every airport in southwest Alaska was closed (or virtually so) because of low ceilings and snow.

About two hours out of Elmendorf, almost 14 hours into a crew day that had started with an oh-dark-thirty wakeup, we were peacefully droning along on autopilot. I was minding the store while the copilot and navigator dozed off in their seats. The engineer was back at the galley reheating the inflight kitchen's offering of mystery fowl a la grease. Suddenly there was a sharp bump and the airplane began to vibrate violently. I seized the control yoke but was barely able to hold onto it. At the same time I grabbed a handful of throttles and yanked them back while I punched off the autopilot.

As we slowed down, I prayed for the shaking to quit before the airplane came apart. I looked frantically around for help from the crew. Without so much as a whisper from me, the engineer had left his chicken on the deck and was in his seat in about three nanoseconds; I'd never seen him move so fast. The copilot looked as if he'd just mainlined a gallon of campfire coffee and was backing me up on every movement while he notified Anchorage Center we were having a bit of difficulty. The navigator was already plotting courses to the nearest airports. The loadmaster had his flashlight out and was in the cargo compartment scanning for any obvious problems.

The shaking continued unabated until we had dropped below 140 knots—super slow for a C-130 unless you're thinking about landing or making an airdrop. Even then an ominous rumble hovered in the background, localized in the aft section of the plane. Satisfied that we weren't going to disintegrate immediately, I asked the copilot to fly the plane while I brainstormed with the engineer.

The trouble wasn't in the autopilot, which was now off with the circuit breakers pulled. It might have been structural failure, but we had no way to tell; the navigator couldn't even see the tail through his sextant (which we could use as a sort of periscope) because of the dark and clouds. It might have been icing, but all of the usually very effective anti-icing systems seemed to be working perfectly and we couldn't see any ice buildup on the leading edges of the wings.

The culprit could also have been an accidentally deployed 20-man life raft, of which the C-130 carried as many as four in compartments on top of the wings. When water seeped in and froze and expanded at altitude, these beasts could spring out of their compartments like giant rubber tarps. Sometimes a deployed raft would hang up on the tail section, disrupting the airflow until it slipped off. On the possibility a raft had deployed, the copilot waggled the rudders per the flight manual procedure to help it slip off, but nothing changed.

There might also have been a problem with the hydraulic actuators for the flight controls, specifically the rudder or elevator. A spate of these had plagued the fleet in previous months, culminating in a fatal accident in the lower 48. The loadmaster and engineer couldn't find anything out of the ordinary, but we still couldn't rule the hydraulics out. We just didn't know what was wrong.

After a few minutes of fevered troubleshooting, the copilot said quietly, "You'd better give me a hand; the controls are binding up." Indeed, fore-and-aft movement of the yoke was almost impossible, even with two of us straining hard. This indicated something seriously wrong with the elevator or its hydraulics, reinforcing our worst fears. I told the navigator to tell Center we had control problems, and we'd let them know how things worked out.

The loadmaster checked the elevator actuators again, but didn't find anything. The pressure was steady and in the green on the gauges. We tried the elevator with each hydraulic system separately to see if one was causing a problem, but nothing happened. Not knowing anything else to do, the copilot and I slowly forced the yoke back and forth, hoping to ease whatever was causing the binding. After an agonizing five minutes or so of roller-coaster altitude fluctuations, the stiffness relaxed enough to allow one of us to manage unassisted. We still didn't know the cause.

We were a long way from the edge of the woods, since the winter storm had devoured all of our possible destinations except home base, and our drastically reduced speed ensured us of at least three more hours of fun. We managed to do some controllability checks and found the airplane didn't want to fly very well with flaps, or much below the 140 knots we were holding to keep down the shaking.

Of course, we now had ATC's undivided attention. Apparently everybody at Elmendorf was on the line as well, and we did our best to keep the command post there up to date. They called in all their standby experts and went through the same ideas we'd already covered. We thanked them for their concern, but there wasn't a lot anyone could do at that point.

About then, we all suddenly became aware of a loud banging in the tail from outside the airplane, as if something was beating wildly against the aluminum skin. Our first reaction was that the airplane was finally starting to come apart, and we passed the word directly to our listening public. We slowed down as much as we dared, but nothing seemed to help.

After an eternity (really only about 15 minutes) the banging abruptly quit. We were still in one piece. On we staggered, white-knuckled and sweat-soaked. We thought briefly about our parachutes, but we were over jagged mountains and frozen boreal wilderness, and none of us relished the prospect of going quietly into the arctic night without survival gear.

Finally we slowly began to let down into the Anchorage area. Center told us a rescue HC-130 was nearby and was being vectored in behind us. The HC-130 pilot offered to pull up and take a look at us as soon as we hit a break in the weather. Soon enough, we hit a "sucker hole" in the clouds and the other plane closed in. Almost immediately we slipped back into the soup, but he was close enough for his landing lights to illuminate the murk around us. We politely asked him to back off, since we didn't fancy making it this far only to have a midair collision.

Anchorage Approach cleared everybody out of our way as we set up on a 40-mile final approach for a screaming no-flap emergency landing at Elmendorf. We figured we'd only have one shot, because a go-around in our apparent condition was unthinkable. We were in and out of the clouds all the way to touchdown, but the landing was mercifully anticlimactic and we managed to get stopped without blowing any tires.

As we turned off the runway into a sea of flashing red lights, we saw everyone on the ground pointing excitedly at our tail. After we shut down and straggled out the crew door on rubbery legs, our first sight was of a giant, tattered yellow amoeba draped over the left horizontal stabilizer, nearly covering it. The life raft had literally wrapped itself around the stabilizer and elevator. Part of it had wedged solidly between the elevator and the fuselage, causing the binding that we'd finally managed to loosen up by brute force. It wouldn't have come off with any amount of rudder work.

The metal inflation cylinder and the various survival kits, all attached to the raft by stout tethers, had worked loose and flailed a dozen fist-sized holes in the side of the huge vertical fin before they finally snapped off. The area around the raft looked like it had been near-missed by an antiaircraft missile. Adding it up, the airflow over the left half of the tail had been almost completely disrupted, and had pushed even the stout old Herc to the edge of its safety envelope.

We all just shook our heads and silently thanked whoever was watching over us that we'd made it back intact. We felt like a shot-up B-17 crew in a World War II movie that had limped back to the English aerodrome with pieces hanging everywhere.

But we weren't in a war. We'd been caught completely by surprise at our lowest level of alertness. And no one had ever taught us how to handle magnitude-eight airframe tremors or jammed-up controls or unknown objects trying to beat the airplane apart from outside. About all we had going for us was teamwork and crew discipline and maybe a little common sense.

Today's ATC environment is almost suffocatingly womblike at times and often lulls us. But still there are more occasions than we'd care to admit when we suddenly realize with stark clarity that we are ultimately on our own, despite all the helpful voices from the ether. In these situations, we have to remember that we all probably have the skills and the knowledge deep inside to pull through the tightest spots. All we have to do is just keep our heads screwed on straight and not do anything stupid—and never forget that even a milk run can turn into a combat mission.

Wing Walk

MY PRIMARY FLIGHT TRAINING began in July of 1956 and took place at Spence Air Base in Moultrie, Georgia. The 40 flight hours I spent flying the Beech T-34A Mentor were filled with tremendous excitement. My instructor's name was Harold Ackerman, a civilian. He was very tough but understanding and supportive. His nickname among the students was "the axe," mainly because he was the instructor who tested those students who were at risk. He washed many of them out of the program if they didn't have the necessary capabilities.

He also had an impressive walk and always wore dark sunglasses. He also liked auto racing and spent many minutes explaining the finer points of the sport.

Every morning or afternoon, I would be filled with fear in preparation for the daily scheduled flight. Each of the students wanted to fly, but until we got into the air, we demonstrated a nervous reaction to almost everything that took place in the flight room and aircraft parking ramp.

After completing the T-34 phase successfully, we started to fly the T-28 Trojan. It was a larger, heavier and much more responsive airplane, much like the jet (T-33) that I was to fly in Basic Training.

Mr. Ackerman really went to work on teaching me the finer points of flying. He wanted each of us to be the best. He encouraged us to make the aircraft part of our bodies by thinking about what we wanted to do and allowing the body to smoothly achieve the maneuver.

He was especially good when it came to instrument flying; he made me believe that the instrument needles should and did freeze on the proper altitude, airspeed, heading, etc. This approach was successful, and I scored very high on the instrument final. This pleased him very much.

It was now January 25, 1957, and I had just completed my final military check ride the previous day. I had done a good job and Mr. Ackerman was happy. I still had three hours left to fly to complete my training, and it had to be scheduled and completed that day.

We took off and practiced on various items that I suggested for about an hour. He then asked if there was anything else I thought I needed to know. At that point, I was about to make the most naive mistake thus far in my flying experience.

He instructed us to approach an emergency bailout situation using the trim tab escape method, which was not in the flying manual. He had instructed us that we would open the canopy, roll full forward trim to the elevator tab while holding the stick back in the level position, release our seatbelts and let go of the stick. This would cause the airplane to nose down abruptly and throw us out the top of the canopy.

The aircraft flight manual, however, indicated that the proper way to escape from the aircraft was to climb out on the wing and dive down and over the trailing edge. I calmly asked whether the flight manual technique was practical. To my surprise, Mr. Ackerman called over the intercom saying "I've got it," meaning he was taking control of the T-28. He then pulled the throttle back and slowed the aircraft down, dropped the flaps, opened the canopy and said, "Okay, get out on the wing." I indicated that he must be kidding; he wasn't.

I followed his directions, released my seat belt, took off my headset and hat, made sure all my flight suit pockets were zipped closed and began to climb out on the wing. It seemed to take forever to do this simple task. I slowly climbed into the wind stream and out on the wing. The wind was very strong and my hands and arms began to shake. My flight suit whipped around my legs with extreme force.

I paused, standing on the wing for a moment. I could see the puffy cumulus clouds from a different perspective. The edges of the fields and wooded areas seemed much more pronounced as I peered over the edge of the wing. I now became more aware of the wind and the force it had on my legs, my head and my body. My legs were getting a little more shaky.

I looked in the rear cockpit to get his reaction. He was smiling and nodded his head in the direction of the cockpit. I quickly returned to my seat. This only took a fraction of a second. He closed the canopy, and I strapped myself into my seat and put on my headset. All I could say was "Wow, that was something special."

I was quiet during the remainder of the flight. It had been quite an experience. Mr. Ackerman was also quiet and didn't say anything about what we had just done. I felt that he thought that he might have taken a chance putting me out on the wing. What if I had slipped? He would have had a hard time explaining why a student had bailed out of his airplane.

We returned to Spence Field, entered a normal landing pattern, and I made a very smooth landing—his special priority. As I taxied into the parking slot, I glanced into the rearview mirror. Mr. Ackerman seemed to have a broad smile on his face behind his dark sunglasses and didn't return my glance.

After I shut down the engine and climbed out of the cockpit, he congratulated me on a being his student and we walked to the flight shack. He indicated that I had done a good job and chuckled about my wing walk.

If that particular T-28A is still in one piece today, I believe you will find hand and finger prints imbedded on the canopy rail from my extremely tight grip while completing my one and only wing walk that day.

Can a pilot ever forget his first flight instructor? I certainly won't.

Lost and Found

WE'VE ALL HEARD SOME VARIATION of the axiom "Flying is not inherently dangerous, but is extremely unforgiving of any careless act or oversight, no matter how small." I was about to find this to be true even with the airplane safely on the ground with the engine shut down!

I have been a professional musician since age 15, but have always loved anything related to aviation. I finally got my private license at age 29 and soon was able to integrate career and hobby by flying a few of the fellow band members to out-of-town gigs when weather and economics allowed. I had decided not to get an instrument rating until I was able to use it often enough to justify the cost.

A few years and a couple hundred hours later, I flew four members of an eight-piece salsa band I worked with to El Paso, Texas. The weekend was beautiful; a nice early fall day with some puffy cumulus and unlimited visibility. I'll never forget the view from 8,500 feet above Van Horn. We could see the smoke of Juarez, Mexico, nearly 100 miles in front of us, Guadalupe Peak 80 miles to our right and the mountains of Big Bend 100 miles to our left.

Returning to Austin the next day in our rented Piper Archer, we decided to make a stop in Alpine to see some old friends and then take in an aerial tour of Big Bend National Park. There are only two places in the lower 48 one can take off, fly in a straight line and land in the United States but still fly through international airspace. One is in the eastern Great Lakes region and the other is from Big Bend west toward Nogales or east toward Del Rio.

After a delicious Mexican food lunch in Alpine, our friends dropped us back at the deserted airport. The lone attendant who greeted us on landing was nowhere in sight. I was ready to file my flight plan back to Austin but the pay phone outside the office didn't work. None of us had cell phones as this was 1988. With the daring of a satisfied stomach and severe clear weather, I opted to forego filing, breaking one of my personal safety rules for the first and last time. I figured I would request flight following from ATC after our low altitude scenic flight over the Rio Grande River.

And what scenery it was! With cool air, few clouds, almost no wind and no other traffic (air or ground) for miles around, I felt comfortable flying a few hundred feet above the canyon walls and stark desert terrain. As we began our slow climb-out to the east from the flanks of Emory Peak (at 7,835 feet, the high point of Big Bend Park), we were blessed with a brilliant full circle rainbow in the small late afternoon rainshower a few miles ahead.

We settled in for a nice quiet ride, the two guys in back already snoring, my "copilot" conga player flying and me navigating. Noticing the Rio Grande curving away to the north. I suddenly realized I was in Mexican airspace! Checking the charts, I opted to save a little time and gas by heading straight toward the Lake Amistad reservoir and our optional fuel stop of Kerrville. I climbed to 11,500 feet, keeping the river (and the Texas border!) always within gliding distance off our left wingtip. I knew an emergency landing in the desert of northern Mexico could be disastrous, with only a pocketknife, one flashlight, no survival gear, and maybe two gallons of water between four men. But my fears of dying of thirst while fending off rattlesnakes and scorpions were unfounded, and soon we were safely across the Rio Grande again, and only an hour or so from Kerrville.

I did call up flight following, and they watched our backs all the way down, more so than I realized! It was already night as we sank into the Texas hill country, and even though I was not IFR rated, I was very comfortable with night flying, as about 20 percent of my total time was at night (thanks to returning home late after many out-of-town gigs).

However, as I taxied up to the Kerrville terminal, I noticed a little black smoke rising out of the oil check hatch. But as soon as the prop stopped, our collective hair stood straight up on our heads as two men rounded the corner out of the dark, brandishing shotguns and yelling to get out of the airplane! A moment later I realized they were the local sheriff and his deputy. Unfortunately, this was when my two passengers in back woke up!

I had already figured out what had happened as we climbed out of the airplane and they made us stand with legs spread and hands on the wing, but I had not had time to explain it to my passengers and our two armed friends! The elder sheriff was calm, soon sensing our lack of guilt, but I was quite wary of the younger, mid-20s rookie obviously out on his first "big drug bust!" He seemed a little nervous holding that shotgun barely three feet from my heart. He demanded some identification, then hollered at me to keep my hands on the wing. I had to gently remind him that I actually couldn't fetch my wallet from the cockpit without taking my hands off the wing.

As he perused my various licenses, I reached one index finger out to slowly push his shotgun muzzle away from my chest and the fuel tanks in the wing. "Would you mind not pointing that thing at me while you're busy with both hands in my wallet? I'm certain we'd both really hate for it to go off accidentally," I suggested. I could swear I heard the elder cop chuckle. He had already pulled out our luggage, and instead of the pounds of marijuana they were hoping for, he found a trombone, several saxophones, bongos and an electric bass. All were in soft, black, odd-shaped leather cases. These seemed even weirder to the sheriff, although he did agree they were, indeed, legal. "We are a band with no contraband," I sputtered as we all shook hands and headed inside the terminal, where, as luck would have it, the only non-vending machine snacks were donuts!

By flying low over Big Bend and then climbing to altitude over Mexico, the border radar controllers saw only a small airplane rising up out of the desert of Coahuila with no flight plan. In retrospect, I was lucky we went to Kerrville instead of San Antonio International, where the U.S. Customs agents would have been considerably less understanding. We got some gas, took a much-needed bathroom break and flew the last hour to Austin. I was so rattled, I forgot to check on the little smoke plume from the oil filler hatch until after we landed. It turned out to be nothing significant. One band member swore he'd never fly with me again, and he never did. The rest of us had great stories to tell for months to come. I now know that a flight plan isn't just for my protection in the air when I am lost or in trouble, but also when I am found on the ground.

The Best Christmas Gift

I **STILL SIT IN AMAZEMENT** as I think of the cold Christmas Eve day in December 1997 and the fate that I had just been rescued from. Although it was a ground occurrence, it soon would have been an airborne nightmare if it weren't for the unknown visitor.

It was about 11:30 a.m. on Christmas Eve and I was anxious to fly to a noon lunch at the Wausau, Wisconsin, downtown airport, an event that had become an annual ritual with a very good friend. As usual, I was running late and the sight of massive amounts of ice and snow around my hangar only fueled my anxiety for departure.

Our community airport, Y50, is about three miles south of the city of Wautoma, Wisconsin, just east of Oshkosh, in a very rural area surrounded by deserted farm fields and recreational forests. From mid-October through mid-May each year it is virtually my private airport from which to operate my Cessna 182 for business and pleasure use; seldom do visitors come to the airport, especially in the winter months and especially on a day as cold and icy as this.

As I was pushing the aircraft out of the hangar where I had just completed most of the preflight inspection to avoid the cold wind, I was suddenly halted due to the slippery ice outside my hangar. Since time was getting short, I backed up my 4X4 Ford pickup truck to the rear of my plane and hitched on a nylon tow line with a hook to the plane and a hook to the rear loop on the tail of the Cessna. With little effort, I backed the plane into position for taxi and quickly unhooked the tail and tow line, threw it in the back of the truck and got back in the warm cab to park the vehicle. I ran without hesitation from the warm truck to the cold cockpit of my airplane.

As I jumped into the left seat I felt as if I had forgotten something in the checklist during the exterior inspection, but a glance at the list and mental review of my observations seemed to prove that I was ready to proceed with the instrument check, warm-up and takeoff.

Just as the engine was starting to chug and pop, out of the corner of my eye I noticed a minivan pulling up between my hangar and my neighbor's to the east. I thought this was very unusual since I would not expect anyone to be out at the airport during this time of the day and especially in this weather, much less in a non-public area only used by the pilots and some visitors.

As I was just about to increase the rpms, a silvered-hair gentleman in a leather flight jacket got out of the van and came around the front. He had his hands extended out, clenched fists together as if holding a ski rope, moving his arms from right to left.

Suddenly I flushed as I realized that I had left the tow bar on the front strut of the aircraft and that at any moment, it would be hitting the prop— or worse, not hit the prop so that I would take off and try to land with an extended tow bar hanging from the front of my aircraft. The number of thoughts that ran through my mind in a short amount of time was astounding compared with my normal thinking process capacity. This obviously was caused by a massive infusion of adrenaline.

I quickly shut down the engine and walked around to the front of the plane and removed the tow bar. With shaking knees, I turned around to thank the stranger and eat some crow. But there was no van on the airfield and nobody in the area where the gentleman had stood only moments before.

I am not one to dwell on the possibility of miracles or profess to the crowds the wonders of the unknown, but after this occurrence, I thank the Lord in whom I believe that there is some grace for the ignorant and forgetful.

To this day, I can only think that considering the possible consequences of my hurried actions and out-of-routine sequence of events in the preflight preparation of my Skylane, I had received one of the greatest gifts possible in that Christmas season.

The small but time-consuming distraction caused by a minor interruption in my "usual and orchestrated" preflight checklist choreography caused a temporary loss of common sense and precaution. It's a lesson well learned, and remembered each time I use the tow bar.

As for the gray-haired man in the flight jacket who braved the cold that day, wherever you are, whoever you are and whatever your reason for pulling onto that field at that time, thank you! And Merry Christmas.

Scattering Ashes

MY PILOT'S LICENSE was still a stiff new piece of cardboard when my grandmother called and asked, "Would you mind spreading your great-aunt's ashes over the mountains?" Sounds a little bizarre, I thought. But my grandmother reminded me that a pilot had once spread my uncle's ashes over the Sierras. "So," she said, "Why don't you spread Aunt Zette's ashes over the mountains in Utah?" I accepted the mission, feeling it was my duty.

My aunt's real name had been Olive Rosetta, but she preferred to be called Zette—a name which could be said quickly. That paralleled her personality. She'd been bright, lively, impatient, modern, complete with dirty jokes and wild outfits. All the way into her 80s she continued to wear a lot of jewelry and bright red nail polish. And she loved the West, showing her thousands of slides to anyone she could corral.

By the time my great-aunt's ashes reached me, everyone I knew had come up with interesting ways of doing the spreading each guaranteed to work, and each aerodynamically complicated. I opted for the simple solution: Rip a trash bag open so that it becomes a flat sheet of plastic, then dump the ashes in the center and bundle it up with a piece of string. Once the string was removed the whole thing could be thrown from the aircraft, after checking to make sure the ground was clear of all obstacles and/or people to please the FAA. What could go wrong?

The little rented Cessna 152 sat patiently and innocently by the fuel pumps surrounded by the early summer heat. The ashes must have weighed at least 10 pounds; they were thick and granular, not light and fluffy as I'd thought they would be. I carried them in a bookbag, since I didn't feel comfortable about telling anybody at the airport what I was about to do. My mother accompanied me; Zette had been her favorite aunt, so she would be the bombardier. While still on the ground I opened the passenger window and discovered a major flaw in my thinking: The bag of ashes could not fit out the little space any way I tried. Oh well, I thought; we'll just open the door instead. My mother agreed with the proposition, but without realizing that we were going to be 13,000 feet in the air.

We found ourselves above the High Uinta Wilderness area heading east toward Colorado in a cool and stable air mass just over 10,000 feet. In the distance I could see the twin summits of Kings Peak, the highest mountain in the state, rising to more than 3,000 feet above us. Snowfields were present even on the south side, desperately trying to survive under the sun's powerful rays. We kept heading east, letting the ground climb with us, allowing brown scrub oaks to turn into green lodgepole pines. Rivers and streams ran free in a webbed pattern not far below, rising to meet us since the ground was climbing faster than we were.

Eventually we reached 13,000. "Is this okay?" I asked through the intercom. She nodded.

We had verbally rehearsed the procedure many times. I would slow the plane down while she removed the string. When the plane could fly at its slowest speed, minimizing prop wash and wind drag making the door easier to open, she would drop the ashes at a slight angle to clear the landing gear.

I slowed the plane down by gently reducing the throttle and letting the flaps down 10 degrees at a time. When the plane was flying at its slowest speed without losing or gaining altitude I said, "Ready?"

Suddenly there was uncertainty in her voice: "Now how do I do this again?"

"Just throw it down at an angle. Make sure you give it a good push so that it doesn't hit the tail."

"Just throw it down?" she asked timidly.

"Right, but give it a good push."

We checked to make sure her belts were fastened tightly. Then I helped her open the door as she held onto me with her free hand. The split-second Aunt Zette fell out of her hand and I heard the door slam, I gave the little engine full power. I made a clearing turn to the left, desperately scanning the air below, looking for a flat sheet of plastic. I felt like a bomber pilot who had just dropped napalm on a jungle. After two turns I noticed my mother staring down blankly, her hands clamped on the lower part of the window.

"Where is it?" I asked somewhat calmly.

She hesitated for a few moments.

"Where is it?" I asked again, not so calmly.

She pointed a nervous finger straight down. At first I thought the bag hadn't opened at all and my great-aunt had fallen at terminal velocity. "It's where?" I asked, nowhere near calmly.

"It blew back. It's stuck on the landing gear," she said.

"All of it?"

"Some of it."

My mind went ahead to the airport, thinking about the fact that it was Saturday afternoon and everybody would be out. How could I explain six feet of plastic streaming from the landing gear?

I put the flaps up and pointed the nose down, hoping the extra air-speed would tear the plastic. All it did was stretch it the product was living up to its manufacturer's claims of durability. I tried a series of stalls; still it refused to let go.

"Can you stick your leg out?" I asked kindly.

She thought about it for a few moments. "I'll try."

Again we slowed the plane down. Again we checked to make sure her belts were fastened. And again we opened the door. She stuck her leg out in the cool air, but it just wouldn't reach. Two times she tried to no avail.

I said, "We're going to Evanston," in a defeated tone of voice.

Although I wasn't carrying a chart, the Wyoming border was only about 20 minutes away. The plains looked vast and limitless, making the sky seem even bigger, lying there with all the power and independence of an ocean. As planned, we intersected the highway several moments later and followed what looked like a long black ribbon running to the airport.

We landed in Evanston and I stopped the plane on the middle of the runway, allowing my mother to climb out and grab the plastic. With a swift tug the plastic and the remaining ashes broke free, shooting backwards in the stiff headwind (assisted by the propeller wind). Zette's ashes were spread some over the high mountains of Utah, some across the Wyoming plains.

On the way back to Utah I listened to the steady drumming of the engine while following familiar roads and rivers. We flew over, around, and in between mountains and lower foothills, assured they would lead us home. I stopped feeling quite so stupid about the day's adventure. I thought about the way my great-aunt was, the way she acted, the way she lived her life. I came to the conclusion that no matter how odd or complicated the day's events, nothing had really gone wrong. It was actually a pretty fitting memorial to an unusual lady.

Me Tarzan, You Jane

AS AN AIRLINE CAPTAIN, I am amazed when I look back over my 17-year career and realize that most of the truly interesting and unusual flying situations I have experienced occurred during my professional general aviation days. Thumbing through one of my old logbooks the other day, I read over the entries made during the summer of 1980. That was the summer that I taught Jane to fly. Jane was an unusual bird. Not only did she come with her own new airplane (a Cessna 172 XP), she was 64 years old. The first time I saw Jane, she was standing at the dispatch desk explaining to the polite kid behind the counter exactly how she intended to use our services. "I have a Texaco road map and a new airplane. Now I need someone to teach me how to fly it out to the Indian reservations in Arizona so I can deliver some food." I do like a person with a plan. . . so, I offered to help.

Jane was a very intent listener. Unlike most other students, she was very patient with the ground school portion of her training. As she put it, "I've already been around for 64 years, another hundred years of this ground school crap won't kill me!" She called me "Tarzan" (as in Tarzan and Jane), which was pretty embarrassing.

Our first few weeks together were very productive. She would come to the airport prepared for her next lesson and armed with good questions. Jane was motivated—a little wacky, but motivated. Her basic flying ability was above average and what she might have lacked in agility due to age, she made up for with effort and dedication. It was all coming together nicely.

Jane soloed. She even promised the tower that she would bring up a bottle of champagne to share with them as soon as she "tied down her horse." They politely declined, of course, offering their congratulations. They were proud of Jane. We all were. As far as she was concerned, however, soloing was kid's stuff. Jane had a mission to complete. She had Indians to feed. It was cross-country time.

As with any other student, Jane's first exposure to cross-country navigation consisted of a local flight incorporating some basic VOR tracking, etc. But Jane, having cash to burn, a new airplane, a Texaco map and credit card, managed to talk me into combining our cross-country lesson with lunch on Catalina Island (26 miles south of Los Angeles). It took very little arm-twisting. It was a beautiful day and I was a flight instructor, broke and hungry.

When Jane showed up at the airport, she had a new toy. It was the longest, fattest, widest lapboard I had every seen. It was like a spare wing. It had clips for everything, multiple note pads, compartments, pen/pencil holders, chart light, spare lightbulb and fuse compartments, the history of the world printed on the front and back (as if you could turn this thing over in the cockpit of a Cessna without scraping somebody's face off), and quite possibly a secret tracking device installed by the CIA; it was truly amazing. She ordered it through the mail.

We spent a couple of hours planning our great ocean crossing to Catalina. We picked out three VORs to use to practice tracking and plotting cross radials, etc. We took off and flew around the L.A. basin area for a while working on basic pilotage and VOR tracking in conjunction with the L.A. TCA chart. It was a challenging exercise that Jane grasped quickly. Pilotage was her thing. She was born to follow those big Arizona highways. VOR navigation was easy enough to do but it was boring compared with following "those cute little semi-trucks down there."

After an hour and a half of serious navigation work, we were hungry. Jane dialed in the Catalina VOR frequency, identified it, and proceeded direct while climbing to 8,500 feet. It occurred to me that after lunch we might not fit back into the airplane with Jane's family-size lapboard. By the time we leveled at 8,500 feet, we were almost halfway across the channel. Sharks roamed those waters—some of the largest in the world. Killer whales were abundant also. But 8,500 feet allowed us enough altitude to glide to shore should the unthinkable happen.

Then. . . silence. The engine quit dead.

"Tarzan!"

"Jesus. Make a 180, Jane, and hold 70 knots." The turn put the wind on our tail, increasing our glide distance.

"Advise Catalina unicom that we have lost our engine and that we are headed back towards the mainland."

Fuel, mixture, ignition. . . "Ignition! Where's the key, Jane? The key is gone!" As soon as I said it, I saw it. It was hanging off the corner of her helipad-size lapboard. She had accidentally knocked it to the OFF position and dragged it out of the keyhold with one of the lapboards's handy-dandy clips. As I reached for it, she also saw it and grabbed at it. Our hands collided, knocking the key under her seat.

Sixty-eight-hundred feet, descending.

"Do you see it?"

"Fly the airplane, Jane, I'll find it."

"I'll slide my seat back." As she unlocked her seat and began sliding it back, it stopped abruptly. The key was jammed in the seat track. I got down on the floor, but the seat wouldn't budge. The key wouldn't budge. I came up for air long enough to call Coast approach control to advise them of our emergency.

Forty-five-hundred feet, descending.

I removed Jane's lapboard and threw it in the back seat to get better light on the floor. My plan was to get her out of the seat to take the weight off the seat track and hopefully get enough movement of the seat to free up the key. Before trying that, I went back down for one more try. Had this not been an emergency, the fact that my head was wedged down between this 64-year-old woman's knees looking northbound (so to speak) would have been highly inappropriate to say the least. Jane was very cool under pressure. I was starting to get that very sick feeling that we were actually going to get wet.

Twenty-one-hundred feet, descending.

As I struggled with the key, Jane suddenly locked my head between her knees. I strained to look up and saw a wild woman letting out a banshee scream.

It wasn't a scream; it was laughter. "Hey, young man! Do you like what you see down there?"

Honest to God, I could not believe my ears. I'm about to drop a Cessna into the ocean off San Pedro and my student has got my head in a kinky leg lock!

The look on my face was more than she could bear. She threw herself back against her seat in wild laughter, and the key popped out. My shaky hand slid the key into the ignition, I pulled the throttle back, turned the key to BOTH, eased the throttle in. . .

Nine hundred feet, climbing.

We spent the remainder of the summer flying the California and Arizona deserts preparing Jane for her mission of goodwill and her private pilot check ride. She did well. By September, I comfortably recommended her for her ride with the local examiner. She went on to fly many relief missions into the Indian reservations operating from unimproved strips and dirt roads. She was a natural when it came to crosswinds.

These days, as I fly heavy jets across the North Atlantic, I sometimes reflect on Jane and our close encounter with the waves. I hope I never have to experience that feeling again. As far as Jane goes, I would fly across any ocean with her anytime. She definitely had a cool head.

Mine Alone

EVEN THOUGH IT TOOK PLACE MORE THAN 20 YEARS AGO, my first solo cross-country flight is one of my clearest memories. I have had many challenging flights since, but the magnificence of that particular day still resonates whenever I gaze up into a blue summer sky with its wisps of clouds and unlimited distances.

Actually, it was not my first solo cross-country, but the major one required for the private pilot license, a triangular course with one leg at least 100 miles long. I had decided to go from my home airport, Montgomery County, Maryland, to Reading, Pennsylvania, and then on to Salisbury, Maryland, on the Eastern Shore of the Chesapeake Bay, and back. I planned to start early, so I could get back in time to relieve the babysitter of my eight-month-old twins. I also wanted to avoid the rush hour traffic at the small uncontrolled commuter airport.

I chose Reading for several reasons, including the fact that it was my mother's home town. It was also the right distance away, and the airport was the right size—not so large that I'd have to taxi for hours or takeoff in jet wake, but large enough to have gas for sale, a lunch counter and, most importantly, a control tower. Montgomery County Airport was uncontrolled and I still needed to log at least three landings at a control towered airport. I was trying to be efficient in accumulating the requirements for the license. We were moving to Boston soon, and I wanted to finish my license, or at least the flying part, before the move. My plan was to land in Reading, do three complete full-stop landings (and takeoffs), buy gas, eat lunch and then continue on the last two legs of the trip.

I had meticulously planned all of the details, down to the exact expected time in the air and gas consumed, including the extra amounts burned during the takeoffs and climbs to altitude. I calculated the course to steer for each leg, starting with the chart, and then including magnetic deviations and compass corrections.

On the morning of departure, my stomach in a knot, I called Flight Service for the weather report, and worked the winds aloft corrections into my trip plan. All of this was approved by my flight instructor in advance, and then again the morning of the flight when I called him with the Flight Service weather.

Neophyte that I was, I didn't notice anything strange about the fact that there were several Notams (Notices to Airmen) about the Reading airport concerning certain radio frequencies to use when approaching from certain directions. But in retrospect, I think my instructor probably should have caught it.

A newspaper reporter about my age, my instructor was an outwardly laid-back person who was writing a book about a recent commercial airliner crash. He was one of those many who loved to fly and would do anything for a chance to get up in the air, including suffering the trauma of teaching flying and, more scary, landing to any takers, however uncoordinated. Only his bitten fingernails hinted at the possibility that he was not as serene as he seemed. He would sit there casually through all sorts of narrow escapes, always grabbing the controls just in time to prevent disaster as I failed and failed time and again to land the airplane safely. When I finally caught on, he almost immediately jumped out and made me solo that very day.

It was a gorgeous spring day, some cumulus clouds, but no expectations of any "weather." The takeoff and first leg up to Reading were completely uneventful, as uneventful, that is, as flying all alone, thousands of feet up, in a small Cessna with minimum instrumentation can be. Actually I was very busy, always keeping track of the landmarks on chart and ground, scanning the instruments for malfunction warnings and the skies for other planes, and naturally, per my instructor, always noting various pastures and golf courses that might make good emergency landing spots if the engine were to quit.

One of the main challenges of cross-country flying is to locate and identify the destination airport. It is usually a relief to spot the runways that match your chart, but on that day, I felt some vague apprehension when I spotted the characteristic three runways intersecting in their centers, and called the tower for landing instructions. Perhaps it was the fact that a significant percentage of the grassy expanse of the airport was covered with parked airplanes that gave me a subliminal message. It is common to see areas of parking of small planes at airports, but here airplanes seemed literally to cover the whole field.

I said to myself (out loud of course; one of the pleasures of solo flight being that you can talk aloud to yourself anytime you want), "I didn't realize Reading had so many planes." I started to get a little nervous as I talked to the tower. The controller was in communication with multiple planes in the pattern, and I had to ask for repeated assurances about which runway he wanted me to land on. However, since this was one of my first landings at a controlled airport, I still didn't notice anything out of the ordinary, even when the controller interrupted his curt professional lingo to ask if I was a student.

I got down safely, turned into the nearest taxiway, and was surprised to see a small jet whiz along a few feet above the runway I had just vacated. Ahead of me, a man with a flag was waving me in the direction of some other small planes which were filing along the taxiway and into parking places on the grass, much as you see at the state fairground when Pat Boone is due to appear.

Still rather slow on the uptake, I radioed the tower and said I would like to do some takeoffs and landings.

There was a slight unidentifiable sound and some uncharacteristically inhospitable sarcasm in the reply, "You have to either stay or go."

I said I would stay and I followed the leader into a parking spot miles from the buildings, still planning to get some gas before going on my way. As I got out of the airplane, a young woman came along with a clipboard asking for my fuel requirements.

I said, "Top her off." She said fine, you pay over there, pointing to a tiny building about a mile away. I explained that I wanted my gas now so I could continue my trip. She was really very nice, when I think about it now. At the time I was somewhat offended by her reaction when I told her I was a student on a cross-country solo: She nearly died laughing. Then she broke the news: I had flown into the middle of the Reading Air Show.

My trepidation turned to panic. Every student pilot knows about the Reading Air Show. It went on for three days and attracted hundreds, thousands of airplanes, jets, wingwalkers, parachute jumps and military demos. Spectators flew in from all over the country, not to mention the clouds of planes coming to put on the show. It was pure chance that I had happened to arrive between events when they were letting visiting planes land. Just imagining all of the things that might have happened made my knees weak and my stomach clutch. How had I gotten myself into such a disastrous situation?

But then, a flash of insight hit me: I was on the ground. Nothing bad had happened. Suddenly I realized the magnitude of what I had accomplished by actually flying there and landing safely. If I could survive this, the rest of the trip would be a piece of cake. All I had to do was follow the procedures to leave again, go somewhere else for fuel and continue with my trip.

I got back in the plane and cranked the engine. I called the tower, and was instructed to taxi to the runway. Finally, after idling for 20 minutes at the edge of the runway while a squadron of vintage airplanes took off, I got my clearance and got out of there.

As I was taking off, the tower asked if I could take off short and turn out before flying over the runway intersection. I answered like a pro, "Affirmative," and I was off to Harrisburg. This was a smaller airport with a control tower, just a few miles west of Reading. There I made an expert landing, ordered my gas and had lunch at the small lunch counter. As I ate and looked over the chart for the next legs of the trip, the feeling of profound relief that had filled me upon landing at Harrisburg gradually changed to exhilaration.

The rest of the trip was magnificent. I took off and set my course over the Chesapeake Bay for Salisbury, Maryland. The view of the Bay was spectacular. It was early afternoon, and the sun was shining. The sailboats around Annapolis looked like a flock of birds; the bay bridge, with its chronic line-up of frustrated motorists, was a toy. The airplane hummed along, all indicators green. After the crowded skies of Maryland and Pennsylvania, the air seemed to be mine alone, aside from a few cumulus clouds that floated above me.

I felt self reliant and invincible, like one of those solo backpackers who survive on their own resources for weeks in the wilderness. For working mothers, though, one of the advantages of flying is that adventures take much less time. You can live a lifetime in a few minutes, as anyone who has accidentally flown too close to a thunderstorm can attest, but that is another story.

On the return trip, high above the rush hour beltway traffic, and then negotiating the crowded Montgomery County airport traffic pattern, I was as calm as if driving to the mall. When I got home, the sitter and babies were as indifferent to my arrival as if I had just been at my desk all day.

In the twenty years since that day, I have had many flights in small planes, some alone, some not and some to much more beautiful places. But it's that first solo over the Chesapeake that comes to mind when I gaze into the endless sky.

BARRY ROSS is a nationally recognized, award-winning illustrator, who is a contributing illustrator to *Flying Magazine, Flight Journal* and *Aviation International News*. In *Flying*, he has illustrated the "I Learned About Flying From That" column for the last 25 years. His sports illustrations have appeared in *Sports Illustrated, Outdoor Life* and *Running Times*. For over 20 years he has been the illustrator of *Golf Magazine's* famous instructional series, "Private Lessons." In addition to his love of aviation and sports, his interest in the interpretation of technology through illustration led to many corporate commissions by clients including Exxon, Mobil Oil, Martin Marrietta, and Bendix Aerospace.

Born and raised in New York City, he attended the prestigious High School of Music and Art, and graduated from Pratt Institute in Brooklyn with a BFA in Graphic Arts and Illustration. As a New York based illustrator he became a member of the Society of Illustrators, and participated in a number of its Air Force Art Program trips.

Aviation has always been a prime force in his life. One of his earliest memories is of being taken by his father to the Marine Air Terminal at LaGuardia Airport, and looking through the chain link fence at the departure end of the runway as a squadron of Flying Fortresses took off for Europe. The sights and sounds of that moment was the beginning of his love of airplanes and flying.

As a teenager, his bedroom/art studio was a mixture of art books, paints and brushes, and photos and models of airplanes. His first actual flight took place at the age of 18, in a Piper Tri-pacer, at New York's Flushing Airport. A couple of years later, he began flying lessons in an Aeronca Champ at Ramapo Valley Airport in Spring Valley, NY. He subsequently transitioned through Piper's Colt and Tri-pacer, the Cessna 150, 172, and the Piper Cherokee.

His love of the planes of his early years has culminated in his present aviation project: paintings of classic aircraft from 1930 through 1960. They will be part of an ongoing series being published by *Flying* magazine.

Barry presently lives in Fairfield, IA, with his wife, Kate, and flies a Citabria. To see more of Barry's aviation art, including his "Classics" series and his ILAFFT gallery, visit barryrossart.com.